# GODLESS
PAGANISM

# Praise for HumanisticPaganism.com

"Thank you so much for all you have done with HumanisticPaganism.com. This site has been very important in my development as a Naturalistic Pagan and a real motivator to move me past just intellectual theorizing about Naturalistic Paganism into actually practicing naturalistic paganism as a religious path. HumanisticPaganism.com has really helped me feel a part of a wider community and given me a sense that Naturalistic Paganism has real viability as a path."

"Finally, I have a name! Your site more than anything else gives me hope that the term 'Pagan' can be reconciled with humanistic values. I was on the verge of abandoning the term 'Pagan' altogether because of the associations with supernaturalism, until I found this site and this group. Thanks!"

"I just wanted to let you know that you've put into words something I have not found any validation for in the longest time. Your beliefs line up so well with mine and your writing has seriously changed my life. You are literally the first person to ever put into words what I've felt for so long."

"After searching all my life (I'm 51), I have finally found my religion!"

"I am just beginning my real involvement with Humanistic Paganism and am so grateful for this community. I am a humanist chaplain and devout feminist who has found that both the mainstream religious and mainstream atheist communities out there are too firmly rooted in patriarchy for me to feel at home or welcome. Humanistic Paganism is a wonderful vehicle for my ministry to women who work in reproductive healthcare. Thank you so much for this site and the Facebook page!"

# GODLESS PAGANISM

voices of
Non-Theistic Pagans

edited by John Halstead
with a foreword by Mark Green

The views and opinions expressed by the individual authors herein do not necessarily reflect those of the editor or the staff of HumanisticPaganism.com, nor do the individual authors necessarily share the views or opinions expressed by each other.

Published by Lulu.com

Paperback Edition 2016
ISBN 978-1-329-94357-5

Copyright © John Halstead 2016

All rights reserved. No part of this publication may be reproduced or transmitted in any form or by any means, electronic or mechanical, including photocopy and recording, without prior written permission from the respective individual authors.

Cover: The view of Earth was captured by Rosetta OSIRIS NAC RGB view on 2009-11-12 22:27 UTC during its third flyby of the Earth. South is up, roughly at the 10:30 o'clock position. Part of South America is visible at the right, about to go into darkness. Rosetta is currently closing in on its target comet 67P/Churyumov-Gerasimenko. The picture was taken at a distance of 327 600 km and Phase angle of 139 deg. (Courtesy NASA)

Typeset in Palatino and Helvetica

To my son,
for having the courage
to say what he believes,
to my daughter,
for having the courage
to say she doesn't know
what she believes yet,
and to my wife,
for having the wisdom
to know that we are
more than our beliefs.

## Acknowledgements

Thanks to our generous supporters, without whom this anthology would not have been possible:

CUUPS Bulletin
Spiritual Naturalist Society
New Orleans Lamplight Circle
Brock Haussamen
Jon Cleland Host
Mark Green
B. T. Newberg
Denise A. LeGendre
Evan and Sara Robinson
Fantasia Crystals
mudandmagic.com

# Table of Contents

**Foreword by Mark Green** ......................................................... xii

**Preface** ............................................................................................ xv

**Introduction** ...................................................................................... 1

**Part 1: Non-Theistic Pagans: "Yes, We Exist!"** ....................... 13

Pagan Atheists: Yes We Exist *by Stifyn Emrys* ............................. 15

Without Gods: An Interview with Stifyn Emrys ........................ 20

Yes, Virginia, I'm a Pagan Atheist *by Jeffrey Flagg* ..................... 24

Atheopaganism: An Earth-Centered Religion Without Supernatural Credulity *by Mark Green* ........................................................ 29

The Theist/Non-Theist Continuum *by Staśa Morgan-Appel* ................ 35

Why I Am a "Naturalistic Pagan" *by NaturalPantheist* ..................... 37

The Worship of the Gods is Not What Matters *by Brendan Myers* ...... 40

Polyatheism *by Steven Posch* ............................................................ 43

**Part 2: Analyzing with Apollo: Rationality, Critical Thought, and Skepticism** ........................................................ 47

A Naturalistic Creed ....................................................................... 50

The Scientific Pagan *by Allison Ehrman* ........................................ 51

Are the Gods Natural? *by B. T. Newberg* ...................................... 53

What Does It Mean for Gods to Exist? *by Tom Swiss* ............... 59

The Revelation of an Uncaring God *by Scott Oden* ................... 72

The Wonder Amplifier *by Dr. Jon Cleland Host* ........................ 76

## Part 3: Dancing with Dionysus: Emotion, Passion, and Mysticism ................................................................. 81

Emotional Pantheism: Where the Logic Ends and the Feelings Start *by Áine Órga* .............................................................. 84

Anatomy of a God *by Alison Leigh Lilly* ...................................... 86

Letting Go of the Side of the Pool *by DT Strain* ............................. 89

Dancing with Dionysus: Ecstasy and Religion in the Age of the Anthropocene *by Wayne Martin Mellinger, Ph.D.* ....................... 93

## Part 4: Not Your Fathers' God: Non-Theistic Conceptions of the Divine ................................................................. 101

What Is This Whole "Deity" Thing, Anyway? *by Blue* ................... 103

Being Human When Surrounded by Greek Gods *by M. J. Lee* ....... 106

Of Gods and Stories *by Nimue Brown* ........................................ 111

The Disenchantment of the Gods and the Reenchantment of the Archetypes *by John Halstead* .................................................... 113

I Worship the Blind Goddess *by John Halstead* ........................... 118

Faith in the Earth *by B. T. Newberg* .......................................... 121

The Three Kindreds *by NaturalPantheist* .................................... 123

A PaGaian Perspective *by Glenys Livingstone, Ph.D.* .................. 128

Goddess as Process: The Creativity of Change *by Áine Órga* ........ 136

Naming the Water: Human and Deity Identity from an Earth-Centered Perspective *by Alison Leigh Lilly* ................................ 139

Natural Theology: Polytheism Beyond the Pale *by Alison Leigh Lilly* ........................................................................................ 144

Naturalism and the Gods *by Glen Gordon* .................................. 149

"What Do You Mean 'God', Cat?" *by Cat Chapin-Bishop* ............ 153

## Part 5: Who Are We Talking To Anyway?: Non-Theistic Paganism and God-Talk ................................................................ 159

In Defense of Gods *by B. T. Newberg* ......................................... 161

When the Gods Speak *by Áine Órga* .................................................. 170

Thanking the Goddess for Tea *by Staša Morgan-Appel* .................... 175

Mystery as Role Model *by Eli Effinger-Weintraub* ............................ 177

Myth and Meaning: A Non-Literal Pagan View of Deity *by Ryan Cronin* .................................................................................................... 181

Theism, or Down to the Sea (of Limitless Light) *by Cat Chapin-Bishop* .................................................................................................... 187

## Part 6: Just LARPing? Non-Theistic Pagan Practice ........... 193

Why I Pray to Isis *by B. T. Newberg* .................................................. 196

The Three "Why's" of Ritual *by NaturalPantheist* ............................ 198

Why Modern Paganism Is Good for Today's Families *by Debra Macleod* .................................................................................................. 202

Four Devotional Practices for Naturalistic Pagans *by Anna Walther* .................................................................................................. 206

Pantheism, Archetype, and Deities in Ritual *by Shauna Aura Knight* .................................................................................................... 209

"As the Gods Pour, So Do Mortals": An Alternative Conception of Divine Reciprocity *by John Halstead* ............................................ 224

Our Gender-Neutral Atheistic Pagan Wedding Ceremony Script *by Irene Hilldale* .................................................................................. 230

Minimalist Religion *by Brendan Myers* ............................................ 241

An Atheopagan Prayer *by Mark Green* ............................................ 245

## Part 7: Bringing It Down to Earth: Non-Theistic Paganism and Nature .................................................................................. 249

Salt Marsh Goddess *by Michelle Joers* .............................................. 252

Gods Like Mountains, Gods Like Mist *by Alison Leigh Lilly* .......... 254

The Forgotten Gods of Nature *by Lupa* ............................................ 255

I Lost My Religion, and Gained the World *by Lupa* ........................ 259

Place-Based Paganism *by Anna Walther* .......................................... 262

A Daily Heron *by Sara Amis* .................................................................................. 264

The Voice of God *by Nimue Brown* ........................................................................ 267

What Being an Animist Means to Me *by Traci Laird* ............................................. 269

Awakening to Gaia *by Bart Everson* ...................................................................... 272

Lost Gods of the Witches: A User's Guide to Post-Ragnarok Paganism *by Steven Posch* ............................................................................................................ 275

## Part 8: Origin Stories: Becoming a Non-Theistic Pagan.... 285

Godlessness and the Sacred Universe *by Kathleen Cole* ........................... 286

The Sacred *by Dr. Jon Cleland Host* ..................................................................... 290

The Death of God and the Rebirth of the Gods *by John Halstead* ......... 293

How Persephone Killed the Gods for Me *by B. T. Newberg* .................... 302

The Impossible Atheist *by Bart Everson* ......................................................... 307

Adventures of a Non-Deist, or, Why I Don't "Believe" in the Gods *by Peg Aloi* ................................................................................................. 311

Paganism at Home: For the Love of Ritual *by Debra Macleod* ............... 314

## Part 9: Looking Back: Non-Theistic Pagans in History ...... 319

The Forgotten History of Atheistic Paganism *by John Halstead* ............ 320

Exploring the Historical Roots of Naturalistic Paganism *by B. T. Newberg*....................................................................................................................325

Was the Buddha a Humanistic Pagan? *by Tom Swiss* ............................... 330

"A Goðlauss Kind of Guy": An Interview with T. J. Fox ....................... 335

## Part 10: Looking Forward: Non-Theistic Pagan Community ........................................................................................................................ 345

The Care and Feeding of Your Atheist Pagan *by Jeffrey Flagg* ............... 348

Atheopaganism and the Broader Pagan Community *by Mark Green*................................................................................................................................356

Ehoah *by Rua Lupa* ..................................................................................................... 359

Earthseed *by John Halstead*..................................................................................... 364

A Poetry of Place: An Interview with Glenys Livingstone of
PaGaian Cosmology......................................................................................... 374

Non-Theism and Literal Belief in Wicca: An Interview *by Pat
Mosley* ........................................................................................................................ 379

Family, Extended *by Amelia Stachowicz* ....................................................... 385

**Contributors** ........................................................................................................ 389

**Environmental Impact Notice**............................................................. 402

# Foreword

I am delighted to introduce this volume of works by thinkers, explorers, ritualists, and theorists of the non-theistic Pagan community, and to have my works counted among them. I take it as a deep honor to be asked to write this foreword, as well; my respect and appreciation for John Halstead's thinking and courage as a leader among us is vast. Thank you, John, for all you do and have done for us.

For centuries, the principles of reason and critical inquiry have stood at cross purposes to those of religious credulity. Those who *believe* have found those who *question and doubt* to be blasphemous and heretical; those who *question and doubt* have found those who *believe* to be excessively credulous and prone to self-deception. This drama plays out today in international conflict; in the politics of the United States; and, in its own small way, in the Pagan community.

Though there has been debate recently about how—and whether—those of us whose Pagan practice does not include gods fit into the broader Pagan community, in many ways the ideas and approaches described in this book extend back to the Epicureans of Greece. Certainly they were well represented at the time of modern Paganism's flowering, being the very same ways of thinking about gods which were documented as being held by many of modern Paganism's founders in Margot Adler's ovarian* *Drawing Down the Moon*. It is new neither to the world nor to the Pagan community to posit that gods are ideas, or that working with them is psychological—and only psychological—in nature.

However, in recent years, with the rise of an increasing emphasis on belief in literal gods by that element of the Pagan community now known as the devotional polytheists, nonbeliever Pagans—humanist

Pagans, naturalist Pagans, Gaian Pagans and some who self-identify as pantheists—have become more visible as well by inevitable contrast. As a result, we have come to develop our thinking to form organizations, write blogs, and generally to participate in the broader conversation of the Pagan community.

And now, we have this book.

Long ago, we humans invented gods to explain things we did not understand, in the hope that by placating them, we could control the future. We were a young and ignorant species then. While there is much that we still do not understand today, little of it is experienced in the day to day living of an average human. We no longer need the device of gods to explain the phenomena of our world.

Though some of my fellow naturalist, materialist Pagans might disagree, I would suggest that we who are moving forward with religion *beyond* gods, *beyond* credulity in the supernatural are charting a path which could, at long last, bring religion and science into alignment. We understand religion as a phenomenon of the mind, and explore how best to work with the mind, thereby to satiate deep human yearnings as only religion can.

To my mind, we have at last drained the bathwater from around the baby, and we are nurturing it to create a way of being in the world that feeds both head and heart without excessively prioritizing either: a path of critically thinking, skeptical realists who are reverent in their religious engagement with a world they deem sacred, who live in the integrity of that experience while understanding that personal experiences are inherently unreliable as evidence of facts, and who work to better the world as a result.

Do we look back to ancient traditions? Yes, but just as we do not long for 8-track audio players and "balancing humours" in our medical care, we understand that old is not necessarily good. Things can evolve for the better, and that includes spiritual thinking. We can honor our ancestors without believing as they did. We can do homage to their practices without adopting their cosmologies.

Paganism brings core values—feminism, egalitarianism, environmentalism—that can inform a life of service, personal growth, kindness and social responsibility. Coupled with reason and critical thinking, it can break at last the cycle of arbitrary belief in "what gods want." It can begin to heal the deep wound of Belief, while knitting together communities to share observances and rituals, not because gods want or need them, but because *we* want and need them. We can dance around the fire because of the joy in it, and the meaning we make from it.

Because we are humans. We are, remarkably, an extraordinary manifestation of the Universe. Surely, that is more than enough.

Mark Green, 2015

* "Ovarian" refers to the possibility implied in the egg, rather than the seed as implied by the word "seminal."

# Preface

When I woke on the morning of February 13, 2015, I was nervous. I was 2,000 miles away from home, at PantheaCon, the largest indoor Pagan conference in the world. Thousands of Pagans, Polytheists, and others gather for a long weekend in February, in San Jose, California, every year to talk about Paganism and experience Pagan ritual and community. This year was my third time at the conference. I was most excited about two events. One of those was a panel discussion of Patheos Pagan bloggers, which I had been invited to participate in. I was nervous because the moderator of the panel had not provided us with any of his questions, and I am not an impromptu speaker.

Before getting ready, I checked my email. In my inbox was a message from a stranger named "Quinsha." Quinsha was writing in response to a recent blog post, which I had written, about the conflict between some atheist Pagans and some polytheist Pagans in our community. Quinsha wrote:

> "Having been told that I can't be Pagan if I am atheist, I ended up being a solitary. I am pantheistic about the universe, but it is nice to hear that I am not so strange feeling like I am a Pagan *and* an atheist. Unfortunately I can't be at PantheaCon this year, though I was there for the last 2 years. After being told that I could not be both, I really did not feel welcome so did not plan to be able to go this year."

In that moment, my thoughts crystalized. I realized that no matter what else I said at the panel, I needed to speak for atheist and non-theistic Pagans.

At the Patheos Pagan panel discussion, we were asked to say one thing we hoped to accomplish through our blogging. When it was my turn, I read Quinsha's email aloud. I told the audience that one of the reasons I continued to blog was because of non-theistic Pagans like Quinsha, people who came to Paganism, many of them feeling that they had been forced out of their religions of origin, and having found a new home in Paganism, now feeling themselves being pushed, sometimes subtly and sometimes not so subtly, out from under the Pagan umbrella.

Quinsha's email was not the first message I received like this. In the course of writing at Patheos and managing the HumanisticPaganism.com blog, I have learned that Quinsha's experience is not uncommon. I have lost track of how many times I myself have been told that I cannot be an atheist and a Pagan, or that I must believe in literal gods in order to legitimately call myself a Pagan. I have lost track of how many times someone like Quinsha has written to me to say they had experienced the same thing and wondered if there was a place for them in the Pagan community anymore.

I believe that at least some of this sentiment arises from a misunderstanding on the part of many theistic Pagans about what non-theistic Paganism is. And I suspect it is perpetuated by the silence of non-theistic Pagans, who do not feel free to speak up when others, implicitly or overtly, seek to impose a theistic orthodoxy in Pagan discourse and Pagan ritual. This book is a response to both the misunderstanding and the silence. It aims to educate others, including theistic Pagans, about non-theistic Paganism, and it aims to help foster a sense of community among non-theistic Pagans, so they can feel safer claiming their space in public Pagan forums.

The second PantheaCon event I was looking forward to attending was an "Atheopagan" panel discussion, which I had also been invited to participate on, followed by an Atheopagan ritual led by Mark Green. This was, as far as I know, the first ever PantheaCon event dedicated to atheist Paganism. The event was not accepted onto the official PantheaCon schedule, so it was held unofficially in a suite generously shared by Cherry Hill Seminary and the Pagan History Project. During the panel, we talked to a small, but enthusiastic gathering, of like-minded Pagans, who filled the room, about our feelings of alienation within Paganism. Afterwards, during an open house, I sat and talked with other non-theistic Pagans. I can honestly say that I have never felt such a strong sense of community among other Pagans. I wished that Quinsha could have been there. I hope this book inspires other efforts to build community by and for non-theistic Pagans.

I believe that it is a good thing that both theistic Pagans and atheistic Pagans are beginning to carve out spaces for themselves. We all need places, both physical and virtual, where we can gather with like-minded people, to feel both safety and support. This is why I am encouraged both by the flourishing of spaces for Polytheists, like Polytheist.com, the Polytheist Leadership Conference, and the Many Gods West gathering, as well as by the growth of the Humanistic Paganism community, the launch of the Atheopaganism website and Facebook group, and the planning of future Atheopagan events at PantheaCon. I hope that having these spaces for ourselves will also help us be less territorial about the spaces we share.

Having said that, we—theists and non-theists alike—must learn to share common Pagan spaces, like the Pagan blogosphere and Pagan festivals and conferences like PantheaCon. Someone once said to me that we will find acceptance in the Pagan community in direct proportion to our own acceptance of others. I have found this to be true in my own experience. (Of course, acceptance does not have to mean agreement.) What's more, sharing these forums can challenge us and encourage us to grow beyond our comfort zones. Everyone needs safe spaces where they can talk about their experiences, and their interpretations of those experiences, without fear of criticism, constructive or otherwise. But if that's where we choose to stay, then those "safe spaces" become intellectual ghettos.

I believe that both theists and non-theists have something to teach the other. When I was a theist (Christian), atheists challenged me to critically examine my interpretations of my experience, to cultivate a tentativeness or a provisional attitude toward all truth claims, and to look for what I had called "God" within myself and in the natural world around me. Now that I am an atheist, my theistic friends remind me not to privilege abstract thought over direct experience, to have the courage to take emotional leaps of faith, and to always keep a lookout for the divine "Other."

It is my hope that, as we come to understand each other better, we will become more hospitable in the spaces we share under the Big Tent of Paganism, and grow as individuals and communities by virtue of our communion with one another.

John Halstead, 2016

# Introduction

Contemporary Paganism is a general term for a religious movement which began in the United States in the 1960s, with literary roots going back to mid-19th century Europe, as an attempt to revive the best aspects of ancient pagan religions, blended with modern humanistic, pluralistic, and inclusionary values, while consciously striving to eliminate certain elements of traditional Western transcendental monotheism, including dualistic thinking and puritanism. Some of the distinguishing characteristics of contemporary Paganism include reverence for and a sense of kinship with nature, a conception of the divine which takes the form of a plurality of both male and female deities, a positive morality which emphasizes freedom and individual responsibility, and a creative approach to ritual.

## The "Big Tent" of Paganism

Contemporary Paganism is a diverse group with varied beliefs and practices, which includes Witches, Wiccans, Druids, Shamans, Goddess worshipers, Unitarian Universalist Pagans, Christo-Pagans, Quaker Pagans, Pantheists, Animists, Humanistic Pagans, Atheopagans, Heathens, Polytheists, Pagan Reconstructionists, Occultist, and many more varieties. What most contemporary Pagans have in common is that (1) they look to ancient pagan religions and contemporary polytheistic religions (like Hinduism and the African diasporic religions) for religious inspiration and (2) they seek to reclaim the word "pagan." How they make use of these sources and what the word "pagan" means to them varies considerably. Consequently, it is impossible to define contemporary Paganism with any precision.

One way of describing the diversity of Pagan belief is to focus on the question of deity. In 1997, Margarian Bridger and Stephen Hergest published an article in *The Pomegranate: The International Journal of Pagan Studies* entitled, "Pagan Deism: Three Views." Bridger and Hergest stated that Pagan belief in deity could not be accounted for dichotomously in terms of simple belief and non-belief. Instead, they suggested three possibilities, each of which subtly blended into the others. They illustrated this as a multi-colored triangle with three different colored corners—red, blue, and yellow—which blended into one another. The red corner represented the view that the gods "are personal, named, individual entities, with whom one can communicate almost as one would with human beings." The blue corner represented the view that the gods are "humanlike metaphors or masks which we place upon the faceless Face of the Ultimate, so that through them we can perceive and relate to a little of It." The yellow corner represented the view that the gods are "constructs within the human mind and imagination." Many of the non-theistic Pagans who are the subject of this book tend to fall toward the blue and yellow corners of this spectrum.

However, because Bridger and Hergest's model begins with the question of deity, it does not adequately account for those non-theistic Pagans for whom deity plays no role in their spirituality. Pagans themselves sometimes have difficulty appreciating the diversity of Paganism which includes non-theistic Pagans. One helpful metaphor in this regard is the "Big Tent of Paganism."

It is common for Pagans to speak of the "Pagan Umbrella" to describe the diverse community as a whole. Those who identify as "Pagan" are said to be "under" the Pagan Umbrella. The problem with the umbrella metaphor is that it implies that there is a single "center" around which all Pagans gather. But no one can agree on what this center is. The reality is that there are multiple centers of Paganism.

Another, more useful, metaphor is the "Big Tent." Imagine a large circus tent. Unlike the umbrella, which has only one pole, and hence one center, the circus tent has multiple poles and multiple centers. Contemporary Paganism has at least three "centers" or sacred foci around which Pagans may gather: (1) Earth, (2) Self, and (3) Deity. Individuals who gravitate toward different centers may have widely different understandings of concepts like "god," "spirit," "magic," "worship," etc. The people that are drawn to each of these centers answer questions of Pagan identity and authenticity differently. All of them relate to something that transcends the individual, but they have different ways of defining and relating to that "something."

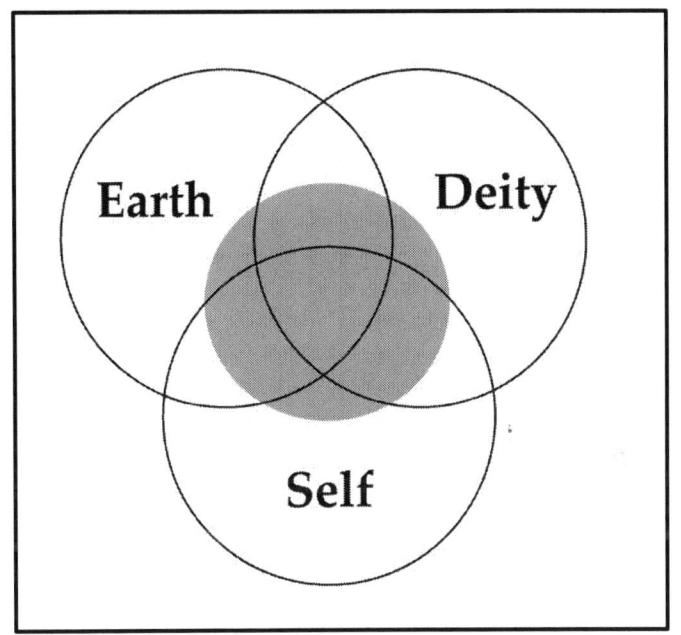

The Three Centers of Contemporary Paganism

Earth-centered Paganism includes those forms of Paganism concerned primarily with nature and ecology, the more local or regional forms of Paganism, and the many forms of Neo-Animism which view humans as non-privileged part of an interconnected more-than-human community of beings. The Pagan identity of earth-centered Pagans is defined by their relationship to their natural environment. Authenticity for these Pagans is defined by one's ability to "connect" with or relate to the more-than-human world.

For earth-centered Pagans, the earth or nature or the cosmos is that "something" which transcends the individual. Earth-centered Pagans seek to enter into a relationship with that nature. A sense of kinship is what characterizes that relationship. The experience of interconnectedness with the non-human or more-than-human world is a core virtue of earth-centered Paganism. This sense of interconnectedness is sometimes called "the re-enchantment of the world," and it refers to an expanded awareness of the nature of reality and of our participation in the natural world.

"Self-centric" Paganism is not to be confused with ego-centric Paganism. The "Self" in "Self-centric" Paganism refers to that larger sense of Self which extends beyond the boundaries of the normal waking conscious identity we commonly call our "self." Pagans sometimes called it the "Deep Self" or the "Larger Self." Self-centric Pagans include Jungian Pagans, "soft" polytheists, many Wiccans and feminist witches, and many of the more esoterically inclined Pagans. The Pagan identity of Self-centric Pagans is defined by spiritual practices which aim at development of the individual, spiritually or psychologically. Paganism is, for some Self-centric Pagans, a form of therapy or self-help. Authenticity is determined by one's relationship with one's Self. To put it another way, Pagan authenticity for this group is measured in terms of personal growth, whether that growth be toward psychological wholeness or ecstatic union with the larger Self.

For Self-centric Pagans, the "Self" is that "something" which transcends the individual. Self-centric Pagans seek to enter into relationship with the Self by disassociating from the ego-self and identifying with the larger Self. Insight is a core virtue for Self-centric Pagans, because insight is what enables us to distinguish the ego from the Self.

The term "deity-centered" is borrowed from Janet Farrar and Gavin Bone's book *Progressive Witchcraft* (2004). Deity-centered Paganism includes many forms of devotional polytheism and "hard" polytheism, and many reconstructionist or revivalist forms of Paganism. The Pagan identity of deity-centered Pagans is defined by a dedication to one or

Introduction | 5

more (usually ancient) pagan deities. Authenticity is determined by one's relationship with those deities. For deity-centered Pagans, the gods are that "something" which transcends the individual. Deity-centered Pagans seek to enter into relationship with the gods. Passionate devotion is what primarily characterizes that relationship. Devotion and piety are core virtues for deity-centered Pagans.

These three centers are not mutually exclusive. They are circles with overlapping circumferences. Individual Pagans may relate to two or even all three centers.

Conflict within the Pagan community occurs when individual Pagans confuse one of the centers with the whole of Paganism. For example, a deity-centered Pagan may conflate Polytheism and Paganism, or an earth-centered Pagan may wrongly assume that all Paganisms are "nature religions." Using the "Big Tent" model of Paganism, it is easy to see that non-theistic Pagans have a place within the Pagan community. It is only from the perspective of those who identify the deity-pole with the whole of Paganism that non-theists are not Pagan.

## Terminology

Many disagreements over religious matters can be traced to differences in definitions of critical terms. In the interest of clarity, several terms which are used throughout this book are defined here.

### "Atheist Pagan"

For some people, the word "atheist" implies a reductive materialism or even an *anti*-theism (think the New Atheists). But atheists are simply people who do not believe in the existence of gods or deities. Some of the authors included in this book are atheist Pagans or "Atheopagans."

### "Non-Theistic Pagan"

"Non-theist" is a much broader term; it includes but is not limited to atheists. Non-theistic Paganism includes:

1. Atheistic Pagans for whom gods and deities play no role in their spirituality. Some examples of these are presented in Part 1: "Non-Theistic Pagans: Yes, We Exist!"

2. Pantheistic Pagans, animistic Pagans, and other Pagans who may believe in "gods" or a God/dess, but who do not believe they are reified supernatural beings. Some examples of the variety of non-theistic Pagan beliefs will be presented in Part 4: "Not Your Fathers' God: Non-Theistic Conceptions of the Divine."

3. Atheists Pagans who do not believe in gods or deities, but who nevertheless use theistic language and theistic symbolism in ritual. The reasons for this will be explored in Part 5: "Who Are We Talking To Anyway?: Non-Theistic Paganism and God-Talk" and Part 6: "Just LARPing?: Non-Theistic Pagan Practice."

4. Agnostic or ignostic Pagans who, in the words of Brendan Myers, are "perfectly happy to shout 'Hail Thor!' with an upraised drinking horn," but "don't care whether the gods exist or do not exist: for as they see it, the existence of the gods is not what matters. Rather, what matters is the pursuit of a good and worthwhile life, and the flourishing of our social and environmental relations."

5. Pagans who believe in the existence of gods or deities, but who do not use theistic language or theistic symbolism in ritual.

## "Theistic Pagan"

In contrast, "Theistic Pagan" will be used to refer to those who believe the gods are reified supernatural persons or "separate and distinct" beings.

## "Secular Pagan"

Atheist and other non-theistic Pagans are sometimes confused with secular Pagans. When we say someone is "secular," it means that they are not religious. So a secular Pagan is a non-religious Pagan, or someone who participates in Pagan culture, but for whom such participation is not religious. This distinguishes secular Pagans from many atheist Pagans, for whom Paganism *is* a religion.

If someone is an atheist or non-theist, they may or may not also be secular. There are non-theistic forms of religion. Some forms of Buddhism and Taoism are non-theistic, for example, as are the various forms of non-theistic Paganism discussed in this book.

The question of whether a person is secular is entirely separate from the question of their belief in deities. So while there are secular atheists, there are also religious atheists. And while there are religious theists, there are also secular theists. What distinguishes people who are secular from those who are religious is their attitude toward ritual or symbolic action: secular people reject ritual, while religious people embrace it.

Of course, there are secular rituals. Holidays, like Valentine's Day or the Fourth of July, birthday celebrations, and social action like Pride Day marches and environmental protests, can be entirely secular and yet involve rituals, i.e., symbolic action. But most people don't recognize these activities *as rituals*. In fact, if someone buying a Valentine's Day card or marching for marriage equality was told that they were participating in a "ritual," they might well be offended. In contrast, most people recognize what happens inside the walls of a church or in a Pagan circle as ritual. The difference between "secular" and "religious" turns therefore, not on the presence of ritual, but on whether the ritual is intentional.

We can think of theism and atheism as existing on a spectrum *of belief*, while "religious" and "secular" exist on another spectrum, a spectrum of *practice*. The theist-atheist spectrum deals with the question of belief, specifically, belief in deity. The religion-secularism spectrum deals with practice, specifically intentional ritual. These two spectrums intersect and create four quadrants.

Religious theism or theistic religion combines the belief in deity or deities with intentional ritual practice. These include most of the people that attend weekly religious services in the U.S. This also includes Pagans who believe in gods and engage in devotions to deities or celebrate the Wheel of the Year.

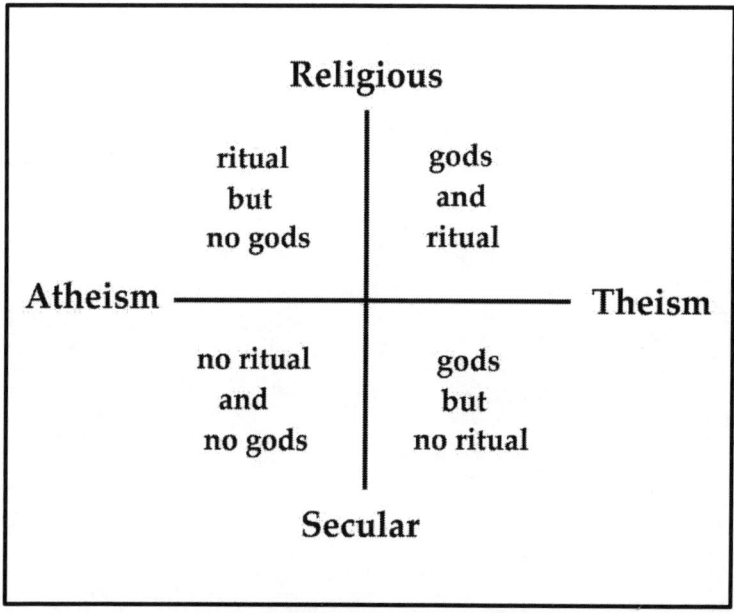

|  | Religious |  |
|---|---|---|
| | ritual but no gods | gods and ritual |
| **Atheism** | | **Theism** |
| | no ritual and no gods | gods but no ritual |
|  | Secular |  |

The Religious-Theism Intersection

Secular theism or theistic secularism includes a belief in deity or deities, but without any intentional ritual practice. These include believers who want nothing to do with organized religion and those who describe themselves as "spiritual but not religious," but don't have any regular spiritual practice. It also includes "spiritual but not religious" Pagans who believe in gods and goddesses, but don't really practice, either privately or with any group.

Religious atheism or atheistic religion includes intentional ritual practice, but without the belief in deity and deities. This includes many Buddhists and Unitarians, for example. It also includes atheist Pagans, who do not believe in gods, but who do celebrate the Wheel of the Year or perform other Pagan rituals in a meaningful way. Much of this book is devoted to explaining how and why Pagan ritual is meaningful to atheist Pagans. It is a mistake, then, to assume that atheist or other non-theistic Pagans are "secular" or that their participation in Pagan ritual is not sincere.

Secular atheism or atheistic secularism involves no belief in deity and no intentional ritual practice. This might include atheists who attend Pagan ritual for fun or for the after party. They may participate in the ritual, but it is not deeply meaningful to them.

### "Humanistic Pagan"

Atheism and humanism have a lot of overlap. Most humanists are probably atheists. Both humanists and atheists tend to be philosophical naturalists (see below). But atheism and humanism are two different things. Atheism is about *disbelief in gods*. Humanism is about *belief in humans*—in human goodness and human potential. Humanists tend to share a human-centered ethics, although increasingly the humanist ethic is being expanded to include all forms of life in a *bio-centered* ethic.

Humanistic Paganism is a form of Religious or Spiritual Humanism. Religious Humanism can describe any religion that takes a human-centered ethical perspective, in contrast to a deity-centered ethical perspective. A humanistic ethic is one that defines the "good" in terms of human experience, not the will of any God or gods.

Humanism adds to atheism a positive ethical component. Not only do Humanistic Pagans not look to the gods to solve our problems, but they emphasize our *human* responsibility to solve those problems. Even if the gods did exist, a Humanistic Pagan would say, we cannot know their will, and so we must base our actions on what we human beings know—our own experience. For Humanistic Pagans, human experience and reason provide a more than sufficient basis for ethical action without supernatural revelation. In fact, some Humanistic Pagans argue that humanistic religion can be more ethical than theistic religion, since the will of inscrutable gods cannot be appealed to to justify actions that cause others suffering.

The term "Humanistic Pagan" is somewhat problematic, since it seems to exclude the more-than-human world, including other animals, plants, and the earth itself. But the term "humanistic" should not be confused with "anthropocentric." Many Humanistic Pagans embrace the notion that we humans are part of a much larger community of beings to whom we have ethical obligations. The adjective "humanistic" is intended to contrast with "theistic"; it excludes gods, but not other living beings.

## "Naturalistic Pagan"

Naturalistic Paganism is a form of Religious or Spiritual Naturalism. The word "naturalistic" refers to a commitment to philosophical naturalism. Philosophical naturalism seeks to explain the universe without resort to *super*natural causes. Just as Humanistic Pagans believe that human experience and reason are a sufficient basis for ethical action, so Naturalistic Pagans believe that the scientific understanding of the material universe is a sufficient basis for the awe and reverence which motivate religious worship. Naturalistic Pagans, who have been referred to as "Sagan's Pagans" (after Carl Sagan), experience a profound and abiding sense of wonder and reverence when considering the process by which the universe and biological life evolved, what is sometimes called the "Epic of Evolution." This sense of wonder, both at what we know and what we don't know of the natural world, deserves to be called "spiritual" or "religious."

The name "Naturalistic Paganism" also can create some confusion. Since many Pagans understand Paganism to be a nature religion or an earth-centered religion, the term "Naturalistic Paganism" may seem redundant. For most Naturalistic Pagans, "naturalistic" means more than respect or affinity for nature. It is more or less synonymous with "scientific." In general, Naturalistic Pagans adopt the most current scientific explanations of natural phenomena and are skeptical of any claims that are not supported by mainstream science.

Thus, Naturalistic Pagans are skeptical about things like magic, psychic abilities, communication with spirit entities, attributing intention to inanimate nature, etc.—beliefs that are common among other Pagans. Naturalistic Pagans tend to be skeptical of claims that have yet to be proven by science. While many Pagans take a "proceed until proven wrong" approach to things like magic and the gods, Naturalistic Pagans tend to take more of a "wait and see" approach. Many Pagans will practice magic or invoke gods until they are convinced that these things do not exist, but many Naturalistic Pagans avoid these things until they are first proven to exist.

## A Note on Capitalization

Except where individual authors have expressed a contrary preference, "Pagan" and "Neo-Pagan" are capitalized herein where they refer to the contemporary Pagan community, in the same way that "Christian," "Catholic," "Mormon," "Hindu," "Buddhist," and so on, are capitalized. When referring to ancient pagans predating the modern era, like the ancient Celts, Egyptians, and Norse, "pagan" is not capitalized, because these peoples did not refer to themselves as "pagan."

Pagan Pentacle and Atheist symbol overlapping

## Part 1: Non-Theistic Pagans: "Yes, We Exist!"

*"'Atheist Pagan' is a contradiction in terms."*

*"All Pagans are polytheists."*

*"If you don't believe in the gods, then you're not Pagan."*

Maybe you have heard statements like these before. Maybe you have even said things like this before.

Or maybe you are a non-theistic Pagan and you've been keeping it a secret because you thought you were alone.

The truth is that non-theistic Pagans exist. Not all of us are vocal about our non-theism, but there are more of us than you may realize. We are a growing and diverse part of the larger Pagan community. If you are Pagan, chances are you already know a non-theistic Pagan or two. You may even circle with them in ritual. How many people identify as non-theistic in any Pagan gathering depends largely on how the question is phrased. (See the Introduction.)

Although non-theistic Pagans have been a part of the Neo-Pagan revival since its early days in the 1960s, we have remained under the radar, so to speak, because contemporary Paganism has always been more concerned about practice than belief. Many early Pagans, both theistic and non-theistic, adopted a "Don't ask, don't tell" attitude toward questions of theology.

At one time, non-theistic Paganism may even have been the norm. Although Pagans routinely invoked deities in ritual, the gods were frequently understood as metaphors for natural phenomena or psychological archetypes. For example, in her 1979 survey of American Neo-Paganism, *Drawing Down the Moon*, Margot Adler cited the Jungian psychologist David Miller for the notion that the many gods of polytheism were "not to be believed in or trusted, but to be used to give shape to an increasingly complex and variegated experience of life."

In recent years, though, all of this has begun to change. Following the publication of Neil Gaiman's *American Gods* in 2001, there has been a growing interest in the Pagan community in deity-centered Paganism or what is now called "devotional polytheism." Although contemporary Paganism has traditionally eschewed any form of orthodoxy, this new enthusiasm for deity-centered forms of Paganism has sometimes developed into a polytheistic orthodoxy which insists that to be Pagan one must share a literal belief in gods as "separate and distinct" beings. Thus, we now hear people making statements like "'Atheist Pagan' is a contradiction in terms." And many times such statements go unchecked. In some instances, the voices of the more dogmatic polytheistic Pagans have become so insistent and so pervasive that non-theistic Pagans have retreated from Pagan forums or from the Pagan community entirely.

Around the same time as deity-centered Paganism began to grow in popularity, we also witnessed the emergence of the "New Atheism," represented by the so-called "Four Horsemen of the Non-Apocalypse," Richard Dawkins, Christopher Hitchens, Sam Harris, and Daniel Dennett. The New Atheism was in fact an *anti-theistic* movement. In addition to being antagonistic toward theists, the New Atheists tended to be antagonistic toward all forms of religion or spirituality. Like some of their religious counterparts, the New Atheists conflated atheism with secularism (see the Introduction), denying space to religious naturalists and other religious non-theists in atheist forums.

As a consequence of these two movements—the one which claims for itself the whole meaning of the word "Pagan" and the other which claims for itself the whole meaning of the word "atheist"—it has become necessary for atheist and other non-theistic Pagans to speak out, to claim our space, and to announce unapologetically that, yes, we do exist.

## Pagan Atheists: Yes We Exist
by Stifyn Emrys

### Can atheists be Pagans?

To me, the answer to that question seems easy. Of course they can. But when I brought up the subject recently, I realized the answer wasn't nearly so clear-cut for many people...and that a few objected vehemently to the very suggestion that these two philosophies were compatible.

One person even suggested that I was doing Paganism a grave disservice by even suggesting such a notion. This person had spent a good deal of effort convincing some folks who identified themselves as Christians that Pagans weren't "godless." To say that Pagans could be atheists, she said, was to prove these Christians right! (I found myself wondering why I, or anyone who holds a non-Christian belief, should care about how a Christian might judge that belief.)

Certainly, not all Pagans are godless, just as not all Pagans are Wiccans. The majority are, in fact, theists—and the majority of those are polytheists, believers in many gods. But there are some Pagan pantheists out there, too, along with some monotheists, some agnostics and yes, even some atheists.

In fact, a survey I conducted online last summer found that the vast majority of respondents identified the most important element in Paganism as "reverence for nature." Given three possible responses, a whopping 87 percent chose this answer. In second place, with just 10 percent of the vote, was "worship of the gods." (The third option, "practice of magic(k)," received a paltry 3 percent.

When asked whether worship of the gods was a fundamental component of Paganism, a majority—53 percent—said it wasn't. While the size of the sample for these questions was significant at more than 600 people, the sampling was not scientific. Nevertheless, it shows clearly that a significant number of people don't think polytheism is essential to Paganism and—even among those who do—most don't think it's the defining element.

Reverence for nature fills that role.

### Sagan's example

Few people showed greater reverence for nature than the late Carl Sagan, an agnostic who made a career of exploring—and marveling at—the wonders of the universe. In fact, he was so astounded by the beauty and complexity of the universe itself, that he saw no need to go seeking gods or goddesses to explain it. His philosophy was that no concept of a creator or overseer could possibly match the awe-inspiring grandeur of nature itself.

This is the way the Pagan atheist views the world, and the universe at large. It's not some dry, clinical and bitter philosophy. It's a vibrant, dynamic view of life and the environment that births and sustains it. In fact, many Pagans view the universe as a sort of living organism—either metaphorically or in actual terms. The parallels are, indeed, fascinating. And, in fact, many Pagans believe that the distinction between natural and supernatural is a false one—that nature is the totality of all there is, and that it's meaningless to speak of anything being somehow outside of nature.

How could we even conceive of such a something in any case? We'd have absolutely no frame of reference for either conceptualizing or experiencing it.

### The role of deities

All of which raises the question of gods and goddesses. What, exactly, are they? Are they supernatural entities—beings outside or somehow above nature? This is certainly the Christian worldview—a view that places its deity outside of nature and, in doing so, casts nature itself in a subordinate role. Nature is but a creation, a tool at the disposal of a superior being who created it either for "his" own enjoyment or for the purpose of allowing other creations (humanity) to exploit it.

I know of very few Pagans who approve of exploiting nature for the sake of human greed and narcissism. Most, in my experience, view humans as part of nature, not separate from it—part of an intricate web of life, not somehow above or beyond it. Gods and goddesses, likewise, are most often viewed as part of the fabric of nature, rather than somehow disconnected from it. On the contrary, they are connected in the most intimate fashion possible. Poseidon is the sea personified. Deities such as Osiris, Aphrodite and Freya exemplify the very principle of fertility. Zeus' lightning and Thor's thunder are in the storm.

The ancients didn't fully comprehend how the forces of nature worked, so they viewed it in terms they *did* understand—anthropomorphic terms. They put a human face on nature, attributing violent storms to an angry god's tantrum or fertile fields to the benevolence of a goddess.

### Sacrificial offerings

One difficulty many atheists have with these conceptions is practical. If we believe that we are at the mercy of a deity's emotions, it's only human nature that we're going to try like hell to influence those emotions. We're going to try to put that deity in a good mood. This is how the concept of sacrifice developed, as an attempt to placate (or bribe) a deity by offering him/her something we ourselves might enjoy—often in the form of food. There were a couple of problems with this assumption.

First off, it was arrogant to think the forces behind the elements needed anything from us, and it was presumptuous to assume that—if they did—they'd enjoy the same sorts of things we did. Second, instead of placating the forces of nature, the assumption led us to actually *destroy* elements of nature itself. We sacrificed things that were never ours to sacrifice. We killed animals and burned them on altars. We even went so far as to kill humans. And if our sacrifices weren't "accepted" (the rains didn't come or the land remained barren), we blamed the priests who conducted the sacrifices and killed them, too.

While we don't conduct human sacrifices today, we still ostracize people who don't believe the way we do on the grounds that they're an offensive to our patron deity or deities. The Christian concept of hell falls into this category, as does the shunning of family members still practiced in some faiths. Indeed, Christian dogma is built on a foundation of the need for sacrifice—both homicidal and deicidal, but it's hardly alone. Those who practice a variety of other faiths still sacrifice animals in the hope of propitiating or manipulating the gods.

### Marvels and contradictions

These are the kinds of practices that the Pagan atheist finds saddening, because they do unnecessary damage to nature itself—something humanity has done far too often. Indeed, the Judeo-Christian tradition, whose god was originally a storm deity in a polytheistic tradition, often justifies brutalizing nature on the grounds that this god gave human beings the right to do so. It seems contradictory (perhaps even sadomasochistic) that a god of nature should have given humans the right to destroy his creation for their benefit. Or his. Or both.

My book, *Requiem for a Phantom God* (The Provocation Press, 2012), was written to expose just such contradictions in the dominant form of monotheism practiced today in the West. Although I think polytheism has an ethical advantage on Abrahamic monotheism—as I explain in that work—I'd be less than fair or honest if I didn't acknowledge similar contradictions where I see them within Paganism, as well.

It is precisely *because* of a love for nature that a person can identify as a Pagan and an atheist with absolutely no contradiction whatsoever. The Pagan atheist views nature itself as the magnificent framework of which we all are a part—and has no need to put a human face on it. To do so is to look at it through a clouded lens, rather than taking it at its own marvelous face value.

"I do not know of any compelling evidence for anthropomorphic patriarchs controlling human destiny from some hidden celestial vantage point," Sagan once remarked, "but it would be madness to deny the existence of physical laws."

## Misconceptions and metaphors

Perhaps the biggest misconception is that Pagan atheists are just a bunch of bah-humbug types who revel in their own bitterness and adhere to a boring and rigid existence devoid of beauty and reverence. There is, of course, plenty of bitterness and negativity out there—but these attitudes can be found in people of all paths. No faith has a monopoly. In fact, Pagan atheists celebrate nature. Though we don't believe in anthropomorphic deities who stand as guardians to the forces of nature, we revere those forces on their own terms and, when others speak of Isis or Demeter, we respect their right to do so. We may even use such divine names ourselves, not in reference to unseen personalities, but as symbol and metaphor—a rich form of human expression—to characterize nature itself.

We don't begrudge others the use of terms like "the Goddess" or "the Lord and the Lady." On the contrary, we see them as a poetic homage to the wonders nature and an acknowledgement of the masculine and feminine principles that are so prevalent across our natural world. We see no contradiction between such poetic reverence and the scientific assurance that thunderstorms aren't the product of a storm god's wrath, but rather the something that occurs when warm, moist air rises rapidly in the atmosphere.

When it comes right down to it, arguing that atheists don't belong in the Pagan world is like arguing that Protestants aren't real Christians or that Sufis aren't true Muslims. It's the opposite side of the coin that argues "All Pagans are Wiccan." No, they're not. You don't have to be Wiccan to be Pagan, but neither do you have to be a theist. It's not a prerequisite. There's room enough in this vibrant community for a wide array of different expressive forms, including Pagan atheism.

## Without Gods:
### An interview with Stifyn Emrys

Stifyn Emrys is an author, journalist, and educator. He is the author of the book, *Requiem for a Phantom God*. He was interviewed by B. T. Newberg in 2014.

**B. T. Newberg:** In the last year, you've become actively involved in the "Atheist Pagan" question, writing numerous blog posts and debating over whether Atheists can be Pagans or not. I find this is often a matter of how you define terms, so could you tell us what "Atheist Pagan" means to you?

**Stifyn Emrys:** To me, an atheist is someone who is "without gods," and a Pagan is a very broad term that comprises any number of earth-based, polytheistic and pantheistic belief systems. I think the conflict comes because some use the term Pagan as a virtual synonym for polytheist. I don't subscribe to this definition. I respect polytheists, but I resist the very human inclination to redefine a broader term in some narrower sense because it happens to fit my particular belief system.

There are many, many people who respect the earth and our universe who do not see it necessary to define these things in terms of deity. I think it's natural to view these things in anthropomorphic terms, because doing so makes them easier for us to understand from a human perspective. I'm also fascinated by ancient myth, because its symbolism offers us a glimpse into how we, as humans, interact with our environment and make sense out of things.

I have great respect for metaphor, myth and symbolism. The difficulty, I think, arises when we forget that these are intended as gateways to understanding. Instead, they are taken literally, because, frankly, it's easier to do so. It also leads to dogmatism and fundamentalism. That's what I'm concerned is occurring among those who insist that Pagans "worship" literal gods. Very much the same thing happened early in the development of Christianity, when the orthodox literalists suppressed mystical or Gnostic traditions that sought a deeper meaning.

There's a huge strand of mysticism running through Paganism that I don't want to see sacrificed to literalism. I'm not using the term "mysticism" in some mumbo-jumbo sense; I'm using it to denote the mysteries of the universe—mysteries I believe we can and should continually seek to understand using science and inquiry. This contrasts with a literalist approach that maintains we've already got it all figured out thanks to our symbols, religious hierarchies or holy books.

I'm aware that the term "atheist" carries a certain amount of baggage. I think the terms Pagan humanist and secular Pagan work just as well. Unfortunately, some of the most vocal self-described atheists and anti-theists tend to come off (in my experience) as bitter or petty. Given the way we're often treated, that's understandable. But I prefer to take a more positive tack. I like Carl Sagan's perspective: that the universe in itself is more awe-inspiring than any god who symbolizes it could ever be. Why spend time revering gods as symbols of nature when you can go straight to the source? I think many non-theistic earth-based Pagans would agree with this approach, and I don't think they should be excluded from a discussion of Paganism.

**BTN:** So when you say an atheist is "without gods," do you mean without literal interpretations of gods, or without gods of any kind, symbolic or otherwise?

**SE:** I mean without literal interpretations. We communicate through symbols; there's no getting away from that. I think it's important to be aware of how we use symbols rather than pretending they don't exist. We don't stop buying tickets to movies involving superheroes because we know they don't exist. We enjoy these movies (at least I do) because they offer an insight into human nature and the world in which we live. Symbols are extremely valuable from that standpoint; I believe they become dangerous when we take them literally and, in doing so, ignore the ideas the symbols were meant to convey.

**BTN:** Your first book, *Gospel of the Phoenix*, re-weaves the story of Jesus with earlier myths like that of Isis and Horus or the Queen of Sheba. After *Gospel of the Phoenix*, you followed up with a critique of monotheism called *Requiem for a Phantom God*, and a further exploration of Jesus-myth issues from your first book in a sequel called *Principle of the Phoenix*. With one foot kicking the "Atheist Pagan" hornet's nest and the other foot pointing in a "Christo-Pagan" direction, you must take a lot of flak in the current Pagan community. What's your stand? Are these legitimate forms of Paganism, and if so, why?

**SE:** I try to see things from different vantage points, which has its advantages and disadvantages. The main advantage is I'm open to gleaning information whatever its source. The primary drawback is, like a referee in football, people who have taken hard stands always seem to think I'm on the other side. As a consequence, it's those hard, dogmatic stands that I seek to soften up. People who say you "can't" be a Christo-Pagan, a Pagan Atheist or whatever generally betray a rigidity in their own thinking and, often, a lack of respect for the principle that people should be able to identify themselves however they wish—as long as they're not deliberately pretending to be something they're not. Spiritual self-identification is, to me, as important as ethnic or racial identification.

Imagine a person telling a person of Native American heritage, "You can't call yourself Native American because you were born in France." Or imagine telling someone who's gay, "You can't identify as gay because you were once in a straight relationship." That's offensive. And to me, it's just as offensive to tell someone, "You can't identify yourself as a Christo-Pagan or Pagan Atheist because those designations don't fit into my preconceived notions about them." It's a matter of respect.

**BTN:** If you could sum up your message to the Pagan community in one sentence, what would it be?

**SE:** Respect one another, embrace diversity and don't be afraid to ask the tough questions.

## Yes, Virginia, I'm a Pagan Atheist
### by Jeffrey Flagg

**Pagan. 'Nuf said?**

I'm an atheist. I'm also Pagan. It's actually not that hard to reconcile.

At the very beginning, it's worth making something quite clear—there is really no rulebook for what makes a Pagan. It's a term that seems to encompass a rather wide and diverse set of people. Generally speaking, Thelemites and Wiccans and Heathens all seemingly share a common set of social concerns and social infrastructure, even if they don't share cosmology or practices. The reasons for hanging together under this umbrella term aren't within the scope of this article, nor is the history of the term. I'm not out to speak about how we got to this point. The fact of the matter is that we're here. And what is Paganism? *It is, effectively, a culture that provides a web of common reference and language for a bunch of different people with different beliefs and practices to hang together.* Paganism, therefore, has no particular theological or religious test.

I actually feel like I could rest the defense there, but I won't. It'd make for a really short article, and outside of that, I've looked on the web and seen a lot of static about Pagan atheism. Some of it comes from atheists that, in my opinion, needlessly deride atheist Pagans for what they consider to be unacceptable levels of religiosity; most of it, however, comes from Pagans who consider belief in the existence of at least one deity to be a necessary quality of a Pagan.

**Really, really there?**

But let's break some things down. Theism is generally accepted to be typified by making a claim of the existence of at least one deity. There are a series of assertions implied in the statement, "At least one deity exists."

For example, it requires a founding definition of "deity." It also requires a founding definition of "existence." Sitting around and indulging in a discussion about what it means to exist would, honestly, turn into a series of articles that would end up rehashing ontology in general. I'm not going to attempt an iron-clad definition of "existence." Generally speaking, though, one of my rules for saying that something exists involves my ability to demonstrate that existence to others in convincing ways, particularly when those "others" may hold views that wouldn't be biased towards accepting that the object in question exists. This actually flows forth, not from some serious position of modernism, but from the pretty practical meat-and-potatoes way that I, and many other humans, handle experiencing strange new phenomena. If I see something strange, I draw others' attention to it, to see if they see it and what they make of it.

Of course, over a lifetime of taking this practical attitude to things, including an admission, upon first encountering something unusual, that I could be hallucinating or seriously confused, I've developed certain rules-of-thumb to help speed up my conclusions. For example, I've found that most things which exist can have machines built which demonstrate and exploit that existence. For example, there was a time when HIV's role in AIDS was not as well-accepted as it is today. The development of drugs which directly assault HIV, and which significantly extend the lives of HIV+ people, has been a major nail in that coffin. Another guideline is observing the biases of those who claim a certain thing exists. There are a bunch of these other sorts of guidelines, and a lot of people who are simply being sensible use them all the time.

Putting a few of these together, I come to the conclusion that no deity exists. Now, we can make some fuzzy definitions of "deity," and there are a few that I might semi-comfortably consider interesting and useful, but I don't grant them the status of, as Feynman once put it, "really, really there." They're not beings in this universe. They're not beings in another universe. They're not on another "dimension" or "plane" or "level" or "realm of ideals," and the existence of those things is also something I do not accept. If I list the properties of deities, existence isn't among them.

That alone is enough to qualify me as an atheist. But I will, for good measure, mention some other things that I don't think exist. I don't recognize the existence of vital life-force, or chi, or ki, or "energy," or any of the other myriad terms used in New Age and Pagan circles. I don't recognize the existence of spirits, of demons, or of angels. I have no reason to conclude that I have a soul that will continue on after my death, which is to say that I also don't believe in an afterlife. There are a lot of things common to the lives of Pagans that I don't recognize in the ontological class of being "really, really there."

And yet, if you find yourself blanching at this, or you're ready to tell me I'm not a "real" Pagan, at least let me tell you my response up front. Stop. You're being obsessed with ontology.

## Putting on the Santa suit

A really wise friend of mine has this great shtick he does about how he'll never tell a child Santa Claus isn't real. It's really a brilliant bit, and I actually love hearing him do it at dinners and parties. Essentially, it goes like this: Santa Claus is more recognizable by more people than your average real person. People know who he is and what he does. People get gifts from him all the time, etc., etc. In fact, if you walked down the street in a red suit giving out gifts, everyone would call you Santa Claus. So, of course Santa is real. He might be more real than most people!

And, of course, this is delivered with a little bit of humor, the sort that says, "Ha, ha!...but seriously!" He, of course, does leave out some really important details that throw wrenches in the works for Santa Claus. For example, we've never found his workshop, nor evidence of his purchasing the raw materials for toys. His employees are elves, and nobody's found those (seriously, not even one crazy whistleblower?!). The FAA has never received a request for an air traffic corridor radioed in from a flying sleigh. Possibly most tragically of all, there are lots of good girls and boys that Santa somehow misses. Most people would agree that this compounds together with lots of other information to suggest that, at a minimum, Santa has yet to be found and his existence would be highly contradictory.

But the whole Santa thing is still a really apt way for explaining how I deal with things like deities and the other ooky-spooky subjects we lump together into Paganism. See, I remember being 13 years old, and because I didn't feel I had any popularity to defend, I played Santa Claus when my Boy Scout troop sang Christmas carols down at the old folks' home. I had a really freaking good time putting on the red suit, going "Ho ho ho!" and giving out candy canes and hugs. Most of the people at that nursing home were beyond delighted to see me. I mean, they were delighted that a bunch of fresh-faced Boy Scouts came to sing for them, but if I'd been passing out candy canes wearing my uniform, it wouldn't have been half as much fun for me or for them. I do suspect that there may have been one or two of them may have been suffering from dementia and possibly really thought I was Santa, but I have no doubt that most of them called me "Santa" because it was fun to do so. And it was fun for me. Everything was more fun for having the living symbol of generosity and happy childhood memories there. Yep. *Santa isn't real, but I was once Santa for a night, and it made the night meaningful.*

## Begging the question

This is generally the place where someone will invoke a sort of fall back cosmology popular within the Pagan community: the Jungian concept of archetypes and the collective unconscious. I've never really been a fan of seeing things that way, either. To be honest, it feels like another attempt at making the gods (or magickal energy, or other such stuff) "real." Hermes no longer lives atop Mt. Olympus, but now lives inside the collective unconscious. The problem is that both Mt. Olympus and the collective unconscious are artifacts of a mythology. This shifts the mythological location, but it doesn't really structurally change things. The other problem I have is that, while we have physical science for discussing phenomena which exist in the world, there is no "science of archetypes." Archetypes are, in a sense, their own mythology, albeit an interesting and compelling one and one that may be a little less supernatural. But as a mythology goes, I don't reach for it often. I also must confess that I don't experience gods or other mystic concepts as being part of my psyche, nor do I use the modality of ritual in such a heavy psychological fashion.

Of course, archetypes are handy descriptors. I will give them that. It's hard to not think about any character without bringing archetypes in. I prefer to see my psyche as mine, full of its own funny idiosyncratic quirks, and to simply explore, as freely as possible, what a deity or a concept or a character means to me. I don't need to hang that on an external framework to do so, at least most of the time.

### Does it matter?

And that's why I honestly feel that, although I'm the atheist, it's everyone else who's being really philosophically uptight. I might not think that Hermes is "real," but that doesn't mean that I can't aspire to be like Hermes, make art that represents Hermes, talk about Hermes, do things and claim Hermes did them, dress like Hermes, act like Hermes, get other people to call me Hermes, or be Hermes, for myself or others, for a time. Just because something isn't real doesn't mean that you can't experience it. If things that didn't really exist had no power, I sincerely doubt that people would go to see Batman or Iron Man movies. People love connecting with those complex symbols of heroism. People just also know that you can't shine a bat-shaped searchlight when you're getting mugged and that you can't trade in Stark Industries on the NYSE. Flynn does not live. "Flynn Lives!" still means at least another $15 for millions of people.

All of this is to say that I find the question of the gods being "real," and indeed discussions of their ontological nature in general, somewhat silly. It doesn't matter if they're "real," if they're meaningful. So, yes, I am an atheist because I don't believe in the existence of a deity. I'm also, however, a Pagan, because I have a personal relationship to the same things that Pagans have relationships to. Once you get past the word games of ontology, being an atheist Pagan isn't so silly after all

## Atheopaganism: An Earth-Centered Religion Without Supernatural Credulity
### by Mark Green

a·the·o·pa·gan·ism *(noun)* \ˈā-thē-ō-pā-gən-iz-əm\
: godless paganism, paganism without gods

I was a Pagan for more than 20 years. At least, I think I was.

I had been raised as a rational materialist in a scientific household, but was introduced to Pagan rituals and community at age 25, and in short order felt at home there. Unlike the mainstream religions, it got a lot of things right. It didn't have a demonstrably error-laden "holy book," and it wasn't as sour and mean-spirited as the various mainstream religions. Paganism's values celebrate the natural world, revere beauty and pleasure and creativity, suspect authority, and encourage gratitude, celebration, humor and enjoyment.

I could enthusiastically embrace all of that. It enriched my life tremendously to join with my friends to ritually celebrate the turning of the Earth's seasons, to remind myself of what each time and season means in the natural world and the agricultural cycle, and what it meant to people long ago.

That said, I believe in critical thinking, in the scientific method, and in the intellectual process. Over time, it became clear to me that in the Pagan community, most of the people around me were not viewing "gods" and "magic" as metaphors and psychological techniques, but as literal, supernatural phenomena taking place in an Invisible Dimension lurking behind the material world and driving its events. This superstitious credulity became more than my intellectual self could tolerate.

However, once I had left its practice, I missed what was right about Paganism: the ways in which religion meets the needs of humans which are not centered in cognitive thought, but rather, which seek community, a sense of meaning in life, and the richness of experience that comes with presence, celebration, gratitude and awe.

So I began to explore for myself what religion is in a functional sense, how these functions correlate with the needs and appetites of the various systems of the human brain, and to ponder how "religion" could be teased apart from "superstition." Because it was clear to me that, though most people assume as a matter of course that a religion must incorporate a supernatural component, there is no particular reason it should, other than as a habit carried over from the days when humans had no better explanations for the phenomena they experienced than the supernatural.

What I decided to do was to create a non-superstitious tradition of Earth-centered religious observance: **Atheopaganism.** As I have done so, I have been delighted to find that many of my friends have acknowledged that they had the same difficulties with Paganism that I did, and have joined my wife and myself in our celebrations.

So…what is a religion, really?

I would contend that, at root, a religion comes down to four elements:

1. **Cosmology:** the accepted understanding of the nature of the Universe and how it works,

2. **Values:** the definition of what is important or sacred,

3. **Principles:** ethical guidelines as operational "rules for living," and

4. **Practices:** rituals, holidays, and other observances.

Now, at this point it bears saying that *my* atheistic religion in no way defines *the* atheistic religion. Entirely different principles and practices could be developed based in other values. But my particular flavor of supernatural-free religion looks like this:

## Cosmology

Cosmology is the easiest one for an Atheopagan: we cede it to science. Science is the best modality we have for understanding the true nature of the Universe, and we allow it to do its job.

## Values (the Sacred)

We can't talk about religion or define a new one without addressing the issue of what is to be considered sacred: what that means, and how it informs the values by which the practitioner is expected to live.

At root "sacredness" is an ascribed quality: an opinion. It is applied to whatever is highly valued by the tradition or practice in question, and to those objects, events and practices which evoke internal narratives which communicate the religion's beliefs and values.

Only four things, ultimately, fall into that category for me:

**The World.** Meaning, generally, the Universe, but most specifically the biosphere: *Life*. It is the Earth and the Cosmos which gave rise to all humanity and which support our ability to survive. All we eat, all we breathe, all we came from is this, and thus it is holy.

**Beauty.** Beauty is that which inspires joy in living and which communicates the inner truth of the creative person. Beauty fills our hearts and provokes our minds, strikes us motionless with the recognition of our good fortune in being alive. Bright and dark, soaring with joy or filled with rage, we know beauty because it sets our limbic brains to singing. It is not optional, trivial or superfluous.

**Truth.** Truth is the only beacon we have to light our way into the unknown future. And the more significant the topic, the more sacred is the truth about it. It is a deep wrong to deny what is true when it affects what is sacred. This isn't about "little white lies." It's about the tremendous and humbling power of Truth to bring down despotism and corruption, to right wrongs, to advance liberty, to build closeness between us.

**Love.** Love lights up the dashboards of our limbic brains and provides us the courage to reach across the great gulf to the Other. It drives our kindest and best impulses, enables us to forgive what we suffer, spurs us to face down the darkness and carry on, to insist that betterment is possible, that the ugly moment needs not be the end of the story. Love brings hope where it has flagged, sometimes for years. It is the redemptive power each of us bears within us to deliver another from hell and into light.

### Principles

Being a moral person is about how you act, not what you believe. These principles are an Atheopagan's guide.

1. I recognize that the metaphorical is not the literal.
2. I honor the Earth which produced and sustains humanity.
3. I am grateful.
4. I am humble, acknowledging that I am a small, temporary being not inherently better or more important than any other person.
5. I laugh a lot—including at myself.
6. I enact regular ritual play, in which I willingly suspend my thinking mind and use the technologies of religious ritual to invoke a state of presence in the moment and heightened experience of the metaphorical.
7. I celebrate diversity and am respectful of difference.
8. I recognize and embrace my responsibility to the young and future generations.
9. I acknowledge that freedom is tempered by responsibility, respecting the rights and freedoms of others and meeting my social responsibilities.
10. I celebrate pleasure as inherently good, so long as others are not harmed in its pursuit and the Sacred is respected.

11. I understand that knowledge is never complete. There is always more to be learned.
12. I conduct myself with integrity in word and deed.
13. I practice kindness and compassion with others and myself, recognizing that they and I will not always meet the standards set by these principles.

## Practices

Religion isn't just belief. It is *doing:* the rituals and observances (daily, seasonally, or for important life events) of a religion bring its community together, lend meaning and ongoing traditions to the lives of practitioners. While my group and I celebrate something like the regular Pagan "Wheel of the Year" for holidays, we have adjusted their meanings a bit to remove any supernatural references, and have added elements of the modern, which the old Pagan holidays do not acknowledge. Highsummer, for example (at the beginning of August) is the celebration of labor, innovation, craft and technology.

Our rituals generally follow a structure, but one markedly different from the standard Pagan rite. It is as follows:

**Declaration of Presence.** Begins with mindfulness practice to calm/center the mind. Then an action or statement is made by one or more participants to declare presence and purpose; e.g., "We are sentient beings of Planet Earth, present in this place, this moment. The Cosmos is above us, the Earth is below us, and Life is around us. Here the wise mind unfolds. Here the playful child creates. Here the wondering human gazes out to view the vast and mighty Universe. We are here, and together."

**Qualities.** Invoking the Qualities participants hope to carry within themselves as they move towards the Intentions: "May we know and embody these Qualities, that our rites guide us forward to achieve our dreams and better the world…"

**Intentions.** Participants express their intentions for what is to be attained/achieved/realized during the ritual, such as to celebrate and give thanks for all they enjoy, to grow closer to one another, or to align themselves with a specific hoped-for possibility in the future.

**Deep Play.** Ritual enactment meant to symbolize and concretize the desired Intentions for participants. Activities which stimulate the metabolism and the expressive self at this time will contribute to the feeling of presence and connectedness. Can include singing, chanting, drumming or other music making; dancing or other movement; symbolic enactment of drama; creation of some kind of art or crafted object in an intentional and allegorical manner; or recitation or spontaneous creation of poetry.

**Gratitude.** Expresses gratitude at having been supported by the Qualities the participants invoked, and for all they are blessed with in their lives. Sometimes expressed with shared food and drink. May also involve expressions of commitment on the part of participants of what they will do to act in accordance with their intent.

**Benediction.** Example: (in unison) "To enrich and honor the gift of our lives, to chart a kind and true way forward, by these words and deeds we name intent: to dare, to question, to love. May all that must be done, be done in joy. We go forth to *live!*"

## Conclusion: What It Looks Like

Atheopaganism provides the fulfilling benefits of a traditional religion, yet is rooted in what is true and open to learning, change, and constant reconsideration of itself. While it does not make promises of eternal existence, a cosmically-determined plan or magical powers, it also does not ask us to sacrifice the unique and marvelous capacities of our cognitive minds in the name of living with a pretty story.

I, for one, find this tradeoff a worthy exchange.

## The Theist/Non-Theist Continuum
### by Staśa Morgan-Appel

There's a big difference between the either/or of theism/atheism and a continuum of theism/non-theism.

When I hang out with people who believe in a creator god who is all-knowing and all-powerful, or with people who toss reason out the window and are satisfied with the explanation "It's God's will/because God said so," it's pretty obvious to me I'm not a theist. When I hang out with people who have no room in their lives for anything science can't prove yet, or with hard atheists, it's obvious I'm not an atheist.

Put another way: if there are only theists and atheists, and if non-theist is a polite way of saying atheist, then I guess I don't exist. (And the babelfish disappeared in a puff of logic, à la Douglas Adams.)

Science and mysticism or spirituality are not by definition incompatible. I'm trained as a scientist. If you can't conceive of what science doesn't know yet, you literally can't do science; you can't use scientific method for scientific inquiry if you can't imagine things that don't yet make sense. Many things that have seemed supernatural in the past make sense now thanks to science. Many things that we don't understand now are simply things science can't explain yet. What's more, many of the scientists I know are deeply mystical people—and some are deeply religious. So to say science and religion are incompatible is factually untrue.

There are no controlled, randomized, double-blind studies, and there are no well-designed scientific experiments, that prove that any specific spiritual practices (such as prayer, meditation, or magic) "work" or "don't work." What little research there is doesn't, or can't, define clearly what "work" means, or completely isolate every variable (such as who is affected). There is some interesting research that demonstrates certain things, such as brain changes during meditation. But anyone who claims science proves spiritual practices do or don't work is factually incorrect.

There's more than one way to conceptualize the Divine/God/Deity/That-Which-Is-Sacred. To insist on conceptualizing it only in certain ways, and to insist on reacting against or defining one's self against only those conceptions, is to give those conceptions primacy and power.

Some non-theists may choose to reject religious and spiritual language completely, because for them it's completely tainted by one conception of Deity. Some of us choose to use it in ways that for us are true, accurate, and have integrity.

I can say, with perfect truth and integrity, that the Earth is the Goddess to me. This doesn't mean, remotely, that I subscribe to a belief in an all-powerful creator deity, or that I'm ascribing such characteristics to the Earth. It means that I name the Earth, exactly as it is, to be Divine.

This also means that being somewhere along the theist/non-theist continuum, or being outright theist, does not automatically mean ascribing supernatural powers to one's Deity. My Deity is nature. You can't get any less supernatural than that. The Sun doesn't do anything supernatural. Neither does the Earth. Nor do the Stars, the Air, the Water, human beings, my cats, or the danged squirrels who have eaten their way into our car's engine. To say, as Witches do, "Thou art Goddess; Thou art God; Thou art the Divine," is to say that the Divine is right here, in this world, is this world, is you and me.

Compared to some folks, this makes me a theist. Compared to others, it makes me an atheist. To me, it's a pretty meaningless distinction, because the concept of Deity that one believes in or does not believe in is not one that has meaning for me. I don't believe in a Deity—I don't believe in the Earth, or the Air I breathe, or the Sun above, or the Water I drink, or the food I eat, or the cats I cuddle, or the rain that falls, or the rocks I carry in my pockets. I experience them.

## Why I Am A "Naturalistic Pagan"
### by NaturalPantheist

Why am I a Naturalistic Pagan? Why do I personally identify as a Pagan, rather than just a humanist, even though my worldview is primarily naturalistic?

Let's start off with why I don't call myself an atheist. I was most definitely an atheist for a while after I left fundamentalist Christianity. In the immediate aftermath of the death of a friend and the searching it led me to engage in, I was first a liberal Christian and then very soon became atheist, thanks to watching many YouTube videos and reading books by prominent atheists. But that wasn't the end of my religious journey. I was hungry for more.

When I found the World Pantheist Movement (www.pantheism.net), I became a Pantheist—one who sees the universe as divine and the earth as sacred. This was religion without the supernatural. I still consider myself a Pantheist. I see the Earth as Mother Nature, something to be honoured, revered and, yes, worshipped. I even pray to the Earth. It is our duty as children of the Earth to honour and look after her. This to me is the essence of Paganism.

I am an animist. Like many in the new animist and deep ecology movements, I see all living things (and perhaps even non-living things) as "persons" we have a duty to respect. Persons who deserve rights. Persons whom we can develop relationships with. Humans are not the superior species on earth; we are just one of many species with no more right to be here than any other. Philosophically I find the ideas within panpsychism/panexperientialism, i.e., that mind is not something that "emerges" from brains/matter, but is something that is inherent all the way down and up—the smallest electron experiences, just as the largest galaxy does. There is no scientific proof for this. It is more an argument from philosophy, and if science ever does prove it wrong I'll have to change my ideas.

Ancestor veneration is also a sacred duty in my opinion. Learning to cope with the death of my close friend and then my grandmother, and without the "comfort" of heaven to believe in, I found the Pagan emphasis on honouring our ancestors to be very helpful and useful. I honour my ancestors regularly. I research them. I have an altar to them. I pray to them. I give them offerings. Can they hear me and are they conscious beyond the grave? I doubt it. The scientific evidence against the existence of a soul is pretty strong. But I venerate them anyway—it helps me remember them, it helps me feel closer to them, it teaches me values like reverence and filial piety. It allows me to feel connected. And if by some miracle there is some kind of consciousness beyond the grave then I'm simply doing my duty as any Pagan should.

What about the gods? First, it is important to acknowledge that modern Paganism has always emphasised that orthopraxy not orthodoxy is what matters. When we stray from this tenet, we only have to look at monotheistic fundamentalism to see what happens. I don't truly know how I view the gods, but I have trouble believing there are supernatural gods. I suppose I'm slightly on the agnostic side, rather than fully atheist.

My religious practice involves regularly praying to the gods, particularly the Anglo-Saxon ones. I give offerings and do devotions. I also follow the Celtic-inspired practice of giving an offering to my local river each Beltane and addressing her as a goddess. When I see the moon each night, I bow my head and say, "Hail Mona." When I hear a thunderstorm or see lightning, I say, "Hail Thunor," and when I see the North Star I say, "Hail Tiw."

I was a member of the hard polytheist organisation, ADF, until recently (I will join again once my travels are over), and so my religious practices and rituals are very polytheistic. In fact, I would say my religious practices are probably barely distinguishable from any polytheist. I would have no problem taking part in a religious ceremony with hard polytheists, praying to the gods, giving offerings or any other Pagan practice. In fact, I find the Celtic and Norse/Saxon Reconstructionist religions to be one of the greatest sources of inspiration for me when putting together my religious practices. But do I believe in powerful literal beings existing somewhere in the universe who are the gods of Paganism? I don't currently see enough evidence to back up such a claim. That said, having read *A World Full of Gods* (ADF Publishing, 2005) by John Michael Greer, I am open to the idea that, because millions have had religious experiences from a variety of faiths, there could well be something I am not seeing.

I follow the Neo-Pagan Wheel of the Year—the eight festivals/sabbats. These help me to stay in tune with nature, to feel more of a sense of the cyclical nature of time, to be aware of the changes taking place in the world around me each season. I love celebrating these festivals, feeling connected with nature, the way they ground my spirituality in the reality of daily life. And that is another reason I consider myself a Pagan.

If these things don't make me a Pagan, I have no idea what would.

Finally, I think it is important to say that I owe a debt of gratitude to hard polytheism. I follow hundreds of Pagan blogs, and most of them are written by polytheists. And that is great! Because I am regularly challenged, made to think, and I learn so much from them. I base a lot of my religious practice on what I read on those blogs, especially those who emphasise scholarship. In a time when it seems like the Pagan blogosphere is becoming more polarised, there is so much we can learn from each other that will improve our religious lives, and it saddens me to see the regular arguments. We need each other. We are better together.

## The Worship of the Gods Is Not What Matters
### by Brendan Myers

"The sacred, I shall say, is that which acts as your partner in the search for the highest and deepest things: the real, the true, the good, and the beautiful."

—*Circles of Meaning, Labyrinths of Fear*

I don't normally see omens or other messages from the gods in the way many other Pagans say they do. I'm not especially interested in ritual or magic or spellcraft. I do not sense auras; I do not feel the energies; I do not read tarot cards or cast the runes. In fact, around ten years ago or so, I hit upon one of the most liberating and life-changing propositions ever to have entered my mind, which is that the worship of the gods is not what matters. What, then, am I still doing in the Pagan community? And if the worship of the gods isn't what matters, then what does?

People and relationships matter. The earth matters. Life, yours and mine, matters. Art, music, culture, science, justice, knowledge, history, peace, and any other similar thing which enriches your relationships with the world and with people, also matter. The extent to which life is worth living matters. Death, yours and mine, matters. And thinking about these things is what matters too.

My path is the path of a philosopher, and it is a spiritual path. It's about finding answers to the highest and deepest questions that face humankind, and finding those answers by means of my own intelligence. It's about not waiting for the word to come down from anyone else, not society, not parents, not politicians or governments, not teachers, not religion, not even the gods. In that sense it is a humanist activity, but it is an activity which elevates ones humanity to the highest sphere. That is what matters. This was the path of all the greatest philosophers through history. It was the path of the great pagan predecessors like Hypatia and Diotima and Plato, and also the path of more recent predecessors like James Frazer and Robert Graves. This is the path of knowledge; and knowledge is enlightenment, and knowledge is power.

Some people, and some religious groups, might see that as hubris. But I see it as humanity's true calling. I've been working for decades to create a philosophical world view which is rigorously rational but at the same time recognizably spiritual, uplifting, accessible to anyone, and genuinely helpful. If I have crafted it well, it will be my legacy. (Although I also want to buy land on which to build a temple. But that's another story.)

This shouldn't be controversial, but it is. But when I said, "the worship of the gods is not what matters," some people demanded my forcible removal from the Pagan community. The statement "the worship of the gods is not what matters" is not the same as the statement "the gods do not exist." It says that, whether the gods exist or do not exist, I have other primary concerns. For there are other things that matter too—and some of those other things matter more. And some of those other things which matter more are sacred things. And some of those sacred things which matter more are things to do with the human realm: such as friendship, justice, and integrity. Thus, the path is a humanist path, yet also a spiritual path.

Suppose the gods do exist. Then relate to them the same way you might relate to anybody else. There's a form of meditation that I still do once in a while, perhaps not often enough, in which I contemplate a certain Celtic goddess whom I shall not name here. My view of Herself is strongly pantheist, and as I see it, speaking of Herself and speaking of the earth is almost the same thing. She also personifies certain moral values and certain relationships that I think are important. There's a bowl on top of one of my bookshelves into which I pour an offering to Herself every time I have beer or wine in the house. And in turn, I like to imagine that She looks after me. But if you think about it, that's a very minimalist kind of religious practice. There's no casting of circles, no raising of energies, no chanting and no invocations. There's just me, doing my thing, and talking to Herself once in a while.

But in my relationship with Herself, I do not bow. I do not obey. I do not "worship." Perhaps this is one of the last remaining strands of my Catholic upbringing, but to me the word "worship" means absolute unquestioning affirmation of the authority of the deity. I'll not have that in my life. If you are wise, neither will you. The gods, if they exist, are just the people who happen to live on the other side. And they shall be friends to me, or strangers to me, the same as any of you.

I was initiated into the 1st degree of a certain lineage of Alexandrian Wicca. I've also followed the Druidic path, co-founded a Druidic community called, The Order of the White Oak, and in 2001, I even followed the Druidic path back to Ireland. I have been a member of the Pagan community for more than twenty years. So I'm not coming to this as a dilettante, or a dabbler. I was once offered my second degree, but we never could find a time to do the ritual, and nothing came of it. But that's okay. Now all I really want to do in the Pagan community is write books, talk about the ideas in them, play guitar, help out at events, and "dance sing feast make music and love" with good people. I want to help create a spiritual culture that is intellectually inquiring, artistically flourishing, environmentally aware, and socially just.

And that, also, is what matters.

## Polyatheism
### by Steven Posch

So, the cat died.

Me, I'm not an Afterlife person. I think that when the breath is gone, we go back into the grand dance of everything, the eternal sabbat of the atoms. And this seems to me both beautiful and good.

But as I move through a house newly filled with absences, stillnesses where I expect movement, it somehow consoles me to think of the Antlered sitting cross-legged with all the animals around Him, and old Mr. Rudycat snugged up in His lap. Or, more likely, draped around His neck and across His shoulders like a black-and-white fur collar, but with a pink nose. Occasionally switching Him in the face with a long, black tail.

Yep, that's the Rude all right.

Emily was the first kid to grow up in the local pagan community, and you couldn't help but feel a sense of investment in her. Smart, talented, charismatic, it was evident to everyone that she was going to be High Priestess of Minnesota someday, if not the first pagan president. When she died unexpectedly at 20, her death shook us all.

In my sorrow, I found it somehow consoling to think of her in that Land where it's always a long, summer afternoon, where cicadas drone and bees boom in the apple trees whose boughs bear leaf and flower and fruit all together.

Odd: though I don't believe in the Summerland, having it as part of my mental repertoire gave me the power to help the healing of my own hurt.

As a rule, witches aren't believing people. If belief is a gift, I didn't get much. My gods are the old gods, the ones you don't have to believe in because their existence is self-evident: Earth, Sun, Moon, Sea, Fire, the Winds. If I speak of the collective plant life of planet Earth as the Green God, or its sum total of fauna as the Horned, well, that's well within ancestral understanding.

So I call myself a *polyatheist*. But don't talk Dawkins to me, please. He and so many of the new Atheists Militant are really *monoatheists*. They don't believe in *God*. Those that I've read are really rather amusing in their passionate fundamentalism.

There's one truth and they've got it.

Sorry folks, that broom never flies. You'd think they'd never met a metaphor in their lives.

Well, it's different for polyatheists. We understand the power (and truth) of the Many.

And we understand the power (and truth) of Metaphor.

Sleep well, Rudy, snugged in the Horned One's lap.

You sure were one fine cat.

*In Memory of*
Emily Susan Lingen
April 22, 1979 - May 16, 1999

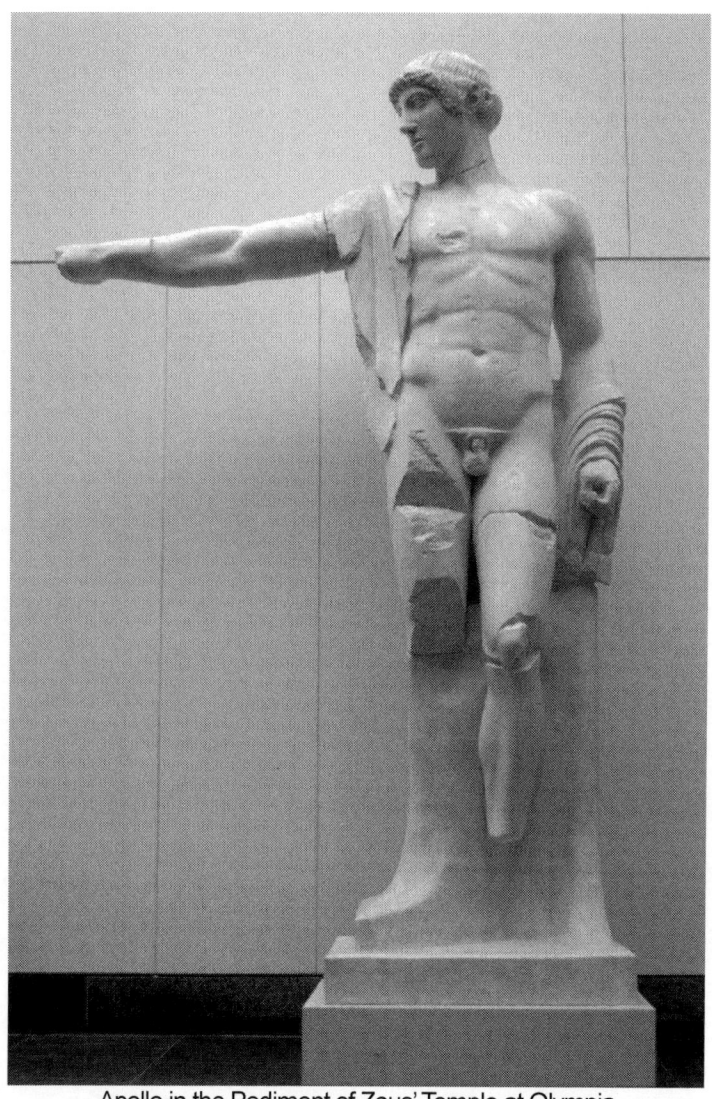

Apollo in the Pediment of Zeus' Temple at Olympia

## Part 2: Analyzing with Apollo: Rationality, Critical Thought, and Skepticism

Many non-theistic Pagans are "Naturalistic Pagans." Naturalistic Paganism is a form of Religious or Spiritual Naturalism. The word "naturalism" here refers to a commitment to philosophical naturalism. Philosophical naturalism seeks to explain the universe without resort to *super*natural causes. Naturalistic Pagans believe that the scientific understanding of the material universe is a sufficient basis for the awe and reverence which motivate religious worship. Naturalistic Pagans experience a profound and abiding sense of wonder and reverence when considering the process by which the universe and biological life evolved. This sense of wonder, both at what we know and what we don't know of the natural world, deserves to be called "spiritual" and "religious."

"Naturalistic" here means more than respect or love for nature. It is more or less synonymous with "scientific." In general, Naturalistic Pagans adopt the most current scientific explanations of natural phenomena and are skeptical of any claims that are not supported by mainstream science. Naturalistic Pagans consider science to be the most reliable guide to understanding reality, more reliable at least than faith in ancient religious texts or the spiritual visions of other individuals. Naturalistic Pagans tend to be highly critical of the misuse of scientific theories to justify belief in non-scientific phenomena, such as invoking quantum mechanics or chaos theory to justify a belief in practical magic, as Tanya Luhrmann has documented (*Persuasions of the Witch's Craft*, 1989). For Naturalistic Pagans, "science" refers to the consensus of the mainstream scientific community, which employs the scientific method and draws tentative conclusions based on the current most compelling evidence available and which are critiqued by a community of experts.

It is probably true that not all questions can be answered by the scientific method. Many issues which concern Naturalistic Pagans may fall into this category. In such cases, humility is what is called for, not faith. The paucity of scientific evidence is not a justification to believe whatever one wants. Naturalistic Pagans believe that, when science has yet to answer a question, we must place the question in the category of the "as yet unknown" and suspend judgment. In the meantime, though, our condition of "unknowing" may be enriched by our individual subjective experiences. But we should remember that we can submit even our own experiences to the scientific method: experiment, observe, draw tentative conclusions, compare with others, and then repeat.

Naturalistic Pagans differ generally from other Pagans in a couple of ways. Recognizing the cultural differences between Naturalistic Pagans and other Pagans can help to avoid conflict between these two groups.

First, Naturalistic Pagans tend to be more skeptical than other Pagans of non-scientific beliefs, like practical magic, psychic abilities, communication with spirit entities, attributing intention to inanimate nature, etc. Naturalistic Pagans tend to be skeptical of claims that have yet to be proven by science, while other Pagans tend to be more skeptical of science—or at least skeptical of the reach of scientific knowledge. While many Pagans take a "proceed until proven wrong" approach to things like magic and the gods, Naturalistic Pagans tend to take more of a "wait and see" approach. So while other Pagans may practice magic or invoke gods until they are convinced that these things do not exist, Naturalistic Pagans tend to avoid these things until they are first proven to exist.

Second, Naturalistic Pagans understand the search for truth differently than many other Pagans. Naturalistic Pagans tend to perceive truth or reality to be less subjective than other Pagans. You might say that Naturalistic Pagans have "faith" in the existence of objective reality and our ability to discover it through the scientific method.

In addition, Naturalistic Pagans, like many in the scientific community, see the search for truth as more of a communal endeavor than do more individualistic Pagans. As a result, many Naturalistic Pagans may seem less reserved about critically questioning other Pagans' beliefs. This sometimes brings them into conflict with other Pagans, for whom such an attitude is felt to be rude. However, if we want to avoid orthodoxies of the mind, then constructively critical discussion is necessary. When we avoid criticism, we become vulnerable to self-deceit and groupthink. For our part, Naturalistic Pagans should remember that a scientific spirit is one of *openness* and *humility*. When done in this spirit, critical questioning benefits both sides in the conversation and the community as a whole.

## A Naturalistic Creed

Inspired by a discussion about Michael Dowd's personal religious credo, HumanisticPaganism.com conducted a survey in the summer of 2014. "A Naturalistic Creed" is the outcome of that survey.

> Life is our religion.
> The Universe is our deity.
> Science is our theology.
> The Earth is our temple.
> Nature is our scripture.
> Evolution is our creation story.
> All truth is our creed.
> A life of compassion and service is our offering.

## The Scientific Pagan
### by Allison Ehrman

One of the few things I lost when I left the religion of my upbringing was the ability to easily define my beliefs in a simple label. I am no longer "Southern Baptist" and everything those two words immediately imply. I don't in any way consider this a bad thing, but when people ask me what I believe now, I don't want to weigh them down with "I'm a Unitarian Universalist Neo-Pagan scientific pantheist humanist who practices Buddhist insight meditation (Vipassana)," even though that's the truth. Sometimes, however, I have the personal need to privately unpack these labels which usually blend seamlessly in my daily life in order to get a better sense of who I am and where I'm going on this spiritual journey.

My degree is in education with a specialization in life and earth sciences. How does my love of science fit into my spiritual life? While I've always been a Pagan at heart (but didn't realize it), I discovered I was a scientific pantheist first. I won't go into all the details of what scientific pantheists believe (for more information you can visit pantheism.net), but in short I have a deep reverence for the universe and believe that science can ultimately explain all phenomena within it. Until that happens, there are many mysteries I can't explain, but I don't believe they are caused by supernatural forces. I believe there are forces and events that are nothing short of miraculous in human terms, but I feel that they are all part of the natural system of our cosmos, that they all obey standard laws of biology and physics, and that we just still have a long way to go in some cases to define these laws. I believe that many of the things we do and do not understand are completely deserving of our awe. Both of the *Cosmos* television series serve as an excellent documentary of what it is I believe as a scientific pantheist.

But then how can I be a Pagan? Don't all Pagans believe in supernatural forces? A brief exploration with Google shows that this isn't the case. Most probably do, and I have nothing but respect for those who do. As an earth-centered Pagan, however, I believe that the universe is worthy in and of itself to be worshiped and honored in my rituals. Science, as the system I trust to explain the universe, is a great tool for shaping and enabling this worship. But it doesn't fulfill my need to interact with the things I don't understand and which sometimes bring about deep emotions and moving mental states. Ceremony and ritual help me meet that personal requirement, and I find that Pagan rituals do so best of all.

When I first participated with the women's Pagan circle at my UU fellowship, I was somewhat uncomfortable using the words "goddess" and "spirits." I've since come to associate the forces and conditions of the universe that science cannot yet explain with those terms. To me, these words are just as good as any others in naming that which cannot (yet) be named. There are also a lot of people who believe that we can be one with, if not the same as, "God" or "Goddess." My spiritual nature can identify with the creativity, love, and sense of power so often attributed to supernatural beings—not that I consider myself to be above others in any way. So I've lost most of the wariness I once had for such terms. When I hear others using them, I often find myself thinking of science promoter Adam Savage's words, "I reject your reality and substitute my own." But this is something all thinking spiritual people do as they evolve.

In the end, I don't feel any kind of disconnect between my love of science and my love of and reverence for nature. And maybe someday I'll drop all the labels I've given to myself and just consider my spiritual beliefs to be what they are. In the meantime, I find them helpful in mapping out just what it is I do and do not believe, and that's an excellent way to continue propelling myself down my own path.

## Are the Gods Natural?
## by B. T. Newberg

Gods, ghosts, spirits, and magic—are these supernatural? Nine out of ten Americans would likely say "yes." And yet Pagans defy the norm.

"No," we Pagans say, *"Our* gods are natural." Is this a joke? A semantic game? A gimmick to get a "100% natural" label on the bottle? What do we Pagans mean when we say our gods are natural?

### Natural and Supernatural

*natural* (adj) : of, relating to, or operating in the physical as opposed to the spiritual world.

*supernatural* (adj) : of or relating to an order of existence beyond the visible observable universe; especially: of or relating to God or a god, demigod, spirit, or devil.

(Merriam-Webster Online Dictionary, 2011)

According to the definitions above, the "natural" is identified as that which is of the observable, physical universe, while the "supernatural" belongs to a realm beyond that. These conventional definitions, however, don't sit well with many Pagans, as we'll soon see.

When a Pagan invokes a storm god in hopes of bringing rain that certainly sounds like a supernatural proposition by normal standards. But many a Pagan would argue that the gods are part of nature, we have a natural ability to communicate with them, and the whole process of producing rain in this way is no more unnatural than any other technology.

Margot Adler (1986) observes in her classic review of Neo-Paganism, *Drawing Down the Moon*, "this naturalistic definition of magic...is common in one form or another" across the Pagan spectrum. In my experience, this is true also of attitudes toward gods.

But you have to admit: calling on gods certainly *seems* supernatural. So what do we mean when we say it isn't? How can our gods possibly be natural? Three things must be understood before this claim begins to make any sense.

## Nature Religion

The first thing to understand is that Pagans are children of Nature with a capital "N." Earth-centered spirituality is our life-blood. Like followers of Shinto, Taoism, and other indigenous faiths, Pagans practice nature religion. The Goddess and the Horned God of Wicca intertwine with the cycles of nature, and the deities of Polytheist pantheons burst from land, sky, and sea. Given this, it would hardly be fitting for Pagan gods to be called supernatural. They are not above, beyond, or outside nature. No, they emerge from the very heart of it.

Some of us go even further to say the gods *are* nature. The whollyimmanent view of deity sees no distinction between the natural universe and the divine. The universe is the divine, and the divine is the universe. The Stoics of ancient Greece and Rome held this view, as did Spinoza in the Renaissance. Humanistic Pagans and Pantheists do the same today. In the wholly-immanent view, gods are certainly not supernatural by any definition.

Yet the majority of Pagans, I would hazard to guess, feel that the gods are both immanent and transcendent (e.g., Starhawk, 1979, as judged by Cooper, 2006).[1] In other words, there is some part of the divine that goes beyond the empirical universe revealed by the five senses. It goes beyond the observable, physical universe described in Merriam-Webster's definitions. Beyond what the most powerful telescopes and microscopes can detect is something else—a spiritual energy transcending matter. How can this part be natural? Isn't this *by definition* supernatural?

## The Undiscovered Science

This brings us to the second thing that must be understood. Many Pagans feel they work on the edges of science, embracing it, but pushing the envelope of what is currently accepted. Gods are natural, they say; science just hasn't discovered them yet. In a similar vein, Isaac Bonewits calls magic an art and a science that "deals with a body of knowledge that, for one reason or another, has not yet been fully investigated or confirmed by the other arts and sciences" (Bonewits, 1979).[2] The concept of the undiscovered science serves to justify the claim of Pagans that the objects of their belief are indeed natural. One day, science will vindicate that claim. Till then, the burden of proof is postponed.

## Convenient Ambiguity

The third and final thing that needs to be acknowledged is that Pagans are comfortable with ambiguity. Are the gods natural or supernatural? "I don't know" is a perfectly acceptable answer. Unlike creedal religions, Paganism places emphasis on practice, not beliefs. This allows Pagans to remain open to speculation and even day-to-day re-evaluation of beliefs. "I'm an atheist on Tuesdays and Thursdays" is a joke you might hear. This ambiguity of belief allows one to interpret the gods according to scientific naturalism one moment and spiritual transcendence the next. According to Luhrmann (1989), it allows the newcomer a long period of trial and experimentation without committing to any specific beliefs.[3]

So, deities can be considered "natural" because anything not immediately fitting that description can simply be stamped "pending review." Ambiguity allows claims to be advanced by way of hypothesis, without binding the person to the claim.

These three things—nature religion, undiscovered science, and ambiguity—help us understand the Pagan claim that god, ghosts, and magic are natural, and *not* supernatural.

## But "natural"? Really?

Yet the skeptic may not be persuaded. Are these arguments satisfying? Or are they just apologetics, rationalizations that *explain away* what really ought to be considered supernatural? Let's investigate them one by one, starting with the last.

The notion of ambiguity appears on first sight to be nothing more than intellectual laziness. However, there's more to it than that. Pyrrhonian Skepticism, one of the great philosophies of Classical Greece, proposes that in the absence of compelling evidence for or against a proposition, the rational thing to do is to carry on in the spirit of inquiry. So, if there isn't enough hard evidence gathered yet to prove or rule out the existence of gods in the natural world, the smartest thing really is to admit, "I don't know."

However, there is a key provision in the Pyrrhonist principle: "and carry on in the spirit of inquiry." That is to say, we shouldn't stop at "I don't know." We should be looking for the necessary evidence.

That leads us right into the notion of the undiscovered science. This argument seems justifiable on the face of it, but may in fact be less than genuine. There have been numerous instances of fringe theories later vindicated by evidence in the eyes of Western science—chiropractics is one, and acupuncture appears set to become another. So, why not believe science will eventually discover magic, energy, and gods lurking in the natural universe too? Why not hope that quantum theory or chaos theory or whatever else will eventually prove it all true?

The simple answer is, if we really believe that will happen, then why aren't we *making* it happen? If mainstream scientists don't take our claims seriously, then why aren't we doing the work ourselves? I know a lot of Pagans, but I don't know any yet who are seriously trying to make the undiscovered science discovered. If they're out there, I would very much like to meet them. (Seriously, I could be way off, so please let me know!)

Suffice to say that I have not yet heard debates about the best methodologies that minimize bias, attempts to formulate falsifiable hypotheses, or experiments designed to decide between two competing theories.

That's what is expected from a scientific community, so why aren't we doing that? It makes me suspect even Pagans do not take the undiscovered science claim seriously. Until we develop rigorous methods to prove our claim that our gods are natural, it seems disingenuous to place much stock in the undiscovered science argument.

That leaves us with the argument of nature religion: Pagan gods can't be supernatural because it just wouldn't be fitting. They emerge out of nature, so they must be natural, plain and simple. We define nature to include gods. This leaves a relativistic taste in one's mouth. Non-Pagans may as well say, "Okay, I get why you say your gods are part of nature, but just the same, what you call natural I'd call supernatural."

Ultimately, the Pagan claim that our gods are natural remains on shaky ground. It is not indefensible, but not particularly compelling either.

### Toward truly natural gods…

The claim could be made completely compelling in an instant. If we adopt a wholly-immanent view, where the gods are identical with the natural universe or aspects of it, the controversy melts away. Whether the gods are seen as archetypes, metaphors, cultural traditions, or some other aspect of the observable, physical universe, the issue is resolved. There's nothing supernatural about these things; they're perfectly natural by any definition. They may not support the effectiveness of magic, but that's another issue that can be settled by scientific experimentation. On the whole, the view of immanence easily renders the gods natural.

So why don't more Pagans take this view? Why do the majority today insist that gods are natural when they really seem quite supernatural? In a sense, Pagans want to have it both ways. They want to have a religion of the natural, but they also want to have the numinous feeling of the supernatural.

At this point, I refer to the nascent work of John Halstead (2011).[4] In his view, the crux of the matter lies in a fear of losing the numinous. Identifying gods as archetypes threatens to reduce them to "just" archetypes. This is why Pagans, after flirting with archetypes for some time, have begun to turn their back on them. We don't want our gods to become mere things, mere mental stuff. As archetypes, the gods are no longer godlike. Their "numinousness" is lost.

The same argument could be made for gods as metaphors or cultural traditions. However you frame it, the mystery is lost. The gods become known quantities.

But it doesn't have to be that way. What we need to do, according to Halstead, is "re-god" the archetypes. We need to recognize the power, the *mysterium tremendem*, of these natural forces. We need to feel the god in them. Then we can have a natural religion of the numinous, without resorting to the quasi-supernatural.

Can we learn to see the awesomeness of archetypes, the mystery of metaphors, and the *tremendem* of traditions? And what of the sun, moon, and seas? Are they not godlike enough just as they are, without us granting them quasi-supernatural powers? Can we accept our gods as both fully natural and fully godlike?

Paganism is supposedly nature religion. Our gods ought to be natural, right? We claim so.

But until we can feel the gods in nature without making them supernatural, that claim remains in jeopardy.

### Notes

1. Adler, M. (1986). *Drawing Down the Moon*. New York: Penguin.

2. Bonewits, I. (1979). *Real Magic*. Berkeley, CA: Creative Arts Book Co.

3. Luhrmann, T. M. (1989). *Persuasions of the Witch's Craft*. Cambridge, MA: Harvard University Press.

4. Halstead, J. (2011). "The Archetypes Are Gods: Re-godding the Archetypes." Retrieved Nov. 9, 2014, from: HumanisticPaganism.com.

*Author's Note: This was among my first essays, published at The Witch's Voice at the inception of HumanisticPaganism.com, and bears the stamp of an earlier and perhaps less-mature voice. The "we" referred to is the larger Pagan community.*

# What Does It Mean for the Gods to Exist?
## by Tom Swiss

### Pagan Atheist???

I have been confidently identifying myself both as an "atheist" and a "Pagan" (among other labels) since at least 1997. Maybe longer, but that's as far back in my e-mail archives that I can find myself stating it explicitly.

In the spaces that I frequented in those days, it was not a controversial stance. My real-world Pagan community was my own eclectic circle where we had Christo-Pagans and self-initiated Wiccans and folks into Druid stuff and I was throwing in bits of Taoism and Zen—who was going to argue?

On-line, we had the net, but the web hadn't become a big thing yet. Most of us were still on dial-up, and blogs were still years away. We didn't even have Myspace yet, let alone Facebook and Twitter. USENET newsgroups and private mailing lists were where the important discussions happened, and regularly posted FAQ ("Frequently Asked Questions") documents were important works of the on-line culture.

And that culture was still weighted towards programmers, engineers, and scientists. We were still griping about "The September That Never Ended," when AOL suddenly let a bunch of non-technical people into our party.

So the "Frequently Asked Questions about Neopaganism" written by hacker Eric S. Raymond had some authority with on-line Pagans. It stated: "[M]any neopagans are philosophical agnostics or even atheists; there is a tendency to regard `the gods' as Jungian archetypes or otherwise in some sense created by and dependent on human belief, and thus naturally plural and observer-dependent" (Raymond, 1992).

(Raymond—or ESR, as we hackers know him—was a Wiccan priest at one point, and also a devotee of Zen, so his 1995 essay-length spiritual autobiography, "Dancing With the Gods," is an *excellent* read for Zen Pagans. Unfortunately he sort of went nuts after 9/11, falling into paranoid conspiracy theories, Islamophobia, and climate change denialism; my citation of his older work here is most definitely not an endorsement of this more recent batshit craziness. May he be healed.)

I got no push-back on my "Pagan atheist" identification more severe than an occasional raised eyebrow—and even those mostly came from Christians upset at my double heresy.

"Pagan" and "atheist" have both been part of my presenter bio for about thirty-five events (counting each year's edition of annual ones separately) spread over a decade and a half now. Neither the Pagan Police nor Atheist Agents have yet come to take me away.

I don't know if times are changing, or if it's an east coast/west coast thing, or something that's mostly in the Pagan blogosphere. Or maybe also including "Zen" and "Taoist" and "Discordian" in that bio have made me seem non-threatening to people, so I haven't been drawn into the conflict. But when I made it out to PantheaCon recently and heard from such prominent atheist/humanist Pagan bloggers as Mark Green (of Atheopaganism fame) and John Halstead (The Allergic Pagan at Patheos), I was surprised at some of the travails they related, people telling Pagan atheists that they are not valid Pagans.

In fact the intersection of atheism and Neo-Paganism goes back centuries. One root of the Neo-Pagan movement was the poetry of British Romantics. Percy Bysshe Shelley was part of a social set that sought a replacement for Christianity and helped shape our Neo-Pagan notions of the deities; he wrote of the "Sacred goddess, Mother Earth / Thou from whose immortal bosom / Gods and men and beasts have birth", and once raised an altar to Pan and wrote of such worship as the "true religion" (Hutton). But he was also a devoted amateur scientist and was expelled from Oxford for writing a tract titled "The Necessity of Atheism."(He was also a vegetarian and an anarchist. I love this guy!)

As happy as I was to meet some other atheist Pagans, I was struck by something about the language that Mark Green uses. He speaks of a distinction between "believing...gods to exist in a literal sense" and seeing them as "meaningful metaphors" (Green). With all respect to Mark, I think that doesn't quite catch it. Metaphor is a literary device; it's something that we recognize intellectually. It seems to me weak tea for discussing the Shining Ones.

I think we need to look deeper and do some philosophy. To answer the question "Do the deities exist?" we need to answer two questions, just two trivial little matters:

*What is a god?*

*What does it mean to exist?*

We have here two fundamental questions of theology and ontology that have had philosophers quibbling for thousands of years.

So, what the heck, there's already so much gibberish on these topics that I don't think I can make the problem any worse!

## Super-Kings with Special Substance

Imagine that we could grab a sample of typical citizens off the streets of various civilizations throughout history, from the Sumerians to today, and quiz them about ontology—the branch of philosophy that studies existence. I think we would get a naïve sort of realism. This brick? It exists, our subject replies, what a stupid question. The unicorn that the town drunk said he saw behind the tavern? It does not exist, it's a fiction or a delusion or a lie. A good story, though, the bit about that unicorn and the blacksmith's daughter is true, even if it's not, you know, "factual." The number three? It exists—see, I have three coins in my pocket. (You think I can't count or something?) People like you and me? Of course we exist; we're standing here talking to each other.

And if we also asked them about theology, if we asked them to describe the primary deity of their culture's pantheon, I think the picture that would emerge is that of a king but even more so—a super-king, a magic king. Indeed, in some cultures, a king could be promoted to godhood.

The idea of kings is central to the hierarchical social structure that has been with us since we became farmers and city-dwellers. Every citizen controls some bit of land, from the peasant's plot to the lord's realm; and each man has power over some number of people, from the head of the peasant household ruling his wife and children to the chief of the whole nation. The kings are the ones on the top of their various heaps, the ones who rule the most land and the most people.

And even though I'm a Zenarchist who looks forward to Universal Enlightenment and the subsequent abolition of the state, I have to acknowledge that a lot of people find that hierarchy very comforting. Someone is in charge. People can know their place in the social order.

But why stop there? It's an obvious extrapolation to follow that curve upward: there must be a ruler of the whole world and everything we see, the sun and the moon and the sea and the rains. It would take power far beyond what any mortal has to rule all that. Magic power. And this ruler would have a royal court, of course. There's your head deity and your pantheon.

And that heavenly king is comforting to a lot of people too. There is not just a social order, but a cosmological order. God is in his heaven and all's right with the world.

Even most citizens of the nominally democratic United States believe in the heavenly King of Kings—and we'll leave for another time the problematic implications of spiritual monarchy in a democracy. (The Athenians at least had Zeus's kingship of the gods be subject to limitations.)

The point I want to emphasize here is that there is a common and unsophisticated notion of deity which I think at least in part comes from projecting hierarchical social structure upwards. As below, so above.

And it's worth pointing out that only as that agricultural social structure has started to fall apart the past few centuries—starting with the humanism of the Renaissance and moving through the birth of modern science in the Enlightenment and the whole-scale social change of the Industrial Revolution—has atheism been able to find any sort of social opening. It would be interesting to trace the parallels between the rise of philosophical atheism and the rise of philosophical anarchism. Maybe as we're figuring out that we don't need kings on earth, we don't need them in heaven. Again, as below, so above.

Put this "common sense" ideas of deities and of existence together you get the gods—and goddesses, but let's be honest, the power dynamic in religion has historically been as sexist as it is in politics—as super-powered super-royalty. Kings (and Queens) and Princes of the Universe, Lords (and Ladies) of All, possessed of the power to bend and shape the world to their liking, as real and as independent of human beings as bricks are (at least according to our common sense), but made of a more rarefied sort of substance not subject to the constraints of normal matter.

Under that set of definitions, I confidently assert that reason leads us to conclude that no gods exist, that they are like the town drunk's unicorn: fiction, delusion, or lies, perhaps useful as metaphors, but not real. Not only that, but not being a big fan of kings, I'm downright glad to say that no such gods exist. Ha! I thumb my nose at the empty heavens!

But these are not the only notions of "realness" or of deity out there.

I want to look at some alternative ideas, but I want to be clear that I'm just pointing out a vast range of possibilities, not claiming that I have the True Understanding of the nature of existence and of the gods. (Not yet, at least.)

### What Does It Mean to Exist? Anatman...

Existence is a weirder thing than we think of in our day-to-day life. Let's consider for a moment the existence of a subject near and dear to my heart: me. According to the teachings of Buddhism, in a sense, I do not exist.

I don't mean that there's some conspiracy to present a fake author, or that everything we experience is a dream or a simulation à la *The Matrix*. The teaching called *anatman* (Sanskrit) or *anatta* (the Pali equivalent) says:

okay, your physical body exists, you have emotional reactions and senses like sight and hearing and touch and time, and you perceive the world and you have memory and intellect. But nowhere in these piles of stuff, these *skandhas*, is there a self that's separate from it all, an *atman* (Keown; Hanh). If you take me apart there's no self in there, any more than if you disassemble an old style mechanical watch you'll find the "watchness" in there somewhere.

The "watchness" of the watch exists only as a relationship of the pieces and of the external world—mostly the owner who keeps winding it and uses it to tell time, but also the watchmaker, the owner's wife who gave it to him as a gift, and so on. The "me-ness" of the thing we call by convention "Tom Swiss" exists only as a relationship of the pieces—body, memories, perceptions—and of the world, both physical and social. "Dependent arising," as the Buddhists say.

"I" exist only as a set of relationships that includes the food I eat, the air I breathe, the sunlight that powers the photosynthesis that makes all that possible; and also all the other humans with whom I participate in the social interaction that makes thought possible. (No interaction, no language; no language, no thought as we usually understand it.) The Zen teacher Thich Nhat Hanh often speaks of "interbeing" (Hanh).

It's like the punchline of a famous Mullah Nasrudin story: "I am here because of you, and you are here because of me" (Shah).

If "my" existence is so conditional on the world around me and on other people…what should we expect about the deities?

### …and the Ouija Board

And if that's a puzzler, consider for a moment the Ouija board. Or any sort of automatic writing controlled by more than one person at the same time, but Charles Kennard's good old "talking board" (a brand originally made in Baltimore, hometown pride) is probably familiar to American Pagan readers (McRobbie). Odds are good that you played around with one a little when you were a kid, or at least knew someone who did.

If you're using a Ouija board solo and holding a conversation with some sort of Other, from a skeptical perspective, it's easy to say that the Other is an aspect of your own subconscious mind, that you've worked yourself into a dissociative state. It's weird and tells us some interesting things about the mind, but doesn't bring up any ontological issues.

But if you've ever experimented with using one with a partner (or several people, a Ouija-à-trois) and you've been able to have some sort of sensible conservation with some sort of something…what was it?

If, as skeptical atheist types, we discount supernatural disembodied spirits, and if we assume our fellow Ouijaers weren't engaged in some conspiracy to fool us, what was on the other end of the line? It seems that these conversations were held with a mind whose physical correlate was not a single brain, but a shifting collection of the neurons of two or more brains, linked not only by the usual synapses but by non-conscious verbal and non-verbal communication between the people holding the planchette. A weak sort of group mind—"weak" in the sense of not absorbing the participants. Not a mob, not a Borg.

I don't mean that this "group mind" is anything supernatural or paranormal or telepathic, just more subtle than we usually encounter.

So, consider: what sort of weak group minds might arise in the subconscious minds of an entire society over a long time? Could the right sort of ritual function as a talking board to let them communicate?

## And What About Numbers?

When we asked our hypothetical typical citizens about the existence of various things, we went from bricks to numbers to people. The discussion of anatman and group minds shows us that the question of the existence of personal "selves" is blurrier than we thought, but surely we can put our faith in the existence of numbers. Mathematics is the purest of the sciences. Right?

Actually, there is a long-standing debate here.

In general philosophy, there are two sides (more or less, not counting some fringe positions) on the question of the reality of abstracts. There are the Platonists who take the position attributed to Plato, that abstract ideals exist, that in addition to (for example) coins existing, there also exists the universal of circularity, which exists independently (Hawton). And there are Nominalists like Thomas Hobbes (Duncan) and John Locke (Hawton) who believe that what exists are particulars, and that general, universal terms are just convenient names.

The debate found its way into mathematics in the 20th century, and so we have Platonists, who argue that numbers and the other entities of mathematics objects really exist, though they do so outside of space and time; and Nominalists who say that numbers are just conventions of thought or language, not real things (Bueno). It's important to understand that this is a contemporary controversy, not something belonging to medieval times or classical antiquity.

If we can't agree on whether numbers exist, how can we say anything about the gods?

### And What About the Brick?

Well, numbers are for egghead mathematicians anyway. At least we can say with 100% solid certainty that the brick is real. Right?

Well…

Richard Feynman was one of the most brilliant minds of the 20th century, a Nobel prize winning physicist often said to be the greatest mind since Einstein. He was a man of broad curiosity, and as a graduate student tried to see how far he could get in various fields. He once dropped by a seminar on Alfred North Whitehead's *Process and Reality*, where the students were discussing the idea of an "essential object." The professor asked Feynman whether an electron was an essential object, but Feynman hadn't read the book and had no more idea what an essential object is than I do.

So Feynman asked the philosophy students, "Is a brick an essential object?" He explained:

> "What I had intended to do was to find out whether they thought theoretical constructs were essential objects. The electron

is a theory that we use; it is so useful in understanding the way nature works that we can almost call it real. I wanted to make the idea of a theory clear by analogy. In the case of the brick, my next question was going to be, 'What about the inside of the brick?' and I would then point out that no one has ever seen the inside of a brick. Every time you break the brick, you only see the surface. That the brick has an inside is a simple theory which helps us understand things better. The theory of electrons is analogous. So I began by asking, 'Is a brick an essential object?'" (Feynman)

Here we have a Nobel Prize winning physicist saying that we can *almost*, but not quite, call electrons real. And saying the same thing about the inside of a brick. According to Feynman, both are theoretical constructs which should be distinguished from reality.

(The philosophy students, as in all good stories about philosophers, proceeded to vigorously disagree and could reach no conclusion on whether a brick was an essential object.)

If we can't agree that bricks are entirely real, what do you want from the gods?

## Questions Need Context

My own answer to this puzzle is contextualism: we can only say that a thing "exists" in a certain context. There is apparently a philosophical name for this (what a disappointment to learn that I'm not the first to think of it!): "ontological anti-realism."

Philosopher David Chalmers has an explanation of that, but first hang tight for some philosophical jargon that we'll need to decode it.

Ontology is the branch of philosophy that deals with what exists. An ontologist is one who practices ontology. A metaontologist, then, is one who gets meta- about ontology and tries to figure out what system (if any) of ontology we ought to use.

We discussed the distinction between Platonists and Nominalists a few paragraphs back when we asked if numbers are real. Platonists say abstract ideals are really real; Nominalists say they're just convenient names.

Mereology is the branch of ontology that deals with the relationships between parts and the wholes that they form. "Mereological sum" means (informally) a whole formed by combining two parts (Varzi). Mereological universalists say that if you take any two things and put them together, you really have a new thing; mereological nihilists say that only the most basic building blocks really exist (Sider).

With that, we can handle Chalmers's explanation:

> "For example, the ontologist may ask: Do numbers exist? The Platonist says yes, and the nominalist says no. The metaontologist may ask: is there an objective fact of the matter about whether numbers exist? The ontological realist says yes, and the ontological anti-realist says no.
>
> "Likewise, the ontologist may ask: Given two distinct entities, when does a mereological sum of those entities exist? The universalist says always, while the nihilist says never. The metaontologist may ask: is there an objective fact of the matter about whether the mereological sum of two distinct entities exists? The ontological realist says yes, and the ontological anti-realist says no…
>
> "Ontological anti-realism is often traced to Carnap (1950), who held that there are many different ontological frameworks, holding that different sorts of entities exist, and that while some frameworks may be more useful than others for some purposes, there is no fact of the matter as to which framework is correct." (Chalmers)

So to deal properly with the gods, perhaps we need several different ontological frameworks. Or "reality tunnels," as Robert Anton Wilson would have called them (Wilson). When we ask "Do the gods exist," we have to ask, "In what framework? In what context?"

Within a ritual, the gods invoked exist—not as metaphors, but in the same way that Hamlet exists during a staging of the play that bears his name. If your Hamlet is only a metaphor, I don't think your play will be very good.

But if I'm working out a physics or engineering or programming problem, or trying to understand a biological process, the gods do not exist.

The gods do not exist when I make my personal budget, and praying to them won't help my checking account, as much as I could use a miracle. But when I try to figure out how to lead my life along lines that bring prosperity to all, maybe I could use a little divine guidance.

If I am doing healing work and the person I'm working on wants me to pray for them—their gods exist. For purposes of that work, I'm a believer, and I will call upon whatever deities work for them: "I am of all faiths in my fashion," as Neil Gaiman's Morpheus remarked.

On the other hand, when I found myself doing CPR on a friend (he's fine now), while I was deeply aware of the gravitas and even the "energetics" of the moment, of the intimacy of my lungs being the breath of life for another, I was not praying. Reductionist biomedicine was the call of the moment.

But when I went to Japan a few days later, while he was still in a coma, I made it a point to visit a temple of the Medicine Buddha and pay my respects. Not because I thought Yakushi is a super-king who could reach out from some other dimension to heal my friend, but because it seemed the aesthetically best thing to do; and because doing so could change my own mind a bit, and telling others about it could change their minds just a bit, and so create a change in our actions: the subtle way that magic works to produce change in the world. And it's natural (in the sense that our brains are wired for it) for us to put a human-like face on that subtle flow of attention, intention, and energy—a flow that exists as more than metaphor.

Some might call this approach cowardly or wishy-washy, but I like to think of it as abandoning a futile quest for a non-existent singular, ultimate, and final truth.

I believe that we can keep multiple views, and build a sort of "depth perception" that can give us a much richer life. I'm an atheist and I'm also a Pagan, and there's no more conflict here than between my right eye and my left eye.

## References

"#1054: Eric S. Raymond." *Encyclopedia of American loons*. 24 May 2014. http://americanloons.blogspot.com/2014/05/1054-eric-s-raymond.html

Bueno, Otávio, "Nominalism in the Philosophy of Mathematics," *The Stanford Encyclopedia of Philosophy* (Spring 2014 Edition), Edward N. Zalta (ed.), http://plato.stanford.edu/archives/spr2014/entries/nominalism-mathematics/.

Chalmers, David J., David Manley, and Ryan Wasserman. *Metametaphysics: New Essays on the Foundations of Ontology*. Oxford New York: Clarendon Press, 2009. https://books.google.com/books?id=6nqzIi16CY0C&pg=PA77

Duncan, Stewart. "Thomas Hobbes," *The Stanford Encyclopedia of Philosophy* (Summer 2013 Edition), Edward N. Zalta (ed.), http://plato.stanford.edu/archives/sum2013/entries/hobbes/#2.3.

"Eric S. Raymond." *RationalWiki*. 9 Feb 2015. http://rationalwiki.org/w/index.php?title=Eric_S._Raymond&oldid=1421750

Feynman, Richard P. and Ralph Leighton. *"Surely You're Joking, Mr. Feynman!": Adventures of a Curious Character* New York: W. W. Norton & Company, 2010. https://books.google.com/books?id=7papZR4oVssC&pg=PA70

Gaiman, Neil. "Ramadan." *The Sandman: Fables and Reflections*. New York: DC Comics, 1993.

Green, Mark. "Why Atheopaganism?" https://atheopaganism.wordpress.com/atheopaganism/ (as of 24 Feb 2015)

Hanh, Nhat, and Peter Levitt. *The Heart of Understanding*. Berkeley, Calif: Parallax Press, 1988.

Hawton, Hector. *Philosophy For Pleasure*. New York: Philosophical Library, 1949.

Keown, Damien, and Charles S. Prebish. *Encyclopedia of Buddhism*. New York: Routledge, 2007. https://books.google.com/books?id=D1pcAgAAQBAJ&pg=PT734

McRobbie, Linda Rodriguez. "The Strange and Mysterious History of the Ouija Board." *Smithsonian.com* 27 Oct 2013. http://www.smithsonianmag.com/history/the-strange-and-mysterious-history-of-the-ouija-board-5860627/

Raymond, Eric S. "Dancing With The Gods." 10 Jul 1995. http://www.catb.org/~esr/writings/dancing.html

Raymond, Eric S. "Frequently Asked Questions about Neopaganism." Version 4.0, 1992. http://catb.org/~esr/faqs/paganism.txt, originally posted to USENET groups talk.religion, talk.religion.newage, alt.pagan, news.answers.

Raymond, Eric S. "Why We Fight—An Anti-Idiotarian Manifesto (2.0)." 26 December 2003. http://www.catb.org/~esr/aim/

Shah, Idries. *The Exploits of the Incomparable Mulla Nasrudin*. London: Octagon, 1983. https://books.google.com/books?id=czZufrUnl0wC&pg=PA2

Shelley, Percy Bysshe. "Song of Proserpine While Gathering Flowers on the Plain of Enna." In Hutchinson, Thomas ed., *The Complete Poetical Works of Percy Bysshe Shelley Oxford edition*, 1914. https://ebooks.adelaide.edu.au/s/shelley/percy_bysshe/s54cp/volume25.html#section213

Sider, Theodore. "Against Parthood." In Karen Bennett and Dean W. Zimmerman, eds., *Oxford Studies in Metaphysics*, volume 8, 237-293. Oxford: OUP, 2013. http://tedsider.org/papers/nihilism.pdf

Varzi, Achille. "Mereology," *The Stanford Encyclopedia of Philosophy* (Spring 2015 Edition), Edward N. Zalta (ed.), forthcoming at http://plato.stanford.edu/archives/spr2015/entries/mereology/ (current URL http://plato.stanford.edu/entries/mereology/ as of 24 Feb 2015)

Wilson, Robert A. *Cosmic trigger : Final Secret of the Illuminati*. Tempe, Ariz: New Falcon, 1993.

## The Revelation of an Uncaring God
### by Scott Oden

I have never had a supernatural experience.

I have never seen a ghost, a spirit, a wraith, or a shade.

I have never witnessed an inexplicable omen.

I have never heard the voice of a god.

When I look at the list above and compare it to the experiences of other Pagans, it makes me wonder what's wrong with me. Am I not doing it right, this faith thing? Do the Gods have no use for me whatsoever, and thus have cut themselves off from me? Did the faith centers in my brain never fully develop? Am I blind to the Gods? Can I not perceive them because my own prejudices get in the way? Do I expect too much from the Divine?

The search for answers to these questions and myriad more like them is what brought me into the sphere of Humanistic Paganism and introduced me to the writings of Humanistic Pagans like John Halstead, where I first encountered a wonderful phrase: "the god box." Far from a negative connotation, I translated this as the space inside a person's head where they perceive the Divine, where they hear and understand the unique voices of the Gods, where they see them in their mind's eye, and where their faith is first given expression. Exploring this notion led me to make a rather predictable discovery: my own god box is empty.

This came as no shock to me. I've always wanted to live under the aegis of a divine pantheon rich with antiquity, to lead a life brimming with mystery and myth drawn from the great spiritual literature of the ancients, from writers like Homer and Hesiod and Sallustius. I've always wanted a cacophony of Divine voices that drove me to the heights of ecstatic madness and filled me with that unbreakable, resolute belief that only the truly faithful can possess.

But that's not what I have. No, that space inside my head where some sense of the Divine resides is empty, nothing but errant cobwebs and dust. I could blame time and location—I am a 21st century American living in a fully Christianized country—or perhaps I could blame my mindset, which is not agrarian, tribal, or yoked to the unknown whims of Nature, but rather is mechanized, urban, and electronic. I think, though, that blame for the emptiness I feel must surely fall squarely on my own perception of reality.

Reality, by which I mean the physical world that exists outside my own head, is where my faith stumbles. I am not bereft of imagination. I write historical fiction and fantasy for a living, and writing is a field that places a high premium on imagination. And while I can imagine all manner of strange and supernatural happenings, there is a great gulf between imagining something and believing that it truly exists in the physical realm.

I can imagine thunder as the wrath of Zeus given voice and offer a sacrifice to propitiate Him, but outside of my imagination I know thunder is nothing more than a sound caused by lightning—itself a complex series of naturally-occurring factors that meld to create an electrostatic discharge. I can fill the divine spaces inside my consciousness with poetic imagery of Zeus in all His multi-faceted glory, drawn from the myths of the ancient Greeks and the writings of the Romantic authors; I can pour libations and ask for divine favor as thunder roars and crashes overhead, but if thunder is merely Nature being Nature and Zeus exists only in my head, am I not, then, simply worshiping a voice in my own subconscious?

It is because I am a writer by trade that I don't credit the voices in my head with divinity, even if there is a great deal of mystery as to how some of those voices got there and from whence they originate. The same goes with some of the imagery I get. One of my strong points, if you believe reviews, is the ability to conjure a place or a time. I could say it's a mystery, that the hand of some God moves me to write of these things I've never seen, of times I've never lived. But that would be disingenuous. I can conjure place and time because I read voraciously about those places and times, and have the good fortune of being capable of relating an image formed of research in a concise and engaging manner. And if I really examine them, most of the voices have their genesis in real-world connections, such as something I see on the street or read in a book. Some, especially the voices of protagonists, are subtle (and not-so-subtle) forms of wish fulfillment: I am not a man of action, so I tend to gravitate toward characters that are exactly that.

What am I, then? An atheist? No, I think not. I have faith that there is something god-like and divine in the cosmos, something greater than me. I used to self-identify as an agnostic, but agnosticism is an unfulfilling stance for someone who desperately wants to experience the Divine.

I was a Hellenic Reconstructionist for a time, but I could never get over the idea that the gods of Hellas behaved in exactly the same manner as the Christian god: because they move in mysterious ways, they can only contact mere mortals via wholly unverifiable moments of personal gnosis or through the most subtle of clues and omens. Was that voice Hermes? Was that swirling zephyr a sign from Apollo? As you might imagine, my tenure as a Hellene ended with me standing in a violent, lightning-laced thunderstorm, daring Zeus to strike me down. He didn't, and that only added more questions to my already burgeoning list.

No, I am a Pagan, and my brand of Paganism is a very simplified form of pantheism. I arrived at this after searching for gods in the physical world, for sources of the Divine that existed as more than subconscious voices and subtle omens. I came up with three: the Sun, the Earth itself, and Inspiration. Sol Invictus, Gaia, and the Muses, if you will. Sol Invictus gives life; he creates a synergy with Gaia to create food, water, and shelter; and the Muses give us a needed push in the right direction to populate the world with science, art, drama, and discourse. Representations of each of these three are as old as Humanity itself.

We've filled our god boxes with elaborate personalities and stories; we've crafted rituals and sacraments and offer sacrifices in hopes of gaining favor, but even if we do nothing, the sun will rise, the earth will turn, and ideas will pop unbidden into our heads. If humanity failed to sacrifice or to propitiate the mighty Sun, Sol Invictus would not withhold the bounty of his energy. He doesn't care.

This revelation brought with a weird dichotomy of feeling. On the one hand, there was a sense of absolute freedom from the rigors of attempting to please a divine force whose wishes and desires were forever hidden from mortal understanding; on the other, a profound sense of sadness—sadness in that I could go outside, tilt my face to heaven, and behold the theophany of a God who ultimately did not care if I worshiped Him or not.

John Halstead asked me once if I had a practice. I do not, not in the strictest sense, for in my belief there is no point to it. Instead, I offer thanks: to the Muses for their continued gifts, which makes my day job all the more easier; to Gaia, for Her gift of shelter and sustenance; and to Sol Invictus, for keeping the cold dark of oblivion at bay.

## The Wonder Amplifier
### by Dr. Jon Cleland Host

While intellectual ponderings were important in my path to Naturalistic Paganism, and these still play a major role, the intellect's interaction with wonder is a very, very big and compelling topic for me. Years ago, Dr. Richard Feynman was told he couldn't see beauty. As he explains:

> "I have a friend who's an artist and he's sometimes taken a view which I don't agree with very well. He'll hold up a flower and say, 'Look how beautiful it is,' and I'll agree, I think. And he says, 'You see, I as an artist can see how beautiful this is, but you, as a scientist, oh, take this all apart and it becomes a dull thing.'"

Dr. Feynman goes on to explain how he sees all the beauty in the flower that anyone else does, and that on top of that, he sees inside, imagining the networks in the petal, then down to the cells themselves, and the complex dance of the many intricate molecules working together, and then, even more! Behind all of that is the deep time history, the long process of evolution which—more than 100 million years ago, drew together insects and plants in mutually beneficial teamwork. He describes how he sees all of this, each level adding to the excitement, mystery, and awe of a simple flower! He concludes: "It only adds. I don't understand how it subtracts."

I know that rush. It's incredible. I see it unfold, level upon level, in the blink of an eye, time and again in my life, all around me. That tree, this rock, that cloud, a blue jay, this computer, and on and on! And that's not even getting into seeing other people. I can't imagine living without it, and for anyone who hasn't experienced it, it's indescribable. For someone to suggest to Dr. Feynman that he sees less beauty in a flower, when he sees so much more, just shows that this friend doesn't understand what knowledge can do. When I first read Feynman's flower story, it hit me: Here was someone who sees the world as I do, and experiences that beauty of so many things as I do! Wow, it works with other people too!

I caught glimpses of it in others too. Carl Sagan comes to mind. As does this quote from Charles Sherrington:

> "The brain is a sparkling field of rhythmic flashing points with trains of traveling sparks hurrying hither and thither. It is as if the Milky Way is engaging in a cosmic dance. The cortex is an enchanted loom where millions of flashing shuttles weave a dissolving pattern, always a meaningful pattern though never a lasting one; with a shifting harmony of entrancing subpatterns."

That's why I just simply don't get how anyone could suggest that a naturalistic worldview somehow decreases awe and wonder, when the opposite has been so true for me. Have they never learned anything about the things they see? For me, a naturalistic worldview, coupled with some knowledge, has taken my awe and wonder to undreamt-of levels, drawing from deep wells of spirituality that I hadn't known existed.

We just saw how someone could describe our brain as an "Enchanted Loom." How our brains work, on a basic level, isn't that hard to understand. We can start with our senses that feed into the brain. For instance, well understood cells in our eyes convert light into electrical pulses, sent along nerve cells to the brain. Nerve cells are also called neurons, and each has many long, thin branches connected to other neurons. It takes many electrical pulses from many neurons to cause another neuron to send its electrical pulse, which may then reach many other different neurons. A number of connected neurons make simple "logic gates," similar to those in computers. Many logic gates linked together can process information like a computer does. But how do they get connected the right way? Our genes, built by trillions of our Ancestors over millions of years of evolution, give us the starting structure, and our history builds the rest, ending up with trillions of neurons, and a hundred trillion connections between them!

The incredible realization here is that this shows how the mind works. These basic chemical reactions and electrical pulses, all working in milliseconds, make up your every thought, from "Where did I leave my keys?" to "Yes! I'll marry him!". I don't know about you, but I find that realization to be mind blowing. We are our brains, without a need for the idea visiting ghosts from some imagined supernatural realm. There are no disembodied "minds," and so any damage or chemical change to our brains affects (or even eliminates) our thoughts. My thoughts seem to me to be the essence of who I am. Yet, at the simplest level, they are undeniably made up of basic chemical reactions! And it's not just my brain that is this amazing, but your brain and his brain and her brain, too! We are surrounded by so many of these incredible thinking chemical, biological machines!

And what if we turn our gaze skyward? How can we conceive of the sheer awesomeness of our Sun? As a ball of plasma a million times bigger than the entire Earth, the sun is *not* a ball of fire—it's much too hot for even fire to exist! A few numbers can show us nature more clearly, and for a Naturalistic Pagan like me, practically everything about nature is spiritual.

How about power? The energy output of the Sun produces over 18 million times more energy in one second than the entire worldwide nuclear arsenal! Our local star produces that flood of energy by nuclear fusion, turning 370,000,000,000,000,000,000,000,000,000,000,000,000 (that's $3.7 \times 10^{38}$) hydrogen atoms into helium, which by Einstein's famous $E=mc^2$ equation, directly converts 4 million metric tons of matter into energy each second. If every grain of sand on Earth were instead several whole planet Earths, then the total number of grains of sand on all those millions of quadrillions of Earths would still be less than the number of hydrogen atoms fused every second by the Sun! And all that energy is only just barely enough to keep gravity at bay.

We could go on all day. It's truly mindbending. I find it even more mindbending to realize that all this energy has caused simple molecules on Earth to organize over millions of years to be able to build cities, sing whale songs, understand DNA, and even to love a new baby. Knowing these facts, and so many more, make it a wonder to be alive, and a joy to be part of our Universe.

Dionysian Bacchantes
Roman Terracotta plaque 27 B.C.–A.D. 68
(The Metropolitan Museum of Art)

## Part 3: Dancing With Dionysus: Emotion, Passion, and Mysticism

"Reason is great, but it is not everything. There are in the world things not of reason, but both below and above it; causes of emotion, which we cannot express, which we tend to worship, which we feel, perhaps, to be the precious elements in life. These things are Gods or forms of God: not fabulous immortal men, but 'Things which Are,' things utterly non-human and non-moral, which bring man bliss or tear his life to shreds without a break in their own serenity."

— Gilbert Murray, *A History of Ancient Greek Literature*

"Even under the influence of the narcotic draught, of which songs of all primitive men and peoples speak, or with the potent coming of spring that penetrates all nature with joy, these Dionysian emotions awake, and as they grow in intensity everything subjective vanishes into complete self-forgetfulness...There are some who, from obtuseness or lack of experience, turn away from such phenomena as from 'folk-diseases,' with contempt or pity born of consciousness of their own 'healthy-mindedness.' But of course such poor wretches have no idea how corpselike and ghostly their so-called 'healthy-mindedness' looks when the glowing life of the Dionysian revelers roars past them."

— Nietzsche, *The Birth of Tragedy*

"Why not just be atheist?" some Pagans might wonder. What does Paganism add to scientific naturalism? For some of us, it adds an emotional or aesthetic quality. It speaks to the parts of our being that a sterile rationalism and reductive materialism does not reach. Some religious naturalists find that humanism and science, while intellectually compelling, are emotionally or psychologically unsatisfying. They lack the symbolic resources of theistic religions, and Paganism is well-suited to fill that void.

On the other hand, contemporary Paganism can seem prone to irrationalism and superstition. Scientific naturalism can counter this tendency. Together, they balance each other. Naturalism can help keep Paganism true to the empirical world around us, while Paganism can enrich naturalism with symbolism and myth.

It's not uncommon to hear theists—Pagan and other—compare atheists or non-theists to people who are tone-deaf or color-blind. In some cases, this is intended, not as an insult, but as an attempt to defuse conflict. Nevertheless, it is inaccurate to suggest that non-theists are constitutionally incapable of seeing what is there to be seen.

Many atheists—including atheist Pagans—unwittingly play into this misperception when they respond to theists on the basis of reason and scientific evidence alone, leaving out their personal, subjective experience. Listening to many atheists, one would think they've never had a religious experience in their lives. Naturalistic Pagans often see themselves playing the role of the Apollonian counterbalance to the Dionysian excesses of contemporary Paganism, which can make it challenging for some of us to suspend disbelief when it is appropriate and to surrender to religious experience. As a result, theists (both mono- and poly-) can end up believing they have a corner on religious experience.

In spite of this, the fact is that non-theists do have numinous and mystical experiences, too. In fact, some non-theists have had experiences which are very similar, if not identical, to those of theists—they just have come to different conclusions about those experiences. Religious experiences do not occur in a vacuum; they are always interpreted from within the context of one's personal history and culture. This is true of the experiences of both theists and non-theists. The historically and culturally contingent nature of our religious experiences does not invalidate them— in fact, it is what gives them their meaning. But it may create the illusion that our religious experiences are more dissimilar than they really are.

When we get past all the interpretation and down to the pure phenomenological experience, we see that a theist and a non-theist may experience the same kinds of epiphanies and encounters. The difference is that the theist may interpret the experience as evidence of the reality of their god(s), while the non-theist may interpret it merely as evidence of the reality of a dimension of human experience different from ordinary waking consciousness. Thus, a Christian, a Pagan, and an atheist may have nearly identical experiences, but one of them will say they heard Jesus, the second will say they heard Zeus and the third will say they heard a voice. For all of them, the experience will be meaningful, but the meanings each attaches to the experience may differ.

## Emotional Pantheism:
## Where the Logic Ends and the Feelings Start
### by Áine Órga

**Logically, I am an atheist.**
**Emotionally, I am a pantheist.**

I am the kind of person who does not really *believe* in anything unless it can be empirically proven in some way. I do have a lot of scope for entertaining theoretical constructs that can be logically laid out—I have an imaginative analytical brain, and I love to theorise and philosophise. And certainly, not everything that is even self-evident can be properly accounted for empirically. The universe as we know it and experience it is not by any means fully understood. But although there are theological and philosophical theories and intangible concepts that excite me and are meaningful to me, I'm not sure that I could be said to *believe* in divinity in any real way.

But when it comes to how I resonate emotionally, I have very strong pantheistic feelings. Although I may not see divinity as something that can even be defined, let alone proven, I *feel* as though the universe is divine. It is not something I believe in the way that I believe in science and physics and the physicality of my day-to-day existence. But it is something that I feel at my very core. It is an emotional response to awe, to beauty, to mystery. And that emotional response is very strong in me.

### My spirituality is built on emotion.

I've come to the understanding that this emotion is what is most important to my spiritual practice. My need for ritual and a spiritual practice and belief is reinforced by my logic and intellect—the mysteries of the universe are certainly awe-inspiring to even the most sceptical. But its seed is in emotion, in an inherent response that is so natural as to be almost a reflex.

My beliefs and therefore my practice are certainly naturalistic. I leave room for the unexplained, and engage in practices that might seem empty or pointless to some naturalists or atheists. But I don't take many leaps of faith intellectually, everything is based in reason. In this way I am a naturalistic Pagan.

Where I do take those leaps of faith is in the emotional sphere. By engaging in this spiritual practice, I open myself up to experiencing things beyond the mundane. In many ways, it is in exercise in allowing myself to feel without judgment. My spirituality is my way of allowing my pantheism a space in my life.

## I have chosen to not choose between naturalism and theism.

I am aware of a certain amount of paradox within this spirituality that I am carving out for myself. I could be accused of being, illogically, a theistic atheist—of holding onto the two concepts or labels. As I've previously pointed out, the two are semantically opposed.

But I am comfortable with this duality within my personality and within my spirituality. I think sometimes we get too bogged down in trying to narrow ourselves into one particular fit—we try to pare away the inconsistencies in an effort to build up an ego that is simpler and less challenging. But we are too complex as individuals to ever hope to accomplish this. Paradoxes will always abound, and I'm learning that it's important to embrace the different facets of your personality, to incorporate it all into your life.

So when I perform ritual—when I light my altar candles and utter words of dedication and devotion—I am not merely marking a changing season or an astronomical event. I am, emotionally, reaching out to the divinity that I see in the Cosmos.

## Anatomy of a God
### by Alison Leigh Lilly

Theology is a tricky thing. It's no coincidence that the history of religion is just as full of heretics and apostates as it is of saints and theologians. Sometimes, it's almost impossible to tell which is which.

Imagine, for instance, the human body. Laid out on the table, splayed open, its skin peeled back, its heart exposed and raw. What does this valve do here? Well, nothing now. And this webbing of veins and arteries, furry with capillaries, rooted in flesh, wrapped around bone—now they are all limp with the loss of blood, deadly still and pale on the autopsy table. We imagine that when this body was alive, it quivered and thumped with the rushing pulse of life. We imagine that when this dead heart quickened at the sight of its beloved, a great deal might have happened within these dried up vessels.

This is the dilemma of theology, too. We want so very much to understand our gods, to know them intimately, to see how they work in our lives. It is tempting to dissect, to analyze, to categorize. And sometimes, it is necessary, even beneficial. We are categorizing creatures, we human beings. We pick out patterns as a matter of survival. When it comes to our gods, we reach for them not only with our prayers and offerings, but with our reason and our intellects—we would know them with our whole selves, in all their parts, in part so that we might know our own selves better in all *our* parts. The challenge is to delve into theology without killing its subject, to try our hand at analysis and critical thinking without pretending that the numinous divine is a dead thing that will hold still beneath our careful knives. Theology is not dissection. It is much more gruesome than that; it is vivisection.

For the natural polytheist, whose gods arise in and from the natural material world, this challenge is not even always a metaphor. Our gods not only have transcendent eyes and metaphysical hands. They have antlers and feathers, hooves and scales, fangs and horns and wings and fins and claws. They are in the lands we strip for veins of precious ore. They are in the waters we poison.

Natural polytheism has an intimate perspective on the uneasy tension between science and religion that plays out in much of modern culture. We have seen the harm that religion can do when it remains willfully ignorant of science, stubbornly clinging to antiquated stories about man's privileged place above a wild and dangerous nature. And we have seen the damage that science can do when it rejects the awe and reverence of religion, plunging forward with its drill bits and lab tests, reducing the world to a clean, neat set of variables to be controlled and manipulated. We know the history of exploitation and grisly experimentation that lies behind the scientific knowledge that we take for granted today, the many mistakes and missteps from which we had to learn hard lessons. But we also know the kind of future that lies ahead if we shy away from science in the face of a warming planet and the ever-creeping sludge of pollution.

How do we reconcile this tension?

For me, this is where ecology comes in. Ecology is a science of systems; but more than that, it is a science of *living* systems. Ecology bubbles over with messy, amazing life. It is a science so full of life that it sweeps even inanimate beings up in its wake. Take, for instance, biogeochemical cycles—the spiraling dance of carbon, nitrogen, phosphorus, sulfur and other life-giving substances through the environment—cycles that not only make life on the planet possible, but that incorporate life itself into their most basic processes. Unhindered, these cycles are self-organizing and self-sustaining.

For many Pagans and polytheists, the earth itself is a goddess: the Earth Mother, Mama Ge, the great Gaia who captured Lovelock's heart.

The science of ecology is, in one sense, a study of the Earth Mother's anatomy, her systems and their parts.

The tundra, the grassland, the forest, the ocean—the water cycle, the patterns of climate, the shifting pressures of tectonic plates—her biomes and ecosystems do not exist in isolation from each other, but work together and influence one another as part of a living whole. This is not a warm-fuzzy New Age philosophy. This is a scientific fact, acknowledged by ecologists all over the world.

For the natural polytheist who finds her gods in the rivers and mountains, in the deep-rooted giants looming above the canopy and in the tiny creatures that move beneath them, ecology gives us a glimpse into a kind of living anatomy of the divine, a theology of physical as well as spiritual life.

The challenge is not to reconcile the conflict between religion and science by reducing one to the other, but to hold them in tension in a way that sings. Can we see our gods on the operating table and do the work of analysis with humility and gratitude? Can we see our gods in the wending river and mourn the pollution that flows from upstream, and act to stop it? Can we embrace the best of science and the best of religion, and bear the weight of both?

I think the answer is yes. And I think the worldview articulated by natural (or what I sometimes call, ecological) polytheism can help us. [See Part 4.]

## Letting Go of the Side of the Pool
### by DT Strain

Many times the real essence of spiritually transformative experiences can be difficult to communicate. They involve glimpses of such things as: unconditional compassion, greater humility, extreme empathy, profound experience, a sense of the sacred, revelatory perspectives, and so on. Experiences with several ancient philosophical sources of wisdom and their sincerely applied practice can help to make us something closer to a "different kind of person" altogether.

But I was asked recently to write about what roadblocks might exist for some of us who come from secular humanist, skeptic, atheist, free-thought, and similar backgrounds. Sometimes our own tendencies can create a serious impediment to really exploring these practices properly. Here are some I can think of...

- Always looking at things from the third-person; seeking "objective" descriptions of everything, as though writing an anthropological research paper on it. This, as opposed to greater appreciation and immersion in first-person subjective experience. We cannot achieve greater subjective intuitive experience through greater objective intellectual knowledge alone. We are still holding on to the edge of the pool, scared to float.

- An outward socially/politically focused agenda and perspective, as opposed to an inward-looking focus on personal growth and development (which, incidentally, helps give a firmer foundation to social efforts).

- Talking/writing about the thing rather than putting it into practice (be it meditation or any other practice).

- Appreciating the role of metaphor merely in an intellectual sense, without ever really moving one's perspectives, responses, and feelings into that place.

- Trying to approach the matter in a step by step process, whereby we: (a) note the claims, (b) assess them empirically, (c) decide if they have merit, (d) engage in them, and (e) reap the benefits. Where experiential cultivation practices are concerned, this algorithm will never get us there. We will eternally be stuck on stage (b), as many of us indeed are. In Buddhist practices, for example, we could be an expert in every character of the Pali Canon and more written over the centuries and this would not even constitute the first step. We will never reach a point where we have assessed the practices and decided they are worthy to be engaged in—not fully and not to the extent that matters. This is because they are inherently subjective experiences. The way you investigate them is by engaging in them without reservation.

- The impulse to reject anything with the "taint" of religion upon it, either because of ourselves or because of our fear others might think we are religious.

- The effort to build something "alongside" or "other" than religion—instead of working to help the continued transformation of religion into a naturalistically compatible genuine path. This involves a completely bold and shameless use of their terms, imagery, practices, and manners of speech, whenever they are applicable—without apology. Not because of some effort to steal them—but because these terms convey honest feelings we have a right to and which illustrate the feelings we have about the awesomeness of reality. "a-" words and "non-" words and alternate clinical descriptions (alone) are—when it comes to the realm of spirituality—the "ghetto" of the English language, and we must aspire to better.

- A continuous drive to debunk, critique, or complain about others' beliefs—focusing on telling others what they ought to believe and do, rather than leading by living example.

- A failure to appreciate or trust the full power of universal and unconditional love, forgiveness, and compassion; a generally harsh demeanor instead of loving-kindness, and an underestimation of the importance of such a demeanor to one's well-being.

Many of us rationalists, Humanists, etc. who aim to approach naturalistic spirituality sit against the wall at the dance, talking with one another about the dancers out on the floor. We analyze their movements and critique their techniques. Then we speculate about the biological underpinnings of their enjoyment of the dance. We might even present studies on the neural correlates of dancing. We imagine that this discussion and knowledge somehow gets us closer to being good dancers or to sharing in that enjoyment. Then the lights come on, the party is over, and we go home completely failing to have ever danced or even understood what the experience of dance is like or how it really feels.

In the Houston chapter of the Spiritual Naturalist Society, we have covered topics like meditation, compassion, spiritual progress, awe/wonder, Taoism, Paganism, Buddhism, etc. I have found that many attendees love talking about "how it is" as if we are a bunch of aliens floating over Planet Earth, assessing the humans. But when I ask them to share their experiences, feelings, and how these practices affect their lives, I sense a resistance to "getting personal." The former kind of intellectualizing and rhetoric is not even a "lower level" of spiritual practice—it is another kind of thing altogether, and will not be sufficient to the practitioner.

There are other doors yet to be entered for many naturalists. And they must be if we are to truly heal the schism and reunite the natural and the sacred.

## Dancing with Dionysus: Ecstasy and Religion in the Age of the Anthropocene
### by Wayne Martin Mellinger, Ph.D.

My goal in this essay is to explore a form of "Godless Paganism" I refer to as Dionysian Naturalism—an approach to religion grounded in scientific evidence, but imbued with reverence and awe, and centered around spiritual ecstasy. It is an "earth-centered" spirituality which searches for sacred ways to experience altered states of consciousness. The importance of ecstatic experiences in religious behavior is highlighted, and I briefly mine the history of what has been called the "Western Mystery Tradition" (by Caitlin and John Matthews) for shamanic elements, mystical experiences, and consciousness-transforming practices to briefly summarize their "base elements." The interests of Dionysian Naturalists in reclaiming embodied ecstatic rituals is not just to infuse intense pleasure and passion into their religious lives. Through such mystical experiences, pre-established ways of seeing the world are dissolved, ego-less realms of becoming are entered, and spiritual connections with the natural world are greatly enhanced. These new-found spiritual connections with nature and fresh ways of thinking are essential if we are to develop sustainable ways of living on our planet as we enter the age of the Anthropocene.

### Sacred Journeys and the Western Mystery Traditions

Through years of deep study of the Western Mystery Traditions, I have identified some "base elements" in the "Sacred Journey", in which earlier Paleolithic shamanic practices become re-articulated and re-adapted through subsequent traditions, including the paganisms of the classical age (Greek, Roman, Celtic, Teutonic, Norse), Hermeticism, Alchemy, Medieval Witchcraft, as well as other "esoteric traditions." These base elements are also found within the Western Christian mystical traditions (Hildegard von Bingen, Saint Francis, Meister Eckhart). Broad parallels in the underlying structure of this formulation might be seen in such diverse traditions as Carl Jung's archetypical psychology, Joseph Campbell's Hero's Journey ( or "monomyth"), Ralph Metzner's Green Psychology, and Michael Harner's Core Shamanism, although important, substantive differences exist, which I won't discuss here due to space constraints. I believe these sacred practices are at the heart of nature religions, as they serve to make the natural world a sacred place and strengthen our spiritual connections to our planet.

## Base Elements of the Sacred Journey

(1) Individuals begin with an experience of psychological crisis verging on insanity. Included here might be intense feelings of isolation, fragmentation, nihilism, alienation and despair. In this state of misery, ego blocks intuition; attempts at healing, wellness, and wholeness are thwarted; and traditional ways of seeing prevent the new perspectives needed move forward or change. In this initial state, people often feel separated from the natural world and thirst for a unifying wholeness.

(2) Individuals participate in "Sacred Journey" in which they "travel" beyond the realms of their culture's pre-established and accepted ways of knowing, through an ecstatic state in which they reclaim a forgotten gnosis. This is a journey of death and re-birth, for the old Self shall die and a new Self will emerge. While physical pilgrimages to real places have long been essential forms of Sacred Journeys, other types of "travel" have equally long lineages. While many traditions in the Western Mystery Tradition see this journey as a literal voyage to another realm, for Religious Naturalists, the notion of a journey is more symbolic and denotes inner transformation more than actual travel to another place.

(3) All Sacred Journeys involve a change of consciousness. The techniques used to achieve such transformations are many, and might include the real-world trials and tribulations of a life lived, overcoming physical limitations through disciplined training, sensory deprivation, "shadow work" (in which psychological "demons" are confronted), entheogenic sacraments, mystical experiences, contemplative practices, or other trance-inducing methods. Some of these transformational processes may be virtually unmotivated and spontaneous, while others involve intensely motivated effort, arduous study, and greatly focused attention. Rejecting mind/body dualisms, I envision all these vision quests as involving the full human.

(4) These processes of non-ordinary states of consciousness dissolve the subjective mind, deflate the ego, and re-connect the human with nature. The outcome of these Sacred Journeys is a new way of viewing the world, other lifeforms and ourselves. Individuals enter a state of egoless becoming, personal integration, and transcendence. A universal vision, in which individuals experience themselves as part of ongoing humanity embedded in the very processes of creation, may also result.

(5) Having found their Holy Grail—a new way of seeing the world, a new and transcendent sense of identity, and new ways to bring healing to their community—individuals return to re-integrate into mundane social life with numerous gifts and forms of wisdom. The recovery of the numinous leads to a state of wholeness and health.

Humans have an innate need to alter states of consciousness. This need has evolved in our species over hundreds of thousands of years and serves evolutionary purposes. These purposes include the generation of new ideas and perspectives, psychological integration, health and wholeness, re-connection with nature and other living beings, and numerous other religious functions. These practices have been institutionalized and enculturated in diverse shamanic and other spiritual practices throughout history.

My focus has been on locating these practices in the traditions of my Northern and Western European ancestors, although clear parallels exist among other traditions, including those of indigenous people of the American, African and Asian continents. This focus on the spiritual traditions of my European ancestors avoids many of the ethical problems involved in the cultural misappropriation of non-European practices, in which, for example, "white shamans" enormously profit from stealing Native American spiritual practices.

In the language of the soul, we might state that the individual, prior to the Sacred Journey, has lost contact with the sacred. To re-establish our connection to the soul, direct experiences of the sacred are necessary. The Sacred Journey is a form of soul retrieval. Everything, both animate and inanimate, is imbued with spirit. We need to re-populate the woods, rivers, and mountains with numina, for our dis-ease is linked to our dissociation from the natural world. I hold that all of the Universe (by which I also mean "Nature") is sacred. For me, this "sense of the sacred" is invoked by (1) the incredible mystery at the center of our understanding of the cosmos; (2) our absolute dependence on the natural world as a source for all life, and for our very sustenance, survival, revelation, and fulfillment; and (3) the awareness of our humble human fragility in the face of nature's awesome power.

Humans seem to naturally distinguish between that which is sacred and that which is profane, and to say that nature is sacred is to insist that it must be treated with respect and reverence and never violated. It is of utmost important. It is holy and ultimate. This conception of the natural world as sacred is intended to change our relationship to the planet. Even if it is built upon a somewhat mythic metaphor, this radical leap of imagination can be a purposeful act which promotes ecological consciousness.

While elements of these Sacred Journeys are at the heart of most nature religions in the Western Mystery Tradition (such as Wicca, reclaimed Paganism, Druidry, etc.), thus far, Religious Naturalists have not embraced these "base elements" of the Sacred Journey. Enter Dionysian Naturalism.

## Dionysian Naturalism and the Quest for Ecstasy

Unitarian-Universalists and Religious Naturalists are both groups of people concerned with infusing reason and science into modern religious life and practice. In social worlds often replete with supernaturalism and superstition, this itself is a noble goal. And while, in so many ways I am with them in that pursuit and definitely want a religious cosmology grounded in scientific evidence, I follow Friedrich Nietzsche in seeing modernity as expressing the triumph of the Apollonian. Instrumental rationality and cold calculation have almost killed the soul of the world—the Pagan notion of anima mundi—and we desperately need a Dionysian revival.

Dionysian Naturalism, while grounded in a scientific worldview and in the practices of critical thinking and skeptical inquiry, maintains a healthy place for the passions and the emotions. Moreover, our human impulses and instincts are seen as related to our sacredness. "Dionysian," for me, invokes the Earth-centered Pagan traditions of the ancient world and their corporeal form of communion. Dionysian Naturalism reclaims the Sacred Journey at the heart of Western nature religions. And it celebrates these forms of ecstasy as ways to re-sacralize the natural world. Thus, I want to bring together Pagan and Naturalist traditions.

In ancient Greece, *ekstasis* meant "standing outside oneself," and referred to the flight of the soul from the body. While I originally associated the "Dionysian" with wild states of frenzy, profane experiences of "partying," and drunken orgies, I now know that the "Dionysian" essentially involves being transported to a spiritual realm, in which even calm and meditative, but no less profound, states of consciousness may be experienced. While reclaiming ecstatic religion and the potential of sacramental entheogen use, Dionysian Naturalism also explores other alternative non-entheogenic spiritual practices, which may equally serve to re-sacralize nature and create transcendent experiences.

Personally I have learned that, because of my prior abusive experiences with drugs, I must be vigilant about sobriety, for my mind will tell me that all recreational drug use is equivalent to entheogenic sacramental use ("Go ahead and get high! The 'Will to Party' is a sacred instinct!"). When that happens I tend to lose everything in my life. Being someone with bi-polar disorder with a history self-medicating with high-powered stimulants leading to repeated bouts of homeless, I must continue to discover new ways to "dance with Dionysus." This has opened up my spiritual journey in greatly enriching ways, and has led to deep study of meditation, yoga, and tantric sexuality. Elsewhere, I have detailed "The Amethyst Path" of recovery I follow, in which I seek Dionysian spirituality while maintaining sobriety.

## Enchanting Naturalism

I describe much of contemporary naturalism as "disenchanted," that is, as a deterministic, mechanistic and reductionistic scientific worldview in which everything can be explained through natural laws and mechanisms, with no mystery left behind. Disenchanted naturalism observes the natural world through a detached objective perspective, in which any notion of wonder has been removed. The consequence of this way of thinking has been near ecological collapse. By conceiving of nature as mere "inert matter," with the central purpose of serving human needs, we set up a situation ripe for human abuse and exploitation of the biosphere.

To "save our planet," we must re-sacralize nature, for no people who truly revere our natural world would allow it to become destroyed. Thus, "enchanting" naturalism is essential to the survival of our planet. To change from a disenchanted naturalism to an enchanted naturalism one, one need only acknowledge that one is in the presence of the sacred. We must open ourselves to the mysteries of the Universe, with ways of knowing that integrate imagination, aesthetic sensibility, and religious intuition. As stated, the Pagan notion of *anima mundi*—the soul of the world—is being revived. Through acts of enchantment, our alienation from the natural world can be removed, and we can again feel the magic of a spring morning, a shooting star on a warm summer night, and the majesty of a snow-capped mountain. Without doubt, Dionysian Naturalism is an enchanted naturalism!

A paradigm shift is occurring, in which the Universe is now imagined, not as a clocklike mechanism, in which wholes are reducible to their parts, but as a sacred living system with emergent properties. This new worldview brings together the wisdom of religion and science to change our relationship to the cosmos. By re-enchanting nature and reviving *anima mundi*, we re-affirm that we are an intimate part of the web of life and kin to other species. The resulting sense of belonging to this planet is required if we are create a new global ethic in which all are valued and respected and choose to live responsibly. Our ancient Pagan roots are still alive, and we must graft our modern spirits onto them to protect our sacred living planet.

Overhanging Rock in Yosemite National Park 1902

## Part 4: Not Your Fathers' God: Non-Theistic Conceptions of the Divine

"O thou that dost support the earth and restest thereupon, whosoe'er thou art, a riddle past our ken! Be thou Zeus, or natural necessity, or man's intellect, to thee I pray."

— Euripides, *Trojan Women*

"I worship nature. Don't laugh. I can prove it exists."

— author unknown

"The one place Gods inarguably exist is in our minds where they are real beyond refute, in all their grandeur and monstrosity."

— Alan Moore, *From Hell*

All three of the understandings of deity above—agnostic, naturalistic, and psychological—can be found among non-theistic Pagans. This kind of diversity of belief is not new. In the 1st century BCE, the Roman philosopher, Cicero, wrote a treatise entitled, "On Nature of the Gods" (*De Natura Deorum*), in which he observed:

> "There is in fact no subject upon which so much difference of opinion exists [as on the nature of the gods], not only among the unlearned but also among educated men; and the views entertained are so various and so discrepant, that, while it is no doubt a possible alternative that none of them is true, it is certainly impossible that more than one should be so."

One might think that non-theistic Pagans would have little use for gods, and that is certainly true in many cases. However, for a surprising number of non-theistic Pagans, "gods" or "deities" still play a role in their spirituality, even while they reject the belief in reified spiritual beings. Some of these non-theistic Pagans have developed truly radical conceptions of what a "god" is. Non-theistic Pagans include animists, pantheists, Gaians, naturalistic polytheists, and more.

## What Is This Whole "Deity" Thing, Anyway?
### by Blue

You know, I don't have a good answer to that question above, and if I claimed to in all seriousness, you should probably just walk away now. Despite the fact that I have had a 25 year relationship with Aphrodite, it may be of interest to know that I don't actually consider her to be an "entity" or being or power outside of my own existence, although it's not quite that simple either. I know this position is troubling for some people. I also do not see her as an archetype or psychological projection. In fact, I think that many of the archetypical constructions of deity are extremely confining and prescriptive and don't allow for revelation or long term growth. I think that seeing Aphrodite as an archetype is very limiting, and I think that except for some rare, short term circumstances, working with her in that way can do more harm than good.

I identify as an atheist/pantheist. Both are true for me. I tend to see the world and everything in it as sacred to the core and made of sacred stuff. That includes me and you! So why do I choose to identify as an atheist? First, I think it can be an important thing to do culturally and politically. I was raised an atheist, and my ideas about deity (or lack thereof) are perfectly compatible with many forms of historical atheism. There are many different types of atheist. For instance, I identify as a "soft metaphysical" atheist, that's just one form; there are many others. I'm frequently frustrated with Pagans and other folks who are merely informing their ideas about atheism based on Christian discourses. Unfortunately, there are also a lot of prominent atheists who also do this, and who seem to be operating purely from a reactive space. While I admit I am not wholly unsympathetic to their cause politically, I find their world view just too reductive. The fact is, in the great big world of religious practice and spiritual experience, there is a whole bunch of cool stuff that happens and many different ways to talk about those experiences. I have found that in the West we are pretty limited in our spiritual vocabulary, and tend to filter our experiences through the monotheistic, Abrahamic, generally Protestant lens.

So, how do I see and work with Aphrodite then, and why would I choose to do something that seems so contradictory to many people? Well, I choose a deity practice because it is awesome, fun, beautiful, challenging and rewarding. It allows me a wonderful vehicle for making real change in my life.

But how do I conceive of her? What is my reality? As I stated, I don't see Aphrodite as a projection of my own mind, not exactly anyway. I had this wonderful conversation with a dear and respected friend one night, where we spoke of deity experience rather like tuning a radio dial into a frequency. When you tighten that focus, you hear things, you see things. The relationship is really about connection and awareness. To be perfectly honest, in my work with Aphrodite, she is rather an outer layer to wider contemplations and practices designed to cultivate awareness of love, compassion, desire, change and action. She is a form that we can see, understand and work with, very effectively too, and for a lot of work, having an external form to work with is essential in helping to articulate your process. But the deeper you go with a deity practice, the more the form gets in the way (especially with Aphrodite), but I'm getting ahead of myself…

For a lot of work, the form is important. Sure, we are all made of sacred stuff, but sometimes you need an external Other in order to get the message you need to hear and do the work you need to do. Aphrodite has a huge, rich history throughout the centuries of myth, devotion, cult, relic and practice. For me, these things help to bring form and focus to a wonderful, beautiful Other, made of sacred stuff that is also me. Sometimes I need to take her form out of myself and then I have her "out there" to listen to, learn from, contemplate, enjoy, yet always with the awareness that I am she, and she is all, and I am all.

Ok, so I guess that part is a bit hard to explain. It's complicated, but you know, the multiverse is rather complex and there are a lot of experiences, resonances and worldviews that don't fit neatly into any box and that simply don't lend themselves to particularly coherent, linear explanation. Life is filled with fuzzy lines, not neat, clean ones, and I'm pretty comfortable with that, although a lot of people genuinely aren't. I think Tantric understandings of deity and deity yoga practices which focus on the union with deity tend to resonate best with me and best approach my perspectives on how this all works. Historically, in the West, we have done this with theurgy, which suggests that we have mostly just forgotten that we are made as the same stuff as the Gods; we just need to remember (although that is somewhat simplistic). Theurgy gives us the techniques for doing that. I find theurgic practices essential to modern deity work. Ultimately, though, over time, every breath becomes a prayer to your own divine self and you don't need the reminders quite so much. Until you do.

## Being Human When Surrounded by Greek Gods
### by M. J. Lee

The center of the world for the ancient Greeks was Delphi, and at the entrance to the Delphian Temple of Apollo were the words *Gnothi Seauton* (Know Thyself). This, according to many scholars, was a command to remember that one is human, to remember one's place as a human.[1] In its most basic form, humanism is simply the focus on the human, and the Greeks were certainly focused on this, as can be seen in their art, literature, philosophy and also their religion.

Many people see humanism as opposed to traditional religion, and in fact use humanism as a synonym for atheism. Humanism is seen as the rejection and replacement of God with the human, who then becomes the center of interest and the source of values and ethics. The history of humanism is often begun with the ancient Greek philosophers and Sophists, who we are told questioned and rejected the traditional view of the gods. Evidence for the rejection of religion is also collected from epic and dramatic poetry, where the gods are sometimes portrayed in a less then noble light, and even sometimes comically. This is especially true of the works of Euripides.

### The human in the god

Euripides is one of the three great tragedians from ancient Athens. He is considered the most "modern" of the three, for questioning the assumptions of his society, for his anti-war stance, and for championing the downtrodden—women, foreigners and slaves. It is often difficult, if not impossible, to discern what Euripides' own position might have been on the issues he raises, and this is especially true in the realm of religion. Many scholars, particularly from previous generations, have found his portrayal of the gods so negative that they thought he must be making fun of religion, showing people how foolish conventional beliefs were. This may be so, but that is not the only way to read him. I think in many ways he gives an old-fashioned, archaic view of the gods.[2]

Euripides' last and most famous play is the Bacchae. In the Bacchae, Dionysus returns to the place of his birth, Thebes, to establish his cult, but he is met with resistance from King Pentheus. Pentheus refuses to recognize the divinity of Dionysus and tries to prohibit his worship, this running wild of decent women, wives and mothers. To punish Pentheus for his arrogance, Dionysus has the women of Thebes in their Bacchic madness tear Pentheus limb from limb as if he were a wild beast, after which Agave, Pentheus' own mother, leads a triumphal procession with her son's head on a stake. It is during this procession that Agave comes back to her senses and realizes with horror and disgust what she has done.

What are we to think of this god Dionysus? If one sees the gods as conscious, supernatural people, then the Dionysus of the Bacchae can only be seen as the worst monster, for only a monster would force a mother to kill and dismember her child. If one thinks that gods are supposed to be good, to care about and for humans, then one will find much amiss with Euripides' gods. It is clear that many of the ancient Greeks did come to believe the gods were supposed to be perfectly good and just stewards of humanity, and therefore became increasingly uncomfortable with the old myths of amoral gods.

If one defines a god as that which is perfect, perfectly good, perfectly wise, perfectly just, then it seems perfectly clear that there are no such gods, or at least none that take an active interest in us. But these are not the gods of Homer, Hesiod or Euripides. The gods that they portray are both kind and cruel; they are in fact capricious. This to me seems more realistic, for this is what matches our experience of nature, not just the nature outside ourselves, but also our own nature, our un-chosen instinctual nature. Sometimes the earth is a gentle, pleasant place, with sweet fruits ripe for the taking, and sometimes it is not.

## The god in the human

The gods are for me metaphors for nature, or more precisely the names, images and stories are metaphors, allegories and archetypes of our relationship with nature. I see the gods—the names, images, stories—as the poetic encapsulation of our human experience, our relationship with the ineffable forces that shape human life. While this makes the gods *no thing*, it does not make them *nothing*. I see the gods as representing very real, powerful, even dangerous forces. I believe the gods are real. It doesn't matter what we call them or don't call them. They are real and dangerous, and we will contend with them. This for me is the message of the Bacchae.

In the Bacchae, I believe Euripides was warning the men of Athens that to ignore a god like Dionysus can bring disaster. Let us not forget that for a woman, the ancient world was a repressive place. The only time a "respectable" woman may have left her home was to participate in religious rites. The Bacchae was written at a time when attitudes about the gods were changing, and no doubt many patriarchs would have preferred to ignore gods like Dionysus and keep their women at home and in their control. Better by far to be like Cadmus, Pentheus' aged grandfather, and show proper reverence. Cadmus, conscious of his status as a human, accepts straightaway the divinity of Dionysus and goes to join the Bacchic revelry. Human beings can't be in control of everything all the time. Better to show proper reverence for gods like Dionysus, to allow a safe outlet for those forces which if bottled up too tight can be explosive.

The Dionysus of Athens was Dionysus Eleuthereus (The One Who Sets Free). He was the giver of ecstasy, which literally means "standing outside of oneself," and those activities which cause this—wine, drama, dancing—were under his patronage. There is a time for working hard and a time for letting go. What I like so much about polytheism is how almost every aspect of life on some level participates in the sacred. There seems to be literally a deity for everything. I see the purpose of religion as the cultivation of reverence, the development of right relationship with self, community and the world.[3] It seems to me that we need if not gods, then something like them, to be the focus of this reverence, to encapsulate this "right relationship."

I can't leave the topic of Euripides without commenting on his play Heracles. In this play, Heracles on returning home from his labors is made mad by Hera, who of course does not like Heracles because he is a bastard son of Zeus. In his madness, Heracles kills his wife and children. When Heracles returns to sanity and sees the carnage of his family, he is devastated, to say the least. In the traditional tale, Heracles, a mortal son of god, is made fully divine, but in this story he is made fully human. No god comes to save Heracles; instead it is the love of his father and especially the friendship of Theseus which redeems him.

## Know thyself

Euripides' Heracles brings us back to the place of the human. I think cultivating respect and reverence for nature, both the nature outside and inside ourselves, is very important, but in the end it is not the place of nature, of the gods, to save us, to give our lives meaning or purpose. I believe that what gives our lives meaning, what redeems us, is *philia*, human love and friendship. Knowing this is part of knowing what it means to be human, *Gnothi Seauton* (Know Thyself). Greek humanism was not about rejecting the gods and elevating humans to that place, but was rather about understanding the place of the human and the god, and giving to each the credit and honor that was due.[4]

## Notes

1. For the conventional interpretation of Gnothi Seauton, see Elizabeth Vandiver's Teaching Company course, "Classical Mythology," Lecture 9 (http://www.thegreatcourses.com) and Donald Kagan's Open Yale Course, "Introduction to Ancient Greek History," Lecture 1 (available for free at http://oyc.yale.edu/classics/). Donald Kagan also gives a wonderful summary of the Greek view of human nature.

2. An interesting article on the evolution of gods is available from the Friesian School at http://www.friesian.com/god.htm. At the end of this page is an essay on Euripides.

3. For a wonderful exploration of reverence and its importance in Greek society, see *Reverence: Renewing a Forgotten Virtue* by Paul Woodruff (Oxford University Press, 2001). Woodruff discusses the Bacchae in several places, most notably on pages 94-97, 128-32 and 210-11.

4. Jon D. Mikalson, in *Ancient Greek Religion* (Blackwell Publishing, 2005), examines the Greek view of the place of the human and divine based on actual temple dedication. On this he says, "The thousands of dedications in the hundreds of Greek sanctuaries are certainly expressions of gratitude to the deities, but they are equally monuments of human achievement and usually the human achievement is given considerably more emphasis than the deity's contribution" (p. 159). In his book, *Athenian Popular Religion* (University of North Carolina Press, 1983), he sums up the Athenian attitude about divine intervention as, "In simple terms, opportunities came from the gods. It was up to the human being to make the best of them. If he was successful, he praised and thanked the gods. If he failed, he faulted, if not himself, a daimon or fortune" (page 62). We might say the same thing about nature and chance.

## Of Gods and Stories
### by Nimue Brown

I have no idea how the universe works. Not a clue. Ok, some tenuous grasp of some of the physics, but when we get round to issues of deity and eternity, I make no claims to insight whatsoever. The whole thing confuses and unnerves me, and has since I was about four and started trying to get my head round such things. I've made my peace with not knowing, and have settled into a place of maybeism. Maybe there are Gods. Maybe there aren't. Maybe everything is part of the divine. Maybe there's a grand plan. Maybe not. It's a good way of not getting into fights with people over issues of belief, because, for all I know, they could be right.

From that position, the idea of working with Gods is tricky. I assume you need a very confident, hard-polytheist belief in the literal existence of Gods as autonomous and individual personalities in order to work with them. Maybe they are like that. Maybe the archetype people have it right…

The one thing I do believe in is stories. Not least because so little actual belief is called for. Stories have power, and that is a power I know how to trust and invest in. Religions are, for the greater part, gatherings together of powerful stories that are meant to show us something. The measure of any story, be it religious, historical or fictional, is the effect it has. The greater Truths about living and dying, being human, being good, being effective…these are more important than whether or not a person actually existed, or whether people a few thousand years ago thought they were looking at a God or a fictional character.

We blur the lines between deity and fiction all the time. Ovid's deities might have existed as Gods, or maybe he made them up for that story. We've turned Thor and Loki into modern movie stars, and we aren't sure what of the Welsh myths is ancient tales of deity and what is mediaeval fiction. I have come to the conclusion that it really doesn't matter. If a story moves you, and inspires you, that's far more relevant than whether some people a few thousand years ago thought it was true. If *The Lord of the Rings* is your sacred, inspirational text that has done most to teach you how to live, why should that be less valid than taking up a really old story that might or might not have originally been religious? Why should it matter if the story is about real, historical events? Robin Hood is a powerful icon. So are Lady Macbeth and Captain Kirk, for some people.

Stories change people. They give us shapes in which we can reimagine ourselves. They give us ways of choosing and living we might not otherwise have thought of. They give us ideas, hope and possibility. No, I have no idea if Blodeuwedd was really a Celtic Goddess. What I do know is how that story touched, changed, maddened and inspired me. That's where the power lies.

The truth is out there (*X Files*). In all kinds of places. In galaxies far, far away, in girls who are shot by religious extremists and miraculously do not die, in modern heroes and ancient tales. Whether we believe in deities or not, we can see the very real effects their stories have. There is a lot of reason for honouring the power of stories. It is not where they come from that matters, but where those stories are taking us.

## The Disenchantment of the Gods and the Reenchantment of the Archetypes
### by John Halstead

I often hear Neo-Pagans say that the gods are archetypes, but rarely do I hear the reverse of that idea: *that the archetypes are gods*. The idea that gods are archetypes is not a new one. It dates back to the 1960s at least, when Neo-Pagans began to seize on Carl Jung's concept of archetypes as a way of making polytheism relevant to a modern world. As Margot Adler explained in *Drawing Down the Moon* (1979),

> "Much of the theoretical basis for a modern defense of polytheism comes from Jungian psychologists, who have long argued that the Gods and Goddesses of myth, legend and fairy tale represent archetypes, real potencies and potentialities deep within the psyche, which, when allowed to flower permit us to be more fully human."

In the process of psychologizing the gods, though, we have lost the sense of the gods as something which transcends us. We have humanized the gods and lost the sense of gods *as gods*.

### Psychologizing the Gods

Pagans often talk about the disenchantment of the modern world. The phrase, "disenchantment of the world," derives from Friedrich Schiller, who described the *Entgotterung der Natur,* literally, the "de-godding of nature." Neo-Pagan myth and ritual are seen by many Pagans as a counter-cultural response to this disenchantment, a re-enchantment of the world or a "re-godding" of nature. Ironically, though, some of the pre-modern cultural forms which Neo-Pagans attempt to reconstruct may actually be transformed in the process, so much so that the "enchantment" is lost in the translation. For example, Wouter Hanegraaff has argued that occultist magic survived the disenchantment of the Enlightenment by becoming disenchanted.

In contemporary Neo-Paganism, we can see this "psychologization," not only in discussions of magic, but also in explanations of the nature of the gods, specifically the reduction of the gods to "archetypes." In the 1960s and 1970s, as the claims to historical continuity with an ideal pagan past began to come under attack, Neo-Pagans turned to Jungian psychology as a means for legitimating Neo-Pagan practice. Unfortunately, as the Jungian interpretation of Neo-Pagan gods was popularized, it was also oversimplified. The archetypes were reduced to mere ideas or metaphors, ideas which with we can consciously play. This "psychologization" of the archetypes was something that Carl Jung himself was actually critical of.

When we talk about the gods as archetypes, we often contribute to the ongoing disenchantment of the world, because we lose the sense of the archetypes as gods. In other words, the "numinous" quality of the archetype is lost. The archetypes become disenchanted. One of the most conspicuous examples of this is the practice of "using gods" in Neo-Pagan magic, also sometimes referred to as "plug-and-play" gods.

The gods may be a part of us, but we have forgotten that they are also *other* than us—if by "us" we mean our conscious mind or ego-self. This is why Jung called the archetypes "gods." We experience the archetypes as gods in the sense that they are beyond our conscious control and they have the power to transform our lives. Jung wrote that we are dominated, even "possessed," by the archetypes, which "function exactly like an Olympus full of deities who want to be propitiated, served, feared and worshiped." A true encounter with the gods is not only an experience of re-enchantment (what Rudolf Otto called *mysterium fascinans*), but also an experience which shakes us to our core (what Otto called *mysterium tremendum*).

While the gods are part of the human psyche, we should remember that the Greek term *psyche* is better translated as "soul" than "mind." Too often, in discussions of the psychological nature of Neo-Pagan gods, the modifier "just" is inserted immediately preceding the word "psychological," as in, "The Neo-Pagan gods are *just* psychological." It is as if to say, "They are figments of your imagination." This is not only a profound misunderstanding of Jung's theory of the psyche, but it also contributes to the disenchantment of the Neo-Pagan concept of divinity. In effect, the Neo-Pagan psychologization of the gods has *de-godded* the archetypes.

### Re-godding the Archetypes

In *Sign of the Witch: Modernity and the Pagan Revival* (2008), David Waldron writes how, in the 1980s, the Jungian approach to the gods began to decline. Since the turn of the millennium (perhaps not coincidentally, after the publication of Neil Gaiman's *American Gods*), a literalistic polytheism has become more popular among Neo-Pagans. This may be in reaction to the disenchantment of the gods or the "de-godding" of the archetypes. Many Pagans, in search of communion with the numinous Other(s), have rejected Jungian Neo-Paganism in favor of a more literalistic polytheism which sees the gods as beings existing independent of the human psyche. It is an attempt, if you will, to put the "god" back into the gods. But Naturalistic Pagans like myself are not comfortable with a literalistic conception of the divine. Perhaps it is time we re-examine Jung's ideas and see if we can put the god back in the archetype.

The de-godding of the archetype in Neo-Paganism is a consequence of a fundamental misunderstanding of Jung's ideas, namely a confusion of *symbol* with *archetype*. As David Waldron explains:

> "It is one thing to acknowledge that symbols and archetypal images have a deep impact on the human psyche through religious experience. It is a profoundly different thing to believe that one can consciously and arbitrarily create and ascribe meaning to symbols, based upon that which is seen to be suited to consciously designated psychological needs."

Jung differentiated between consciously constructed symbols and numinous archetypes. According to Jung, symbols refer to, but are not identical with, the archetypes located deep in the unconscious. While symbols have a conscious and known meaning, an archetype always transcends our attempts to understand it. Thus, the archetype retains a numinous quality. Our comprehension of an archetype by consciousness is always necessarily partial, never total. The meaning of the unconscious archetype is inexhaustible. The claim that any one symbol exhausts the archetype it refers to is the substance of what John Dourley calls "psychological idolatry." If a symbol can be totally explained or rationalized by the conscious mind, then it ceases to be an archetype. While a symbol may masquerade as an archetype, it actually is merely an expression of our ego-self.

Neo-Jungian James Hillman writes, in *Re-visioning Psychology* (1975): "Just as we do not create our dreams, but they *happen* to us, so we do not invent the persons of myth and religion [i.e., the gods]; they, too, happen to us" (emphasis Hillman's). It is no coincidence that, historically and cross-culturally, the gods have spoken to mortals in dreams. As Neo-Pagans came to consciously construct and "plug-and-play" their gods, we have lost the sense of the gods as something that happens *to* us. We might say that we overemphasized the immanence of the gods and lost the sense of their transcendence.

## The Modern Hubris

In ancient Greek tragedy, heroes who were guilty of the sin of hubris, disregarding the existential gulf between themselves and the gods, were invariably punished for it. In contemporary Neo-Paganism, hubris takes the form of confusing the creations of the conscious mind with the numinous aspects of the unconscious psyche.

On the one hand, this modern form of hubris results in the loss of our experience of the gods, a further disenchantment or de-godding of our world. But on the other hand, it invites the retribution of gods, who can be repressed in the unconscious, but will not be ignored. Above the door to his home in Zurich, Jung had inscribed the words: "Called or not, the god will be present." We can ignore the gods, but their effect in our lives is unavoidable. If they are not given their due honor, the gods will make themselves known forcibly and often with disastrous results for our lives.

In *A History of Ancient Greek Literature,* Gilbert Murray explains the meaning of Euripides play, *The Bacchae*:

> "Reason is great, but it is not everything. There are in the world things not of reason, but both below and above it; causes of emotion, which we cannot express, which we tend to worship, which we feel, perhaps, to be the precious elements in life. These things are Gods or forms of God: not fabulous immortal men, but 'Things which Are,' things utterly non-human and non-moral, which bring man bliss or tear his life to shreds without a break in their own serenity."

To confuse Murray's "things not of reason" with the conscious creations of our own mind is hubris, and we do so at our own peril. The gods may be archetypes, but we must also always remember that *the archetypes are gods*.

As Neo-Paganism moves increasingly in the direction of literalistic polytheism, those Neo-Pagans who find literalism untenable may find themselves marginalized in the Neo-Pagan community. The pendulum which previously swung to the humanistic extreme by reducing the gods to symbols is now swinging to the other extreme of transcendental theism, denying that the gods are part of the human psyche.

When properly understood, Jung's theory of archetypes offers us an opportunity to find a golden mean between these two extremes, one which may simultaneously satisfy the humanist, who sees the gods as products of the human psyche, while also satisfying the mystical longing of the theist for contact with a numinous Other, which is greater than any creation of our conscious mind.

## I Worship the Blind Goddess
### by John Halstead

*You weary Nations, perhaps I am some new being you've never encountered before. Yet there is nothing about me you can't recognize. I live in the place where you perceive nothing. Look again!*

—Geoff Bartley, "The Language of Stones"

I was once accused of worshiping a "blind" God. I'm a Naturalistic Pagan. I worship nature. Which can seem pretty strange to theists, people who worship personal gods. Nature does not "care" about us—at least not as individuals, and not as a species either—at least not over and above any other species. And making offerings to earth and singing the praises of nature do not avert catastrophe or bring down the blessings of Providence. So why worship nature?

But Nature is not exactly indifferent to us. In the fantasy author Terry Pratchett's humorous Discworld series, the head of his fictional pantheon of gods is named "Blind Io." Pratchett describes Blind Io this way:

> "On this particular day Blind Io, by dint of constant vigilance the chief of the gods, sat with his chin in his hand and looked at the gaming board on the red marble table in front of him. Blind Io got his name because, where his eye sockets should have been, there were nothing but two areas of blank skin. His eyes, of which he had an impressively large number, led a semi-independent life of their own. Several were currently hovering above the table."

Blind Io is blind, *but he's not*. In fact, he sees everything. That's my Goddess too. She is blind—in the way that Lady Justice is blind—having no favorites: neither sports teams, nor combatants in war, neither saints, nor sinners, neither little children, nor parasitic wasps.

At the same time, my Goddess sees everything. As the Christians say, "not a sparrow falls..." But my Pagan Goddess sees all, not because she sits on some Archimedean point beyond everything, but because *we are all her eyes*. She sees through us (and through other animals and every other sensing living being). As Augustine said, "God is closer to you than you are to yourself." As a Jungian Pagan, I would say that we are the consciousness of the Goddess. People sometimes wonder if we are God's dream. Jung would probably say, rather, that we are God waking from his dream.

You might wonder how interaction with such a God is possible. But I wonder how one could avoid interacting with such a God. Every breath we take is an interaction with the Goddess. She shapes us. By everything that touches us. And we shape Her. Through everything we touch. As the science fiction author, Octavia Butler, writes: "We are God's victim, God's prey, but...

> *A victim of God may,*
> *Through learning adaption,*
> *Become a partner of God.*
> *A victim of God may,*
> *Through forethought and planning,*
> *Become a shaper of God.*

Dancing the Wheel of the Year does not avert global warming—no more than the Aztec sacrifices raised the sun each day. But then, neither will praying to any other god. No god will save us from disaster. The hurricane will still come and the bear will still eat us. But praying helps keep us in balance when these calamities happen. It's not the wheel of nature's seasons that I turn with my ritual dance, but the wheel of the seasons within me.

For some Naturalistic Pagans, "worship" is a problematic word. Octavia Butler writes:

*We do not worship God.*
*We perceive and attend God.*
*We learn from God.*
*With forethought and work,*
*We shape God.*
*In the end, we yield to God.*

But, speaking for myself, I *do* worship the Goddess that is the world. I worship nature. There is a definite element of devotion in my practice. I ask: *Is not this world worthy of love?* I hear the world calling me with the voice of a waiting lover, calling me out of my self, calling me to passionately embrace it. And worship is my way of affirming, encouraging, and sustaining that embrace.

So yes, I worship nature. I worship a blind Goddess. For me, she is the only worthy object of worship. She will never care that I worship her. She will never answer a single prayer. But she is always with me… shaping me as I shape her. I will struggle with her to the last gasp of my life. And in the end, in my final act of devotion, I will yield to her.

## Faith in the Earth
### by B. T. Newberg

It is important to believe with as little force as possible. It is only in non-nature-based religions that faith must overwhelm natural instincts and sensations.

In nature-based religions, we need only look and see what is there. Faith in the Goddess is no more difficult than faith in the solidity of a stone. You can tap it, touch it, strike it, weigh it, toss it, drop it, pick it up, and feel its weight against your skin.

The Goddess too can be touched and felt, though she is not one thing but many, indeed everything around you and in you, and more. Thus, there is no need to strive for faith. Faith is given to you as naturally as your body.

Having a vision is no more difficult than looking and seeing what is in your mind's eye. Touching the Goddess is no more difficult than touching your own flesh.

And yet, there may be times when you feel your faith is being tested. For whatever reason, you may feel that the Goddess is not there. You can no longer believe in her. Thus you feel your faith threatened. But actually this is an illusion.

Even if you become an atheist, still nothing has changed, because the Goddess appears in many forms. First she came to you as "Goddess" and next she came as "there is no god." You stop calling her by any name, you stop calling yourself Pagan, you do whatever it is you feel necessary to root out religion in yourself, yet your body abides. Your world abides. Your life abides.

That is what is meant by the Goddess—she is that which goes on. In the wake of all change, she abides. And no matter what you call her or don't call her, she remains with you.

And even if you spit on her and curse her, she remains with you. The Goddess cannot be blasphemed. Hers is a purity no abuse can stain.

But you can make things harder for yourself. You can take such a cantankerous attitude that she can only appear to you as hostility, misery, and boredom—because you refuse to see anything else in the world. So you can make her fight you. Yet even so, you cannot offend her so terribly as to remove yourself from her being.

You may try to conquer her. But try as you might to conquer her, all you can do is change her. It is she that conquers you, by changing with you.

How much easier is it, then, to embrace her than fight her? How much more livable is it to care for her than neglect her? She does not require us to call her by any special name, or think of her in any particular way, yet how much more enchanting is it to call her by an enchanting name? How much more loving is it to know her in a loving way?

And so we celebrate the seasons, and perform our rituals, and tell our stories.

But let's be honest: if the last Pagan ceased calling back the sun at Yule, would the sun cease to rise? Nothing would change but the enchanted feeling of things, which would be lost.

Yet she would not be lost. Nor would hope of regaining that enchanted feeling.

This is the mature reality of the Goddess: responsibility for the earth and its livability. It is childishness to think we can divorce ourselves from the earth. To be Pagan is to take responsibility for our relationship with the world. When we embrace the Goddess, our mother, we give up the illusion of separateness. Such is little more than adolescent rebellion. This childishness we surrender.

And yet, even as we accept responsibility and grow toward adulthood in the earth, we also grow the other way. As we return to enchanted ways, and allow ourselves to be suckled by a loving mother earth, we become children once more.

## The Three Kindreds
## by NaturalPantheist

I've been investigating and studying Druidry for some time now and one of the ideas within this philosophy (as well as other Pagan religions) is the idea of the Three Kindreds. Essentially this is another way to talk about the idea that there are three supernatural groups—the gods, the spirits of nature, and the ancestors.

Obviously, being a Naturalistic Pantheist, I do not believe in anything supernatural. However, does taking this stand mean I must reject all ideas of gods, spirits and ancestors, or does the concept of the three kindreds offer something to a Naturalistic Pantheist?

### The Gods

Let's start by discussing the idea of "Gods." Most Pagan religions are polytheistic, which means they believe in many gods. In fact, throughout much of human history, most people have believed in a multitude of gods. Monotheism is a fairly recent and limited phenomenon that grew out of ancient Persian Zoroastrianism and its influence on Jewish and later Christian and Muslim faiths. Undoubtedly, the ancient believers in polytheism believed that there were supernatural gods and any reinterpretation we might do must acknowledge this.

So what does a Pantheist believe? Well, the key idea of Naturalistic Pantheism is that the Universe is divine. "Divine" here doesn't mean supernatural, but it does mean that it is worthy of the same awe and reverence a believer would give to their own god or gods. The universe shares many of the same attributes we might normally ascribe to the gods—might and power, omnipresence, eternity (it has been there since the beginning of time and will be there until the end), majesty, awe-inspiringness, creativity, destructiveness, beauty, etc. It can also be seen as the web of life, as in the modern scientific idea of Gaia.

Personally, I refer to the universe and the amalgamation of all its forces, i.e., ultimate reality, as "Mother Nature." For me she is the "Supreme Goddess." Although this looks like having one god, and therefore monotheistic, it is not. This is because monotheism believes in a single transcendent god (outside of or greater than the universe), while Pantheism does not believe there is any transcendent aspect of Mother Nature. Similarly, monotheists tend to see their god in personal, anthropomorphic terms, while pantheists see Mother Nature as impersonal, more akin to a force.

Is there still a place for polytheism in Naturalistic Pantheism? Well, it depends on your definition of polytheism. There are two types—the first is hard polytheism, which sees each of the deities as literal, supernatural, distinct beings with their own personalities. This type of polytheism is not really compatible with pantheism. However, there is something called soft polytheism, which is the idea that either all gods and goddesses are really just parts of one god/goddess, or that they are archetypes (elements inherent in the human psyche), or they are personifications of the forces of nature. All three views of soft polytheism offer something to Naturalistic Pantheists.

If I said to you, "Thor" or "Zeus," the image that would probably come to your mind immediately is of thunder and lightning. If I said "Aphrodite," you would probably think of love, and if I said "Ra," you would probably think of the Sun. The point is that these are all forces of nature, either physical nature, or human nature. Through science we may have a much greater understanding of them than the ancients did, but they are still forces that control and have an impact on our lives, and they are uncontrollable. Most of the ancient "gods" were simply natural forces personified. If we removed the names of these gods from the equation, we would simply end up with Sun, Moon, Rain, Storm, Thunder, Friendship, Courage, Love, Justice, Wisdom, Fear, etc.

These are not supernatural things; they are natural. They are not personal; they are impersonal. They don't exist separately from these forces or control these forces; they are the forces themselves. They are the powers that touch our lives and affect our survival; they are able to destroy or create. They are neither good nor evil; they just are. However, by personifying them and giving them names as the ancients did, it may help us to connect with different aspects of nature on a more personal level—to interact with them and show them (and therefore nature as a whole) gratitude and respect. Using the mythology and stories behind these gods can help us to feel a deeper relationship with the forces of nature and tap into our mind, emotions and spirit in ways science normally does not. It does not mean believing in supernatural entities, but it does mean using the names, symbols, and mythology to enhance our relationships with, and connection to, the great whole, the universe, Mother Nature. And just as Soft Polytheists see all "gods" as aspects of one god/goddess, so Natural Pantheists see each "god," i.e. force of nature and human nature, as an aspect of the one god/goddess: Mother Nature.

By using the poetic and symbolic language of Deity to describe both Mother Nature and the forces of physical nature and human nature that control our lives, we can connect more deeply with the natural world.

## The Spirits of Nature

Ancient pagan cultures were animistic. They saw everything in nature as being "alive" having its own soul or spirit. Rather than believing that everything has a supernatural spirit behind it, Neo-Animism is about seeing each thing in nature as a "person" worthy of respect. In this way, we can re-interpret "spirits of nature" to mean all the living creatures of the earth, sea, and sky: plants, trees, birds, animals, insects, fish, micro-organisms, etc. These are the "spirits of nature" that live with us and around us (and even within us as some bacteria does), both great and small, seen and unseen. It doesn't mean that all these "spirits" are friendly towards us, but it does mean that we should see them as having "personhood" in an other-than-human way, and therefore we should be aware of them and treat them with respect.

We can also use the word poetically to describe "spirits of a place." In Japanese Shintoism, there is a concept called "Kami," which literally means "outstanding." Viewed from a naturalistic perspective, anything in nature, whether it be a waterfall, a great mountain, a rainbow or anything else that evokes within us feelings of great awe and wonder, we can call a "spirit" or "kami." We are not saying that there is some sort of supernatural ethereal being controlling the place, but we are saying that there is something very special, something awe-inspiring about the place and that it has an effect on us. Like the story of Moses and the burning bush in the Old Testament, we realise that we are standing on sacred, holy ground and must show this place ultimate respect. When we go into these places, we must remember that this is home for those "spirits" of nature and place, and we should act like guests, showing respect and kindness as we enter and perhaps even leaving offerings.

By acknowledging the "spirits of nature," the other creatures, plants and animals, as well as places in nature that evoke awe and wonder in us, we can learn awareness of and respect for those that live around us.

## The Ancestors

The Ancestors play a big part in my own faith and practice. I have researched my family tree to get a better idea of where I have come from. Throughout human history, most human cultures have (and still do) venerated their ancestors. Showing respect and reverence for ancestors, even though as Naturalistic Pantheists we don't believe they live on as beings, is an important spiritual practice.

There are various groups of Ancestors. The first are ancestors of blood—every person in your family tree and bloodline right down throughout the ages. But it goes further. What about the fact that evolution teaches us that we have many other descendants: animals, plants, dinosaurs, fish, even single-celled bacteria. These are all our ancestors. And if we consider the reincarnation of atoms, if everything we eat and drink becomes a part of our bodies, then the plants and animals we consume must become part of us, and surely that too makes them ancestors!

Secondly, there are the people who have influenced our lives, friends and people we know who have inspired or had an effect on our lives, making us the people we are today—surely these too are our ancestors, especially if they are people we have loved and lost.

Finally, what about people we don't know, those who have influenced and affected our culture, our local area, the places we go and see and experience? All of these things become a part of our lives, so perhaps they too are our ancestors.

By venerating Ancestors, whether of blood, culture, or influence, we can connect with the past, heal emotional wounds caused by someone's passing, and give thanks that they have made us the people we are today.

## A PaGaian Perspective
### by Glenys Livingstone, Ph.D.

*This is an edited excerpt from the author's book* PaGaian Cosmology.

I long considered the practice of my spirituality to be Gaian, encouraged by Charlene Spretnak's use of the term[1]: that is, it is an Earth-based spirituality, which requires only birth, not baptism, for belonging. We are all native to Gaia; all humans are indigenous to Her, though as Primordial Mother She does have many names around the planet. We do all issue forth from the same Origin. Gaia, as I understand Her however, is not only Earth; She is Cosmos. The same Creative Dynamic[2] that flourishes in Earth is assumed to be the same Creative Dynamic present throughout the Universe. Earth-Gaia is seed and jewel of a larger living Organism. Earth-Gaia is our Mother, but She is Daughter too, of an essential sentience that seethes through the Universe. The only faith required in this spirituality is in the Teeming Abundant Creativity (a name for Deity?) that has been manifesting on this planet in a particular way for some billions of years, and throughout the Cosmos for about thirteen point seven billion years. This is not a flimsy track record! Perhaps, as James Lovelock has said, this is "as near immortal as we ever need to know"[3]; or as Susan Griffin said more poetically, "at no instant does She fail me in Her presence."[4]

Essential to Gaian spirituality is the development of relationship with Earth, entering into Her consciousness, expanding awareness beyond the human-centered perspective. It requires a remembering of the "real" — the actual situation of "all human thought, social or individual…in the processes of body, nature and place."[5] As Thomas Berry describes, it requires a return to our "native place," the recovery of a feeling of intimacy with "the earth community," which he describes as the recovery of

> "a sense of presence, a realization that the earth community is a wilderness community that will not be bargained with; nor will it simply be studied or examined or made an object of any kind; nor will it be domesticated or trivialized as a setting for vacation indulgence…"[6]

He says it requires remembering

> "our sense of courtesy toward the earth and its inhabitants, our sense of gratitude, our willingness to recognize the sacred character of habitat, our capacity for the awesome, for the numinous quality of every earthly reality."[7]

This kind of presence may be enabled by an identification of ourselves (the human) with the entire cosmic process—Gaia's story, which is also ours; and by an identification with the cosmic powers that sustain us—such as Air, Sun, Water and Earth: that we are this, we depend on this, we come from this and we return to this.

Earth-Gaia is not separate from Universe-Gaia. There is no seam that separates Earth-Gaia from Universe-Gaia…She is One. There is no "up" and "down." There is no "out there." Gaia is "in here," as much as anywhere, or She is nowhere. Gaia can be known, felt, in any single articulation of Herself—within any Self. We are *in* it, Earth is *in* it. Earth floats in the "heavens"—the "heavens" are where we are. This *is* it. Gaia is a nested reality—manifold, but at least, Universe-Earth-Self; and inversely Self is Earth, is Gaia. Many spiritualities and most language imply that Earth is a world apart from the heavens—and even that the heavens are "higher' and thus "better." Yet we know that Earth is a Jewel in the Womb of Space—we have seen Her. We know that "Earth" is stardust—Her dirt is transfigured stuff of the stars. We know that we and all of it, are made from the same stuff—that we come out of the cores of stars, that a significant percentage of our "stuff" comes directly from the

Origins, albeit recycled many times over. Spiritual language must catch up, if we are to stop killing ourselves and other beings with our words. "Higher" indicates "out there," in "loftier" realms beyond the earth, transcending lowly earthly nature. "Deeper" indicates "within," the depth of the earthly realm, enriched awareness of the multivalent numinous earthly nature/reality. The use of language such as "higher levels" by spiritual traditions in particular, and even by ecological texts, and the worldview that accompanies it, has created and goes on creating a sense of alienation from what is here—the stuff we inhabit and where we dwell.

In 1926—long before the human eye had actually seen Earth from space—Russian scientist Vladimir Vernadsky, was able to hold a vision of Her in her "cosmic surroundings."[8] He developed a hypothesis of the biosphere "as a unitary agent molding the earth's crust as a primary geological force"[9] that was in relationship with the cosmic energies of radiation, particularly solar radiation.[10] Throughout his work, Vernadsky scientifically and poetically describes a holistic vision of Cosmos and Earth, and at times refers to humankind as a "geological entity."[11] And he asserted:

> "The biosphere is as much, or even more, the creation of the Sun as it is a manifestation of Earth-processes. Ancient religious traditions which regarded terrestrial creatures, especially human beings, as 'children of the Sun' were much nearer the truth than those which looked upon them as a mere ephemeral creation…"[12]

Vernadsky understood scientifically that the phenomena in the biosphere are "related to the structure of atoms, to their places in the cosmos and to their evolution in the history of the cosmos."[13]

Earth does not need to be named Gaia—Charlene Spretnak refers to "Earthbody"[14], and the Primordial Mother has many names[15]: but it is a name that now has large appeal in the West, due to James Lovelock and Lynn Margulis's scientific theory named thus, first published in 1974. The name "Gaia" now not only invokes the ancient Greek myth of the Creator-Goddess, but also the present scientific inquiry. Lovelock points out that the Gaia theory is now

> "spurring a great deal of scientific research into the geophysiology of our living planet (and) it is also spurring philosophic conceptions of what it means to our species to be part of a living planet. Some of these conceptions stay carefully within the accepted limits of science; others have a religious bent."[16]

The naming of a spirituality as "Gaian" today, signifies the integration of scientific knowledge gained by humanity into the vision and metaphor of that spirituality. For Charlene Spretnak, knowing Gaia is knowing that we are "inextricably linked at the molecular level to every other manifestation of the great unfolding. We are descendants of the fireball…glimpsing the oneness of the sacred whole."[17]

As participants in Gaia, we may understand ourselves as Gaia, holons of the Large Self, as a drop of the ocean participates in (the whole of) the ocean. I regard the concepts of holons and holarchy[18] to be a crucial model for understanding a participatory universe. Willis Harman and Elisabet Sahtouris define a holarchy as "the embeddedness of living entities within each other (e.g., cell, organ, body, family, community, ecosystem, bioregion, planet, star system, galaxy, etc.)"[19]; and they define a holon as "a living entity or system."[20] They describe the entire Universe as a vast living entity or holon, and also as "a holarchy containing smaller holons in continual co-creation."[21] A most significant feature of a holarchy is that every layer/level has as much importance as any other, because they are embedded in each other—and actually the layers of simpler life forms are not dependent on the more complex, though the more complex are dependent on the simpler earlier layers. Within the context of holarchy, it may be possible to explain by physical principles how a quality of living systems "may apply all the way from the most simple single-cell life form to Gaia."[22] The cut between the self and the "natural" world is artificial in fact—all the "way out" and through the Cosmos.

James Lovelock refers to the human as Gaia: "She has seen the reflection of her fair face through the eyes of astronauts...", and speaks of a "commonwealth of all creatures that constitutes Gaia."[23] He has spoken of his relationship with Gaia as possibly kin to the relationship of some Christians to Mary: he said "What if Mary is another name for Gaia?"[24] and later wondered if

> "...hearts and minds could be moved to see in her the embodiment of Gaia, then they might become aware that the victim of their destruction was indeed the Mother of humankind and the source of everlasting life."[25]

Some Gaian researchers, scientists who study the global metabolism, generally tread more carefully, riding a fine edge in regard to Gaia's sentience, applying the principles of science, yet "without postulating a global organism."[26] Yet for many minds today, Gaian research and knowledge of the evolutionary story furthers our knowledge of the Mother and, at once, knowledge of ourselves. The restoration of the material reality is a restoration of the maternal reality, is a restoration of the Mother.

> "For so long we've considered the Earth as just a big dead ball of dirt. It shocks us nearly out of our minds when we discover we're involved with something that moves...(that) the whole process is alive."[27]

The entire Cosmos itself has been imagined as something dead and static—the heavens as a vacuous space "out there." Just as Aristotle storied the female body as passive matter, so the Womb of Space has been imagined. The cosmology of Earth-based religious traditions, on the other hand, has always understood Earth as Mother, and the Mother as active Creator. Starhawk writes of Goddess as

> "the living body of a living cosmos, the awareness that infuses matter and the energy that produces change. She is life eternally

attempting to maintain itself, reproduce itself, diversify, evolve..."[28]

Ecologist Stephan Harding, teacher of Gaian ecophilosophy, said that "the whole reason for gathering scientific information is to provide a cognitive basis for developing wide identification with nature," that people love it when they "realize that the planet has life-like qualities of self-regulation"[29]—in my own words, people love to hear news of the Mother, that She is alive.

True self-knowledge includes knowledge of the larger Self: that is, knowledge of Gaia. Scientist Mae-Wan Ho says, "It is in knowing her that we shall have intimate knowledge of ourselves."[30] Just as the prokaryotes, the first cells on Earth deeply affected the planet and its future, so our small organism and the many others affect the planet over long periods of time. This is Gaian spirituality—taking on the mind of the Universe, participating in the dream of the Earth, beginning to *know* from within the perspective of Earth, Moon, Sun, Tree—our home and habitat. I have named such a perspective a "PaGaian" cosmology, to adequately express this integral sense of Gaia as Self-Earth-Universe, combining as the term does, the Pagan/indigenous sense of country/place—that we belong here, with an extended vision of GaiaMother, the larger primordial country of whom we are part.

## Notes

1. Charlene Spretnak, "Gaian Spirituality," *Woman of Power*, Issue 20, Spring 1991.

2. I capitalize this term here because I am implying or offering another name for the Divine.

3. Cited in Connie Barlow (ed.), *From Gaia to Selfish Genes: Selected Writings in the Life Sciences*, p. 42.

4. Susan Griffin, *Woman and Nature*, p. 219

5. Charlene Spretnak, *The Re-Surgence of the Real*, p. 4.

6. Thomas Berry, *The Dream of the Earth*, p. 2.

7. Thomas Berry, *The Dream of the Earth*, p. 2.

8. Vladimir Vernadsky, *The Biosphere*, p. 6. Elisabet Sahtouris questions whether Vernadsky really did perceive Earth as a whole live entity (*Earthdance* p. 118), and refers to Scottish scientist James Hutton, as having such a view in 1785 (*Earthdance*, p. 69).

9. Vladimir Vernadsky, *The Biosphere*, p. iv.

10. Vladimir Vernadsky, *The Biosphere*, p. 1.

11. Vladimir Vernadsky, *The Biosphere,,* p. 2.

12. Vladimir Vernadsky, *The Biosphere,,* p. 8.

13. Vladimir Vernadsky, *The Biosphere,,* p. 9.

14. Charlene Spretnak, *States of Grace*, p. 144-145.

15. "Mago" is a name for Her in East Asia: see Dr. Helen Hye-Sook Hwang: http://magoism.net/2013/07/10/meet-mago-contributor-helen-hwang/

16. In James Lovelock's Foreword to Elisabet Sahtouris, *Earthdance*, p. xiii.

17. Charlene Spretnak, "Gaian Spirituality," *Woman of Power*, Issue 20, Spring 1991, p. 17.

18. Originally they are Arthur Koestler's terms. See Connie Barlow (ed.), *From Gaia to Selfish Genes: Selected Writings in the Life Sciences*, pp. 89-100. Ken Wilber also describes them in *A Brief History of Everything*, p. 20ff.

19. Willis Harman and Elisabet Sahtouris, *Biology Revisioned*, p. 130.

20. Willis Harman and Elisabet Sahtouris, *Biology Revisioned*, p. 130.

21. Willis Harman and Elisabet Sahtouris, *Biology Revisioned*, p. xxiii.

22. Willis Harman and Elisabet Sahtouris, *Biology Revisioned*, p. xxii.

23. Cited in Connie Barlow (ed.), *From Gaia to Selfish Genes*, p. 19.

24. Cited in Connie Barlow (ed.), *From Gaia to Selfish Genes*, p. 41.

25. Cited in Connie Barlow (ed.), *From Gaia to Selfish Genes*, p. 42.

26. Tyler Volk, *Gaia's Body*, p. ix.

27. Brian Swimme, *The Universe is a Green Dragon*, p. 135.

28. Starhawk, *The Spiral Dance*, p. 228.

29. Cited in Connie Barlow, *Green Space, Green Time*, p. 216.

30. Mae-Wan Ho, "Natural Being and Coherent Society" in *Gaia in Action*, Peter Bunyard (ed.), p. 305.

## References

Barlow, Connie (ed.). *From Gaia to Selfish Genes: Selected Writings in the Life Sciences*. Massachusetts: MIT Press, 1994.

Berry, Thomas. *The Dream of the Earth*. SF: Sierra Club Books, 1990.

Griffin, Susan. *Woman and Nature: The Roaring Inside Her*. NY: Harper Colophon, 1980.

Ho, Mae-Wan. "Natural Being and Coherent Society" in *Gaia in Action*. Peter Bunyard (ed.). Edinburgh: Floris Books, 1996, pp. 286-307.

Livingstone, Glenys. *PaGaian Cosmology: Re-inventing Earth-based Goddess Religion*. Lincoln, NE: iUniverse, 2005.

Sahtouris, Elisabet. *Earthdance: Living Systems in Evolution*. Lincoln, NE: University Press, 2000.

Spretnak, Charlene. *The Resurgence of the Real: Body, Nature and Place in a Hypermodern World*. NY: Routledge, 1999.

_____. *States of Grace: The Recovery of Meaning in the Postmodern Age*. SF: HarperCollins, 1993.

_____. "Gaian Spirituality," *Woman of Power*, Issue 20, Spring 1991, pp. 10-17.

Starhawk. *The Spiral Dance: A Rebirth of the Ancient Religion of the Great Goddess*. NY: Harper and Row, 1989.

Swimme, Brian. *The Universe is a Green Dragon*. Santa Fe: Bear & Co., 1984.

Vernadsky, Vladimir. *The Biosphere*. London: Synergetic Press, 1986.

Volk, Tyler. *Gaia's Body*. NY: Springer-Verlag, 1998.

Wilber, Ken. *A Brief History of Everything*. Massachusetts: Shambhala, 1996.

## Goddess as Process: The Creativity of Change
### by Áine Órga

One of the wonderful things about dancing to the beat of your own spiritual drum is that you can constantly change your dance. You can change your practice, change your philosophy, even change your beliefs. And one of the things I love best about my personal brand of Earth-based spirituality is that the way I understand the Divine is utterly fluid.

It's not that I throw my beliefs around willy-nilly. Rather, the Divine is an incredibly complex concept, and the way I see it, there are many, many ways to understand it or approach it conceptually.

### Goddess is existence.

Goddess (or God, or God/dess) to me is the pure fact of existence. She is the fact of being. She is the unmanifest, the everything and nothing that the universe is born of and returns to. In one sense, then, She is immutable. She is what is static in Cosmos.

But She is also change. And the very stuff of the universe is the product of her constant changing.

If I were a monotheist and believed in a transcendent Divine above and beyond the universe, then That Which Is Constant might be Goddess for me; and That Which Changes would be Her creation—the universe. But as a pantheist, I feel that the matter of the universe is divine too. And I believe that everything is one, so there is no divide between the constant aspect of Goddess and the changing one.

## Is Goddess a thing, a being, a force? Or is She a process?

I feel the divinity in the interconnectedness of everything. And perhaps for me that interconnectedness *is* the Divine.

Goddess for me is not a personified deity. She is not a conscious being. She is not even something that is beyond or separate from me, or you, or *anything*. Rather, she is something that runs through us all. She is the way that we are all linked. She is the relationship between all things. She is the force of change and creativity.

But is She really a *force* in the way we traditionally understand it, or is she simply the process of Cosmos? She is many things, many forces—the tendency of Cosmos to behave in particular ways. She is the process of Cosmos.

## So what is the Goddess process?

The Goddess process is the act of change itself. Change is the energy of Cosmos. If Cosmos were not changing, it would not be creative. In fact, it is difficult to imagine how the universe could exist if it were static. Static existence is empty, a void, the unmanifest. It is the ultimate mystery.

Cosmos/Goddess changes because she is deeply connected. She is connected to everything in Cosmos, because she *is* Cosmos. And this relationship cannot happen without her changing, and without her changing it.

## The Goddess process is the act of creation through change.

What happens outside of change is a mystery to us. The universe for me *is change*. Goddess is both the existence that encompasses everything and the change that births the universe.

Cosmos encompasses the universe, but also includes anything that is beyond it. So Cosmos may on some level be static. But because it contains the universe, and the universe is part of it, it is also in constant change.

Goddess and Cosmos are to me somewhat synonymous. But Cosmos is the matter, the fact—Goddess is the process, the creativity, the change. The universe is *part* of Cosmos. But the Goddess *created* the universe.

So on some level, I believe in a creator God. But the way I got there is turned on its head. Rather than deciding that there is a conscious being in charge of the universe who must have created it, I have decided to call that act of creation itself divinity.

## Naming the Water: Human and Deity Identity from an Earth-Centered Perspective
by Alison Leigh Lilly

As a Pagan, my theology is rooted firmly in the earth. To me, the earth is sacred, and so the ecological truths that guide and shape life on this tiny blue marble are sacred truths. One of those truths is that identity is fluid. I can no more name the discrete entity that is "me" than I can name the water flowing in a river. From moment to moment, that identity changes. This was the insight of the Buddhists, too: we are not the same person from one second to the next, and reincarnation is less like viscous soul-substance getting sloshed from one meat-container into the next as it is like a flame passing from one wick to another. Is it the same flame? Yes…and then again, no.

Like a river is defined by its shore, my identity is defined by my limitations, by the extremities of my being. I learned this before I even had the words for it. The first time a wail escaped my infant throat and my mother's breast was not there to soothe my hunger, I knew what it was to be me and not her. I discovered how to move fingers and toes, how odd it was that these unwieldy awkward bits of flesh and bone were somehow responsive to my will in ways that other bits and pieces of the material world weren't. We all experienced this as infants, learning who we are by discovering who and what we are not.

As we grow up, we discover that technologies and material possessions can expand our sense of self-identity as they help us overcome our natural limitations. When we sit behind the wheel of a car and speed down a highway—no, of course we don't believe that we are literally the car, but our ability to drive depends on us momentarily losing that distinction at a subconscious level, being able to respond with instinctual quickness to swerve as that deer darts out in front of us. When we play video games, our sense of identity expands and we know what it is like to be our avatars. Scientific studies confirm this, in everything from our emotional well-being and psychological state of mind, to how we form habits in our real lives. (Did you know playing a video game in which you watch an avatar of yourself lose weight as it exercises can encourage you to exercise more frequently "irl"? Did you know that gamers with obese or unattractive avatars experience bullying and emotional abuse from other gamers that is just as damaging to their health and well-being as real-life prejudice and fat-shaming?)

The fact that material possessions and technologies can help us expand our sense of self is part of the impetus behind the rampant consumerism of modern culture. Accumulating and hoarding wealth can make us feel powerful, less vulnerable to scarcity, less insecure about the uncertainties of the future. Our sense of self-identity is shaped by what clothes we wear, what car we drive, what kind of house we live in, what indie music we listen to, what soda we drink, what organic foods we eat, even who we vote for—all the ways that our limitations are expressed or obscured in the eyes of our fellow human beings. Our personal choices are also ways that we communicate our belonging to different overlapping communities: foodies, conservatives, cyclists, dog lovers, environmentalists, Pagans. Self-identity is a social as well as a physical construct.

There are also ways of engaging with self-identity that are grounded in our sense of the sacred. Spiritual practices and rituals can teach us about the fluidity of our identities through exercises that alter our states of consciousness. Meditative practices of stillness and silence open up an internal space within which we lose our sense of limitation, the discrete boundaries of our being. Without the constant friction and noise of our being rubbing up against the banks of self-consciousness, we forget for a moment where our physical bodies end and the rest of the world begins. Like a river entering an ocean, we flow one into the other. This, too, is confirmed by neurological research into the effects of meditation on the brain: increased activity and interconnectivity among different parts of the physical brain, and a gentle relaxation in the right parietal lobe that is responsible for, among other things, spatial relations. Practices like fasting, contemplative prayer, sweat lodge ceremonies, shamanic trance-work, even time in a sensory deprivation tank can bring on similar effects, altering our sense of our physical bodies and their limitations, allowing us to rejoice in the power and energy that flows in and through us. It is not an accident of history that so many religions throughout the world have traditions of mystical union and ecstasy. The belief in the unity of being arises from the experiences of worshippers themselves as they explore the porousness of the boundaries of self-identity.

But self-identity is also a mystery of multiplicity. Intense, sustained physical activities like dance, martial arts, labyrinth-walking, and sometimes painful acts like scourging or other forms of ritualistic body mutilation—all these can bring the boundaries of our being into sharp relief as dynamic liminal spaces of exchange and communication. Through community rituals of dance and movement, we experience our boundaries not as rigid forms that keep us trapped within ourselves, but as coterminous places of contact with the vast diversity of being beyond ourselves. We experience our extremities, the limits of our being, moving in harmony and grace within the sacred variety of world-being. And like a serpentine river whose banks are worn away by the rushing waters, twisting and changing through the landscape over time—our engagement with our own boundaries allows us to shape those boundaries as well, to craft our self-identity as a vessel of the sacred life-force that flows through us and connects us to all other beings.

The multiplicity of human identity is not just a spiritual principle, it's a biological fact—a basic ecological reality. The cells that make up your body are dying off all the time, replaced by new cells born of the food you eat and the water you drink. We shed skin cells more quickly than it takes for our fingernails to grow out, and we replace the cells of our stomach lining sometimes as quickly as every meal. Even with all this, only 10% of the cells in your body belong to you. The rest are the cells of bacteria and microorganisms that call your body home, and without these symbionts living on and within your physical self, you would be unable to digest and process the nutrients necessary to keep you alive. Your physical body is teeming with a microscopic diversity of life that rivals a rainforest. The insight of the Gaia Theory—that "the Earth system behaves as a single self-regulating system comprised of physical, chemical, biological and human components"—is as much a statement about our own physical bodies as it is about the planet. If we imagine the Earth as the body of a goddess, we can also imagine our own bodies as a sacred home to an ecologically complex and diverse array of microscopic life.

These are the first glimmerings of an earth-centered theology of polytheism. If human identity is complex, both personal and social, physical and psychological, spiritual and ecological—why should we expect deity identity to be any simpler? If our sense of self-identity is fluid and changeable, interconnected, responsive to the teeming, dancing life that permeates and surrounds us—why should we expect the gods to be objective, discrete and separate beings? The experience of spiritual practice and the biology of physical life teach us otherwise—showing us both the astounding unity and the sacred, interconnected multiplicity of being.

According to some, there are only two approaches to a theology of polytheism. There is hard polytheism, which believes that the gods have a definite sense of separate self-identity, and that humans would likewise retain such an identity even after death. And then there is the psychological approach that sees the gods as archetypes, stories that we tell ourselves about ourselves and that, as powerful or moving as they may be, remain little more than make-believe, a fiction. Neither of these approaches seems all that satisfying to me. Both are abstract doctrines, not articulations of our real experiences of the world which ground us in a bone-deep knowledge of identity as porous and complex.

Identity does not have to be simple in order to be meaningful. It does not have to be rigid in order to be real.

I suggest a third alternative, an ecological or natural polytheism. In this natural theology, identity is responsive and creative, and divinity, like everything else in the sacred cosmos, is interwoven, connecting us all to all other aspects of being. We move through a world rife with gods and spirits, and a multitude of gods dwell within each of us. We show up to liminal places of communication—whether they be small altars tucked away in our homes, or the banks of a raging river carving serpentine paths through the wide, rolling landscape—and we open ourselves to experiences of connection in which we discover the porous, flexible natures of our own boundaries. We practice our spirituality through ritual and prayer, and discover that boundaries are not rigid constructs that separate us from the gods, but sacred points of contact, created and destroyed and re-created with every holy act. We rub up against divine being with every turn in the sacred dance, feeling the warm friction of our extremities, the very limits that define our beauty and direct our power.

We show up to the banks of the sacred river. Here the shore curves in such a way that a small pool opens up among the eddies, spiraling and foaming, and we catch glimpses of a presence unique to this place, here and now. Tomorrow, a year from now, a decade, a millennium, the river's banks may have changed. But for now, this place is familiar to us, this presence is a friend. We name this place with the name of deity. The banks of the river define its identity for us, as the unique personalities and limitations of the gods define their identities for us in our worship. They step into our lives as guides, givers of wisdom, inspiration and love, as familiar patterns in the spiraling energies that move the universe. But neither the river nor the gods are static, unchanging abstractions separate from the physical, natural world.

We can name this river, here and now—but we cannot name the water itself. We can name our gods and we can name ourselves, but we cannot name the essence of sacred identity that flows through both, that connects us and sanctifies us.

## Natural Theology: Polytheism Beyond the Pale
### by Alison Leigh Lilly

When exploring polytheism in an ecological context, we quickly find ourselves beyond the pale: out in the wilds shaped by natural forces of forest and river, sea and shoreline, wind and rain, the slow dance of erosion and the sudden violent shifting of tectonic plates. Where do the gods fit into this wilderness? How does our theology grapple with the realities of the natural world that transcend yet include human civilization and our familiar anthropocentric concerns? What does it mean to worship beyond the pale?

### Deepen Your Relationship with the Gods

In theology, as in magic, words have a deep power. They define concepts and construct mental abstracts that we map onto the world, creating boundaries where once there was only the chaotic beauty of what is.

But certain words are particularly powerful. They invoke not only what they mean, but what they do not mean. Words like "fast" or "loud" have obvious opposites that jump to mind immediately. "Hard" is one of those words that is especially potent. When Pagans talk about "hard polytheism," they invoke a theological framework which places hard polytheism in opposition to other forms of polytheism, usually referred to as "soft polytheism." Soft polytheism might include anything from the duotheism of many Wiccans, to a Jungian theology of archetypes among humanist Pagans, from animism or pantheism, to panentheism, monism, henotheism or even syncretic monotheism. Most hard polytheists define their theology as "a belief in many individual deities as separate and distinct entities" and define soft polytheism as a belief that all gods are manifestations of a single Divine source or spirit.

But by choosing to draw this distinction using the language of a dichotomy between hard versus soft, they also evoke another pair of opposites: hard versus easy. There's the unspoken suggestion (or sometimes directly stated opinion) that someone who is "soft" on polytheism (like a politician who is "soft" on crime) is somehow taking the easy way out, reducing a complex issue to an overly simplified solution.

In my essay, "Naming the Water: Human and Deity Identity from an Earth-Centered Perspective," I suggested that ecological or "natural polytheism" might provide an alternative to a theology of hard polytheism that struggles with complex questions of human and deity identity. Where hard polytheism draws hard and fast lines separating the gods from humans, from natural forces, and from each other, natural polytheism embraces a theology of interweaving and interpenetrating boundaries of identity. From a hard polytheistic perspective, this might sound a lot like "soft" polytheism: individual deities as expressions of the complex relationships and patterns of force and consciousness in the cosmic soup of existence.

But natural polytheism doesn't have to be "soft" at all. In fact, you can be a hard polytheist and a natural polytheist—it's just a matter of deepening your relationship with your gods and learning to ask the tough questions.

### Start Asking the Tough Questions

In the introduction to his book, *The Natural History of Puget Sound Country* (1991), Arthur Kruckeberg explores how a text on natural history differs from a guide book or reference book about plant and animal species in the region. His musings lay bare the revolutionary importance of ecology as a science of systems:

> "In probing the natural world, what kinds of questions do we ask? Easiest are the 'what' and 'how' questions. 'What is it?' and 'How does it work?' usually can be given direct answers. The unknown tree or insect gets a name and a place in its family tree to satisfy the 'What is it?' question. Though more demanding of

observation and thought, the 'How does it work?' question also has ready answers. The literature of how things function in the world of life is the product of patient experiment and observation by plant and animal biologists. It is only when curiosity persists to the 'How come?' stage that science reveals its tentative and ever-probing qualities. The answers to 'What for?' questions asked of the color of a flower, the hair on an insect's body, or the slime of a slippery slug, are within the domains of ecology and the study of adaptations."

For centuries, the hard sciences of physics, chemistry and biology have been absolutely essential tools in our exploration of the physical universe as we look for answers to questions like "What is it?" and "How does it work?" It's only in the last few decades that ecology—the scientific study of the relationships living organisms have with each other and with their natural environment—has begun to bring these separate fields of investigation together into a more holistic understanding of the natural world. If we want to understand "how come" the propagation of palm trees affects the mineral and nutrient levels in the surrounding coastal waters of a tropical island, and why this in turn influences the fluctuating population of manta rays, we need to understand not just biology, botany, chemistry and geology, but how all of these sciences work together as a single system.

Ecology does not reject the hard sciences that came before it, but brings together and expands upon them.

In this same way, natural polytheism draws on an ecological approach to theology to build upon the insights of hard polytheism, challenging us to deepen our relationships with the gods by asking more challenging questions about their relationships with us, with each other and with the natural world. Natural polytheism does not reject hard polytheism any more than natural history excludes hard sciences like biology, geology or chemistry by embracing ecology. But it does draw connections and invite us to think about the world holistically, as systems nested within systems, wholes nested within wholes. An ecological perspective can deepen our scientific understanding of the world by moving us beyond the questions "What is it?" and "How does it work?" to the more challenging questions, "How come?" and "What for?"

In the same way, natural polytheism isn't content merely to name the gods and identify their associations, symbols and spheres of influence. It challenges us to ask: How did the gods come to be the way they are? How do the gods relate to each other, within cultures and across cultural boundaries? What is the cultural, physical or spiritual reason why this particular deity manifests in this way but not that way, embodies these associations or symbols but not those?

## Why the Tough Questions Matter

During a conversation with a Pagan friend of mine recently, she mentioned in passing that Apollo wasn't the Greek god of the sun as many people believe—the Greek sun god was actually Helios. For many reconstructionist or hard polytheists, this distinction is an important one and getting a fact like this wrong is a big faux-pas.

But from the perspective of natural polytheism, this kind of distinction is only part of the truth. It brings up many more fascinating questions that can deepen our understanding of deity far beyond just "Who is it?" and "How do they work?" For instance: What is the relationship between Apollo and Helios? Why is one a personification of a physical celestial body, while the other has associations not just with solar energy and light, but also with music and culture? How has the relationship between Apollo and Helios evolved and changed over time, and what might this tell us about changes in Greek culture (and aspects of our own culture today)? What might it tell us about our attitudes towards the sun as a physical object as well as a cultural symbol? What does it tell us about our personal relationship with the sun, and with gods of the sun? And what are those relationships for?

From the natural polytheistic perspective, the question of whether or not Apollo is a "god of the sun" is not nearly as interesting as the question of how he is connected to the sun. After all, there is no plant, animal or ecosystem on earth that does not have some relationship with the sun as the planet's primary source of energy—the real investigation begins when we start to wonder how an entity's relationship with the sun expresses itself in ways that are unique to the local landscape, and how this relationship affects the ways that everything else in that landscape lives and works together as a whole. Accepting that beings in an ecosystem, and the ecosystem itself, have a relationship with the sun, or with global patterns of ocean currents or air circulation, does not make them any less unique or complex—quite the opposite! The same is true for natural polytheism.

Natural polytheism is polytheism beyond the pale: polytheism beyond the restrictions staked out by our grasp of human history alone, embracing instead the whole of natural history and the modern sciences that give us insights into our world in new and startling ways. Hard polytheism demarcates boundaries that separate the gods from each other and from the natural forces and patterns (human and more-than-human) that enrich our world. Natural polytheism does not reject or ignore these boundaries. Instead, it places polytheistic theology in a new, more challenging context and provokes our curiosity to discover more powerful ways of living out our relationships with the sacred. It forces us to ask not just "Who is this god that I have experienced in ritual?" and "How do I worship him?", but also "Why did I experience this god in this way?" and "How does my practice itself shape my beliefs and my experiences of the gods?"

Natural polytheism embraces the science of ecology as a basic metaphor for theological inquiry. In other words, natural polytheism seeks to understand our relationship with the gods as an aspect of interrelated systems of being, consciousness and meaning. Its focus is, first and foremost, on the wildernesses that defy our carefully mapped boundary lines, that penetrate even the most civilized cultural centers and underlie our most cherished notions of what it means to be human.

## Naturalism and the Gods
### by Glen Gordon

Having a naturalist sensibility, I always found supernatural concepts of deities within Paganism difficult to accept. Having been unsure if concepts of deities were valuable, I drifted towards an agnostic humanism. But exposure to the blending of process theism and religious naturalism in Karl E. Peters' book *Dancing with the Sacred* (2002) reawakened my interest in polytheism. By applying naturalistic process theism to polytheism, I now see deities as processes which superimpose and overlap each other in complex patterns of creativity. And I see ceremony as a powerful method of actively participating in these processes.

Process theology moves away from God as an omnipotent being, and describes God as the act of becoming. In this way, God is found in the events which shape our experiences and initiate change in our lives. Religious Naturalism finds value in religious expression and experience and holds the natural living-world sacred without supernatural intervention. Peters combines these two perspectives by seeing God as continuous evolutionary creativity. Thus, God is found both by the experience of the scientist seeking to understand the building blocks of life and in the experience of the religious person longing to understand humanity's place within the cosmos. Upon reading Peters' book, I began to see processes everywhere as God's becoming: in the groupings of atoms that create matter, in the weather cycle, in the evolution of lifeforms, and in human creations like art, literature, and music.

## Into Action

As a member of a group of Pagan and naturalist Unitarian Universalists, I began incorporating these concepts into group ceremonies. One ceremony focused around the planting of native seeds at our UU church. We spent a week preparing the ground with meditative intent. In song and dance, we sowed the seeds under the night sky of the autumnal equinox. These experiences helped me understand myself as an active co-creator with the processes of the natural living-world. As I combined my efforts and will with these creative evolutionary processes, I came to see deities no longer as individual personal beings, but as those processes with which I contributed by active participation.

## Beyond Anthropomorphism

These realizations caused me to question the usefulness of anthropomorphism as a way of understanding deity. Giving deities human-like forms may have made sense at one point of human understanding. Perhaps to understand how deities worked, we gave them human form. But the downside is that these images became the focus of worship. In a postmodern context, with our expanded understanding of the world around us, anthropomorphism feels outdated. It can help us understand those processes which are related most closely to human experience, but it limits us to a human-centric understanding.

I believe there are far more deities than those known from ancient mythic narratives. (How many gods have now been forgotten?) And there are new gods emerging all the time which go unnoticed by neopolytheism. I do not worship gods from ancient narratives belonging to any time or culture I can never know. I am called by a different kind of deity. These deities consist of love, music, evolution, water, fire, electricity, dark matter, food, and the atmosphere, to name a few. They are not gods *of* anything; rather they are the actual processes mentioned above.

## Seeking the Transpersonal

The goal of transpersonal psychology is to explore those experiences which transcend the separation of ego and otherness. A transpersonal relationship with a deity expands our experience of deity through participation. Deity is not a being or a vague idea of the sacred, but a continuous experience of co-creation that is malleable and present within each passing moment. This contrasts with the desire of many neopolytheists to seek interpersonal relationships with deities. In my experience, images of deities may be useful in identifying and understanding the processes which are deities, but they should not be allowed to become static representations, nor should they be the focus of worship. I prefer seeking a trans-personal relationship that allows me to participate in the sacred process that is the deity.

It is the distinction between transpersonal and interpersonal relationships with deities which sets naturalistic polytheism apart from neopolytheism. Interpersonal relationships are between two or more persons and are focused upon individual perspectives. A transpersonal relationship extends beyond the individual perspective, transcending the distinctions of ego and personality. For example:

> A *neopolytheist* has a close personal relationship with a modernized personification of Thor, to whom she prays to daily.
>
> A *naturalistic polytheist* practices breathing as a sacrament which allows her to focus on life's connection to the atmosphere, altering her perception of separateness, resulting in viewing the atmosphere as a deity.

## Naturalistic Polytheism

Looking upon the gods both as relational and as processes, I see that they touch my life in many subtle ways. One form of worship is the simple act of mindful breathing. I call this my sacrament of breath. The continuous transformation of the atmospheric cycle is the focus of this practice. I attune myself to become mindful of how amazing the atmospheric cycle is, and to cultivate a sense of awe at the act of breathing. As I breathe, I worship. And it is not a solitary worship, but a *global* worship involving all within the biosphere. Who would have guessed breathing is such a mystical experience?!

There are other ways I participate in creation with these deities. Cooking can become an act of worship, or picking up litter at my favorite park, planting native seeds with my community, having sex, being involved in environmental justice, or planting my feet in bare soil—the possibilities are endless. I see gods everywhere. I cannot go a day without seeing and interacting with gods in the most subtle and sacred of ways.

Seeing deities as active, creative evolutionary processes deepens my understanding of ceremony and religious experience. I do not see worship as passive, but as an active expression of co-creation with the universe and the natural living world. I refer to this approach as naturalistic polytheism. It has allowed me to see that the scientific and the sacred are not contradictory, but part of each other. By taking a naturalistic perspective of deities and mythology, the traditions of the past can come to life, and we can develop new traditions, appropriate to who we are as human beings today.

## "What Do You Mean, 'God,' Cat?"
### by Cat Chapin-Bishop

I am utterly inconsistent in the spiritual language that I use. One day, I will write "Spirit." Another day, I will write "God" or "gods." Here's why:

Outside my window, I can hear the forest breathe.

It is a hot day—one of the last really hot, humid days of a New England summer. Thunderstorms are predicted for the afternoon, and they will be fed, in part, by the moisture that the trees—swamp maple, sugar maple, white oak and hemlock—are transpiring into the air above the woods.

The forest is breathing, breathing out in a long, deep, sighing exhale, and its breath passes over and through the tops of the trees. And through my window, I hear the breath of the land. I hear the life of the land.

Between the waves of wind that ruffle the leaves, I hear the soft, high music of crickets, singing their death song to the summer. I hear the hawk perched in the top of a white pine. I hear a different set of sighing waves, as traffic passes along the road beside my house. All these things are distinct, and all these things form a whole. The life is in the parts, the individuals; the life is in the whole, the totality.

I am a human. I see myself, almost always, as an individual human consciousness, caught up in my lonely envelope of flesh and skin. But the car I drive breathes out its carbon (as do I; as does my house, the hawk, the crickets) and the trees breathe in what of it they can. The rest rises, on the outbreaths of the trees, into the atmosphere. It traps a little more of the heat of the sun, raises the temperature of the oceans, alters the cycle of the seasons, the patterns of climate…My car, my carbon, feeds the heat that draws out the breath of the trees, feeds the heat that intensifies the power of our storms, brings on the heat and humidity of this morning, and very likely, the flash floods and winds of this afternoon.

I see myself as an individual. But I am still a part of a whole.

Each human, cricket, hawk, and tree has their own life. But they remain a part of the whole. We breathe together, whether we know it or not. We are many—and we are one.

I am a spiritually bilingual writer. As a Pagan, I sense the life within all of the parts. As a Quaker, I listen to the life of the whole.

I became a Pagan (a Wiccan, originally) shortly after the birth of my only daughter in 1986. I became a Quaker shortly after the destruction of the World Trade Center in 2001. Neither of those decisions was "notional," as Quakers would put it; neither of those decisions was a result of a purely reasoned and intellectual process. In a very real sense, my religions chose me; I did not choose them. More than rational Powers have guided my journey.

The more than rational Power I experienced within my body while it was shaping a new human life won me to Paganism. It was the physical, sensual experience of living in a life-bearing woman's body that called me to Wicca. My *body* taught me it was more—I was more—than I thought I was. My body taught me that physical being is holy, and that you can turn to your body for illumination.

What that illumination gave me, as I sat suckling an infant and reading Margot Adler, was Witchcraft. I am a Witch because my daughter's life growing inside my own taught me to be. There were additional, formal lessons eventually. It was not my body alone that taught me these ways…but those are details. It was my body, first, that taught me to notice spirit…everywhere.

As a Witch, I know that there is spiritual force in everything. As a Witch, I know that the deer I glimpse in the woods is a member of the species *Odocoileus virginianus*; I know that it is male or female, young or old. I know that the stag lives alone in the summertime, but that it will den down with others of its kind in winter. I know that it may come and eat my apple trees, killing them—or eat from my yew trees or from the mountain laurels in the woods, taking no harm from leaves that would surely poison me.

Those deer are individuals. And they are part of a shared genetic heritage…and distant relatives of the *Megaloceros giganteaus*, extinct since the last ice age and never present on my continent, and of the red deer and Irish elk that have become so interwoven with European legends and myths—legends and myths that have seeped into my subconscious, and that take shape sometimes as the Spirit of the Deer or the Horned God of the Hunt.

Sometimes the deer that I see is only that individual deer. Sometimes it is that deer, *and* the spirit of the land on which we both live. And sometimes it is a messenger of the god I call Herne, and He has come through a messenger, specifically to speak to *me*.

How do I know which spirit is which? I use my Witch's sight, the same inward vision that first called me to become Pagan. I rely on a form of gnosis…and sometimes I am wrong. Of course, as I have come to understand, seeing the world only through the eyes of reason—that will be wrong sometimes, too.

Likewise, sometimes the earth in my garden is an assemblage of partially composted corn cobs, last year's manure from the farm just down the road, and the teeming host of microbes found in healthy dirt. And then at other times, the earth in my garden is the flesh of our Holy Mother, the living planet Earth.

Sometimes, I understand that the sacred lives within the individual. Sometimes, I understand that it lives in the interrelationships between many individuals—a herd of deer, a forest…a planet. Sometimes, those interrelationships themselves stand out in distinct patterns of individuality—as distinct as you or I. (Are you an individual? Ask the bacterial cells that live within you—ten times more of those than of your own! And yet, you will say yes, and it is true.)

With my Pagan vision, I can see shapes of individuals, of beings larger than we are. These shapes have names that humans have given them over time. For the sake of argument, we can call them gods.

We do not make them, these beings. Perhaps we shape their stories—certainly, we write them down. Who are they, really? More than our imaginations. More than we understand.

I said that I am spiritually bilingual. My Pagan language for my Pagan vision is not the only language my heart can understand. On the day that I became a Quaker, Something large stopped me in my tracks and poured an understanding straight into my heart. I've never been the same since then.

It was Paganism that taught me to listen when the gods spoke. It was Paganism that taught me that the gods are real. It was Paganism, then, that made me a Quaker.

As a Pagan, I learned to listen to the spirit within the parts, and of relationships among the parts. As a Quaker, I learned to listen to the Spirit within the whole.

Eventually, it began to feel labored, even precious, to go out of my way never to call that Spirit "God." It began to seem less than faithful, to change my words to reassure my hearers, "I am not a monotheist!" And I am not. But sometimes, I speak with the same words as those who are.

What do I mean by "God"? Not a white guy with a beard, sitting on a Michelangelo cloud. Not a person at all, though not an *it*, not the mere inanimate, unconscious physical fact of existence.

I mean something much more intimate than that—not a person, but personal. Aware. Large. Interested, and loving. I mean that, because that is what I felt, what I feel, when I sit in Quaker worship. Something there is that lives in everything that is. Something there is that loves us, and wants us to be kind.

What I mean when I say "God" is the wind outside my window. The wind that is more than my body or the woods, that shapes our weather and shapes our world…but is also the living breath of crickets, hawks, and trees.

Pythagoreans Celebrate the Sunrise
by Fyodor Bronnikov (1827—1902)

## Part 5: Who Are We Talking To Anyway?: Non-Theistic Paganism and God-Talk

Non-theistic Paganism can seem pretty confusing to both atheists and theists. To make matters more confusing, some non-theistic Pagans choose to use theistic language, both in conversations about theology and in ritual. For some, the use of theistic language in a ritual context is more productive of certain kinds of religious experience than non-theistic language.

As B. T. Newberg has explained, the words "god" and "gods" are embedded in a complex web of cultural associations. Such language is laden with emotional resonance and has unique potential to evoke powerful emotions of a special character. Because the word "god" lacks an objective referent for non-theistic Pagans, it is like a container that can be filled with many different meanings. Whatever goes in the container takes on the qualities associated with the word, including a sense of sacredness and moral power.

In addition, much of theistic language is also anthropomorphic. Some non-theistic Pagans find anthropomorphic language to be effective in a ritual context, because it stimulates different parts of the brain than non-anthropomorphic language. Anthropomorphic language activates the regions of the brain associated with sociality and relationship, in contrast to the part of the brain that processes objects and abstractions.

This is why we may have a different experience in response to words like "God" or "Goddess" than we do to more abstract or impersonal words like "Being" or "Nature." For example, we may experience "Goddess" as a "Thou" (to use Martin Buber's term) rather than an "it" — even when we are using the word to mean something impersonal like nature. As a result, we can become open to a kind of relationship with nature that would have been impossible had we used more objective (or objectifying) language, and more susceptible to the life-transforming experiences that flow from that relationship.

## In Defense of Gods
### by B. T. Newberg

Why would a naturalist speak of goddesses and gods? What do these words offer that other terms do not?

Whenever a naturalist pulls out the "g" word, there is always the danger of misunderstanding. Others may suppose a supernatural meaning, though naturalists disavow any such thing. Instead, naturalists point to aspects of nature, existence, or the mind. So, why not speak of these things directly? Wouldn't it be better to use some other word, like "nature," "being," or "psychology"?

This essay attempts to show that the word enjoys advantages not enjoyed by competing terms such as these. While some naturalists may use a different term, categorically denying all naturalists use of it throws the baby out with the bathwater. A careful analysis of the word's traits reveals its unique virtues.

First, the context of the discussion must be made clear: we're talking about use of the word as part of a living religious or spiritual path. If precision of meaning were the only criterion, it might be better if naturalists chose some other term. But in religion, experience counts as much as precision, if not more. Both head and heart must be considered. Thus, words must be evaluated for their potential to shape a person's responses to ritual, meditative, and mythic activities. The goal, then, is to find words that offer maximum potential for religious experience while still maintaining a reasonable amount of semantic precision.

In order to demonstrate how "goddess," "god," and "gods" (hereafter just "god") offer a unique balance of head and heart not offered by competing terms, we must consider seven of the word's most pertinent traits:

- variance across and within cultures
- contested meaning
- rich associations
- absence of objective-world referent
- anthropomorphism
- sense of the unpredictable
- narrative

The following is an intellectual argument, but it is motivated by personal empirical experience. I have been agnostic and more or less naturalistic since high school, but upon discovering Druidry, I was surprised to find ritual with deities creating powerful experiences. "This is working," I thought, "but why?!" I believe it has to do with the specific traits of a word like "god," with its cultural context and anthropomorphism. It plays on the strings of human nature to conduce toward a certain kind of experience not easily accessible by other means. The following argument may be abstract and intellectual, but it is meant to explain a concrete, empirical experience.

### Variance across and within cultures

First, "god" is a culturally contingent term, varying across cultures and even within cultures. Some words, like "two" or "circle" are more or less universal, but "god" is highly variable across cultures. This means that precision of meaning is going to be a hairy matter no matter what. The word can only be understood within the context of the speaker's culture, subculture, and personal beliefs. Absolute precision is a lost cause, though it is still very possible for two people to understand one another by defining their meaning. Naturalists can formulate working definitions to improve precision.

## Contested meaning

Second, since the word "god" varies across and within cultures, it is a contested term. Myriad cultural traditions vie to determine its meaning in different ways. It cannot be said to have a single authoritative meaning, and the most common meaning must not be construed as the most authoritative. Supernatural definitions have no greater claim to it than naturalistic ones. The latter enjoy a venerable lineage, traceable through Santayana and Spinoza all the way back to Stoicism, Neo-Confucianism, and other ancient traditions. This shows that naturalistic definitions are not imprecise deviations from supernatural ones; rather, they are precise definitions with their own precedents.

## Rich associations

Third, the word "god" is embedded in a complex web of associations. Considering its proven ability to inspire powerful emotions and myriad creative interpretations over the centuries, we might say that it is particularly rich in this regard. It is critical to note that among its associations are a sense of heightened importance (sacredness), ultimate questions (e.g., why are we here), and a relation to moral values (how we live our lives). These grant it a unique power to evoke experiences of profound importance and moral relevance. When the word is invoked within a ritual, the mind is signaled to take the message seriously and consider it in relation to how life ought to be lived. Using the word thus prepares the mind for a potentially life-transforming experience.

## Absence of objective-world referent

Fourth, "god" is a word that may or may not have a referent in the objective world, depending on one's ontology. Some words, like "unicorn," refer to something recognizable and real (the idea of a unicorn), but not to something that can be found in the objective world (unicorns don't exist). They can be found in the subjective world (in the mind's eye, courtesy of imagination), and the inter-subjective world of representation (in art and literature), but not the objective world of nature. Those who believe literally in gods consider them to exist in the objective world somehow, but naturalists do not believe that to be the case. If the word "god" has any objective-world referent, it must be allegorical, like "Thor" referring to thunder or "Artemis" to untamed wilderness. Yet it must not be overlooked that even in the absence of a real-world referent, the word still refers to something "real"—an internal experience in the mind's eye.

As a word with no objective-world referent, it might be expected to lack a certain *oomf*. Yet the tradeoff is freedom from objective constraints. The individual is able to read a wide variety of meanings and connotations into it, which makes it an extremely flexible mental tool. With a bit of interpretation, it can be brought to bear on any present problem or situation with relative ease. None of this detracts from the "realness" of the subjective experience. Rather, the insight it inspires and feelings it evokes are very real. This reality is made especially palpable by the next trait to be considered, that of anthropomorphism.

## Anthropomorphism

Fifth, the word "god" is anthropomorphic. That is, it suggests person-like associations, though in the naturalist view it does not refer to objective persons. This critical trait means the word enters the realm of sociality, which the human brain handles differently than inert objects or abstractions. This is a controversial claim, so some elaboration is in order.

Some of the most popular theories about why human intelligence evolved propose that the driving factor was sociality (Whiten, 2007). In an environment where the greatest threat was other humans, interpreting other people's intentions was a priority. Large groups competing for mates and other resources had the advantage over those who could guess what others were thinking, and whether others knew that they knew what they were thinking. Thus, it is not an exaggeration to say that the human mind is designed for sociality.

Furthermore, the brain seems to handle language differently than other tasks. It seems to have evolved not as a single general processing unit, but as an amalgamation of connected sub-units or "modules" with different purposes. Mithen (1999) proposes different modules for natural history, linguistics, and other tasks, including sociality. This suggests that the brain responds in a fundamentally different way to persons than to things.

Given these two facts, it is reasonable to assume that an anthropomorphic term activates different brain functions than a non-anthropomorphic term. It activates a special module that has been designed by evolution with particular care. This does not mean the brain is necessarily *better* at dealing with persons, but it does mean that it deals with them differently and with special relevance. (As an aside, this might explain Martin Buber's dichotomy between the I-It experience and the I-Thou experience, the former comprising an objective, analytical stance and the latter a subjective, social stance.)

An anthropomorphic term will therefore stimulate a different range of physiological responses than a non-anthropomorphic term. Those responses will be similar to those evoked by social interaction, and may therefore stimulate such social emotions as empathy, compassion, love, gratitude, etc. It matters little that the term does not refer to an objective person, because recent neurological research has revealed there is no difference in activated brain regions between imagining a thing and objectively experiencing it (Schjoedt, et al., 2009). So, in sum, anthropomorphic terms stimulate physiological responses specific to sociality that are not necessarily accessible via abstract terms like "being," "nature," and so on. We are biologically biased to treat anthropomorphic terms differently.

### Sense of the unpredictable

Sixth, as an anthropomorphic term "god" connotes a certain unpredictability. Persons are assigned the power of will, which makes them complex decision-makers. Whatever tendencies they might exhibit, they may always act contrary to expectations. Thus, there is always an element of unpredictability in the word "god." In contrast, abstract concepts are considered to have meanings that are relatively fixed and predictable. This allows them to be taken for granted, freeing up processing space for other cognitive tasks.

Persons cannot be taken for granted in this way; they cannot be reasoned about like objective things. Persons are ever variable, and therefore ever at the forefront of consideration. This means an anthropomorphic term will occupy more of one's attention; it is privileged in working memory and may thus exert greater influence on the decision-making process. Thus, if one's goal is to influence one's decision-making process toward, say, enhanced empathy or compassion, an anthropomorphic term can be a powerful ally, if only because it commands more attention through its sense of unpredictability.

## Narrative

Seventh and finally, as an anthropomorphic term "god" is also a narrative term. Persons act in ways that we naturally describe in terms of story ("she said this, then I did that, then this happened"). So, "gods" are naturally known through myths (which essentially are narratives of divine actions) and rituals (which essentially are enacted narratives). This is important because narrative is universal among humans. Storytelling is known in every society, from the simplest to the most complex. It is common among all classes, races, genders, and ages. Whereas abstract thinking requires a certain level of maturation, narrative thinking comes easily from a very young age. It continues to be favored by all types of people throughout life, whereas highly abstract thinking may appeal differently to various occupations, subcultures, and levels of education. Thus, anthropomorphic terms are effective across diverse populations.

There is one more crucial point about narrative. More than any other mode of communication, narrative invites suspension of disbelief. It might be argued that many of the qualities of anthropomorphic terms mentioned above depend on believing literally in their objective-world referents. Yet this is not the case, because we are endowed with the power to suspend disbelief. By this power, we can bring imagination to bear and thereby experience a physiological response without necessarily assenting to the reality of the stimulus. Art moves us. Poetry moves us. Myth moves us. Thus, we can be moved to love or gratitude even by a word with no objective-world referent. The only limit is the degree to which we can learn to temporarily suspend disbelief. If one's goal is to train the empathic response, anthropomorphic terms can be valuable by virtue of their narrative quality.

Temporary suspension of disbelief in a word like "god" allows it to come alive for the period of a ritual or meditation, just as it allows theatrical characters to come alive for the length of a play. There is never a moment when we don't ultimately know the characters are really actors, but we allow ourselves to take them as if they were real. This enables us to experience powerful responses not readily accessible by other means. When we are watching a play, we say "Hamlet," instead of the more technically precise phrase, "the actor portraying a Danish prince," because the latter takes us out of the play. The former maintains the personhood of the character, and thereby lets us relate to him as if he were a real person for the duration of the drama. The same is true of "god," "goddess," or "Zeus." By preserving a sense of personhood, invoking "Persephone" in ritual lets us relate to her in a way that we could not by invoking "being," "nature," "psychology," or other such terms.

It should be emphasized that the power of a word like "god" operates by our consent—we must willingly suspend disbelief in order to take it seriously. Art may entice us, but it cannot compel us against our will. Thus, there is no chance that the word may dupe, deceive, or brainwash us. We have to *want* to be enchanted by it. Control remains firmly in our grasp.

Yet the word *is* dangerous. There exists a crucial difference between the suspension of disbelief in art and myth. In art, the disbelief is temporary. Movies engross us in another world for an hour and a half, but then we return to objective reality. Myth has the potential, if we allow it, to maintain its sense of reality beyond the narrative's conclusion. This is the essential difference between a naturalist and a literalist. The naturalist *temporarily* suspends disbelief; the literalist chooses to do so *permanently*. This is a genuine danger involved in using a word like "god" that must not be understated.

For this very reason, it is all the more important that naturalists not give up the word. It has been shown to have powerful advantages, and relinquishing the term to literalists hands over exclusive control of a potentially destructive weapon. Instead, naturalists can continue the age-old tradition of contested meanings by affirming naturalistic definitions alongside supernatural ones. Naturalist usage of the word "god" subverts literalist dominance, reclaims the word, and evolves it in directions compatible with modern scientific discovery.

## Conclusion

The words "goddess," "god," and "gods" are not simply replaceable by other terms like "being," "nature," or "psychology." Even a term like Brendan Myers' "Immensities," which seems able to evoke a sense of awe and inspiration, does not enjoy the advantages of anthropomorphism (and in any case, Myers states that "gods" and "Immensities" may overlap but are not identical).

The specific traits of the word "god" make a significant difference for those who invoke it. The difference involves both culture and biology, calling up cultural associations as well as biological predispositions. The anthropomorphic quality of the term is particularly decisive, activating brain modules designed for social interaction. This may explain why Druidic ritual with deities somehow works for me. In light of these observations, it seems justified to allow a place at the table for "gods" within naturalism.

There is no need for *all* naturalists to speak of "goddess" or "god," of course, but it is unjustified to categorically deny the use of these words to those who respond well to them. Such would be tossing the baby out with the bathwater. It would be unnecessarily iconoclastic, and would diminish the richness and potential of religious naturalism.

These terms function to evoke positive experiences not easily accessible by other means. Those who respond well to them, and seek those experiences, ought to be able to use them. In sum, they offer an appealing combination of semantic precision and potential for shaping religious experience. They balance head and heart.

## References

Mithen, S. J. (1996). *The prehistory of the mind : a search for the origins of art, religion, and science*, London : Thames and Hudson

Schjoedt, U.; Stodkilde-Jorgensen, H.; Geertz, A. W.; and Roepstorff, A. (2009). "Highly religious participants recruit areas of cognition in personal prayer." *Social Cognitive and Affective Neuroscience*, doi: 10.1093. Note: The study compares prayer to a God considered "real" to prayer to a figure considered unreal (Santa Clause), but does not consider prayer to a figure treated as "real" for the purposes of prayer.

Whiten, A. (2007). "The evolution of animal 'cultures' and social intelligence." *Philosophical Transactions of the Royal Society*, B(29), April, Vol. 362, No. 1480, pp. 603-620.

## When the Gods Speak
### by Áine Órga

I don't know about you, but when I read or listen to people talk about their experiences with their gods, I get very curious about what their experience *really* looks like. Particularly in the Pagan and Polytheist communities, but I think perhaps in religious communities as a whole, there seems to be a fair bit of shorthand used when describing communion with deity. It can be hard to tell whether the person actually sees and hears full-blown corporeal presences or voices, or if a feather fell in a certain way at their feet and they had this gut feeling that they associate with Odin and so they came to the conclusion that he was saying…you get my drift.

Despite being a pantheist and an agnostic, I do spend a fair bit of time thinking, talking, and writing like a polytheist. I talk about the Morrígan as if she is a real, conscious entity. I talk about Odin as if he is a person—albeit quite a mysterious one—who is attempting to make contact with me.

I use this language because it is quicker, easier, and metaphorically accurate. But perhaps I should also spend some time talking about my experience of deity as it actually happens.

For the most part, I'm going to refer to my experiences with the Morrígan, because She is the deity with whom I have the most history, the most experience, and the best rapport. But most of what is true for her is true for other deities with whom I work, too—such as Odin, Ganesh, Cailleach, Brigid, and to some extent Gaia.

I experience the Morrígan in several different ways, through several different facets of my consciousness. It's difficult to narrow down and label all of these, but they include: mythologically, creatively, imaginatively, archetypally, and in nature.

## Mythological and Creative Connection

This level of my connection with the Morrígan is the most intellectual, and the most logical. This is the level on which I connect with Her as a story, as a myth. Her stories strike a deep chord with me—and in turn, they inspire me to create my own artwork or stories in Her honour.

This kind of response requires absolutely no faith or belief in divinity of any kind. You can certainly apply a mystical interpretation onto your response to a deity's myths—but it's not required to have that strong response in the first place.

I grew up to a soundtrack of Irish folklore and mythology, and so when I finally came to the Morrígan's stories as a Pagan, She was already in my bones. But this kind of mythological connection is mostly mundane. Her stories resonated with my personality, with my experience of life, and most of all with the folkloric backdrop of my upbringing. The stories are where I encountered Her symbolism.

From that mythological connection arises the creative one. Because the symbolism of Her mythology is so potent for me, it inspires vivid imagery, and creative ideas. The Morrígan is, in many ways, my Muse—because Her image is so strong and vivid in my mind. Again, this kind of creative connection and creative expression of the Morrígan feels strongly devotional to me, but it exists whether or not you want to put a mystical framework over it.

## Imaginative Connection

I have called this an "imaginative" connection because for the most part, this is what I believe is happening. As such, this is very closely connected with my creative connection with Her. Here, I am referring to my experiences with Her while doing active imagination or pathworking.

As a skeptic and a rationalist, my logical and objective mind sees these experiences as simply a wandering of my imagination. I enter a meditative state, close my eyes, and allow visions to come. Sometimes I deliberately ask to see Her. Most often, I move about an imaginative landscape and come across Her in it.

Mostly, when She appears, She is very clearly just a product of my conscious mind. This often results in a predictable appearance, predictable speech or behaviour, and a general lack of movement. But sometimes, and usually when I'm not really so certain who or what I'm talking to, She appears in stranger forms. She shape shifts, moves about erratically, says strange or cryptic things, and most often appears as a hag. At these times, I assume that I have gone a level deeper—something a little more unconscious within me is bubbling up. I have much less conscious control in this case.

It might sound exciting, and when I remember particularly visceral experiences it thrills me, too. But honestly, when it's happening in the moment, it usually doesn't feel very grand. The visions are generally no clearer than anything I can usually conjure in my mind's eye—certainly nothing approaching the vividness of a dream or lucid dream. I feel as though my conscious mind is in the driver's seat, and I take everything I glean from these pathworkings with a grain of salt. I always assume in the first instance that the only person I'm talking to is me, my ego, in a dressed-up form.

### Archetypal Connection

With this theory, I am straying somewhat from objective reality into the realm of subjective experience. Jung's theory of the archetype comes closest to defining this feeling, but while this is a respected psychological theory, it is by no means scientifically proven or even provable.

Mythology is creative expression of archetypes—and through the mythology and folklore, we receive a particular symbolic system or image of an archetype. But the archetype itself is more overarching and runs much deeper in the psyche than the projected image ever can.

The archetypal theory of deity also suggests that the deity we meet— through all the ways I have outlined thus far—is a projection of a part of *ourselves*. We each contain all of the archetypes within our own psyches. In some ways, they are symbolic structures, a means of understanding the world we live in. But personified archetypes can also represent or speak through certain aspects of our selves and our personalities—often suppressed aspects of our psyche.

This is the primary way I understand the Morrígan to operate. I assume that when I engage with the mythology, when I am creatively inspired by Her, when I meet her in my imagination, I am tapping into some hidden aspects of my own being.

### Natural Connection

But for me, the Morrígan also exists outside of my Self, outside of my mind. I sometimes extrapolate on the ways in which She might exist beyond my or other people's psyches—as a connection to the All or to God—but also, I see Her literally embodied in the landscape.

The Morrígan's myths (and most other deities) can be read as a description of a historical figure, or a mythical anthropomorphic figure or archetype. However, they can also be read as a personification of natural forces or events in nature and the landscape.

For me, She is both. Her archetype is reflected as a personhood within our psyches; and as natural occurrences and tendencies in the natural world. I see her, particularly, in wilderness and in the wild and wet weather of coastal Ireland. While Irish weather is rarely extreme, we frequently experience combinations of gusting wind with rain, and a stormy turbulent sea. Parts of the West Coast, in particular, are a juxtaposition of fertile farming land and fishing waters, and a wild and treacherous ocean. I see her in the life-death-life cycles of the earth, in carrion birds, in rain, in storms, in the poignancy of a misty day or a single open flower.

When I say that I experience the Morrígan in these places and times, I simply mean that these experiences in nature remind me of Her, or conjure a similar emotional response as her imagery, symbolism, and mythology. Sometimes I will feel that something has been conveyed to me through nature, a message of sorts from Her. I understand this to be the Morrígan archetype within my psyche interpreting patterns so as to express itself.

### Mystical Connection?

All of these means of connection to the Morrígan can be understood from a logical, objective perspective. And for the most part, there is nothing to compel me to understand it any differently. When I say that I feel the Morrígan has asked something of me, or that something that has come into my life is a gift from Her, what I am factually referring to is either something that came to me through my imagination, or just a niggling feeling from a part of me that I associate with Her. There are no trumpets and fanfares.

But I choose to use the polytheistic language that I do because sometimes when I think of Her, when I have an experience of communion in any of the ways outlined above, I briefly touch the numinous. Sometime there is something Other in that moment, a kiss from God Herself.

I originally expected that these moments of mystical connection would increase over time—so far, they haven't. I still expect that my relationship with Her will continue to change and flux over time. But while I get a lot out of using personified language and treating Her as a god, I also sometimes feel the need to keep it real, to be really honest about just how mundane my experiences really are.

But this is what I have learned so far about spirituality. The transcendental moments are few and far between. For the most part, it is an exercise in finding the sacred in the mundane.

## Thanking the Goddess for Tea
### by Staśa Morgan-Appel

Yesterday, I posted to Facebook: "TEA. Thank You, Goddess."

Today, while making my tea, it occurred to me to ask myself: Can I thank the Goddess for tea, when I don't believe in the Goddess?

I have said many times that I don't believe in the Goddess; I experience the Goddess. And I do.

I live on this planet, so I experience the Goddess—the Air, Fire, Water, and Earth that are Her breath, energy, blood, and body. That are literally and metaphorically these things.

Air, Fire, Water, Earth in my everyday experience: I breathe air. I listen for the wind in the trees, down our chimney, against the walls of our house, against the sides of the bus. I feel the wind against my face, against my body, as I walk; it blows my hair in my face these days. I love sunny days; I depend on sunlight even on cloudy days, for the food I eat, for my mental health, for vitamin D, for so much else. I revel in how our cats luxuriate in the sun shining through our living room windows. I love how our back patio is a little sun-trap. My neurons fire, a near-infinite number of tiny points of tremendous energy. I love the moon. I drink water. I drink tea.

I am, myself, more than half water. My blood pumps. Making my tea, I had a clumsy moment which reminded me that I definitely experience gravity, and if that's not an Earth power, what is? I have a body. I walk on the ground. There are trees in our communal back garden, and flowers, shrubs, and other plants in both front and back gardens, and so many of our neighbors' gardens. I can walk down to the end of the block I live on, look east, and see Arthur's Seat, one of the "mountains" in town. Another few steps, and I can see Salisbury Crags. I can go climb them. I can walk across the green at the end of my block. I can go sit on our back patio and listen to the birds and the wind in the trees, and feel the sunlight on my face.

These days, I feel very estranged from that fifth element, that something more, the Spirit which binds all the elements, all life, together.

But I can experience the Air, Fire, Water, and Earth in the everyday.

I can thank the Air, Fire, Water, and Earth—including humans—responsible for my tea.

Thank You, Goddess.

## Mystery as Role Model
### by Eli Effinger-Weintraub

Did I ever tell you about the one real encounter I ever had with a named Mystery*? It was one of the most profound spiritual moments of my life—and it was the experience that helped me accept once and for all that I'm an atheist.

It was during a Reclaiming ritual, and we were singing "Oh How Sweet," a beautiful song by Reclaiming teacher and songwriter Matt Sweet, to invoke Brigit, a Mysterious One from the Celtic pantheon.

*Come now, Brigit*
*Come we call you*
*Mistress of the Forge and Well*

As often happens in ecstatic ritual, we reached a point where we left behind most of the song's beautiful, evocative and repeated only the plea:

*Come now Brigit*
*Come now, Brigit*
*Come now, Brigit*

I had closed my eyes and was dancing to the beat, joining my voice to the call:

*Come now, Brigit*
*Come now, Brigit*

I felt a change come over the room. I opened my eyes, and I knew: Brigit was there. We had called to Brigit, and she had come.

*Come now, Brigit*
*Come now, Brigit*

I felt her presence as surely as I felt my own, or of my wife's beside me. Then I realized that was because they were the *same* presence. Brigit had come not as some outside force invoked by our pleas, but as an internal awareness *evoked* by our need for those energies. We called Brigit as sacred beekeeper and brought forth the part of ourselves that loves and nurtures community. We called Brigit as mistress of the forge and well and brought forth the part of ourselves that could create with great passion and heal even the deepest emotional wounds.

*Come now, Brigit*
*Come now, Brigit*

I keep theistic Mysteries (in other words, gods and goddesses) out of my personal religious practice. I feel no connection to them, even on an archetypal level. I'm very good at devotion and very bad at belief: moon but not moon goddess; river but not river god. And it strikes me as the height of disrespect to take on and off like cheap costume jewelry that which to devotional polytheists is powerful and real, especially those from marginalized cultures that aren't my own.

However, I often participate in ritual with theistic Pagans, who usually invoke named Mysteries. In order to participate fully in these rituals, I can't shut off whenever those Mysteries are mentioned; I'd be mentally, spiritually, and emotionally checked out for half the ritual. I've had to come to an understanding of what deities mean to me, and how I can interact with them in meaningful ways that allow me to participate in and contribute to mixed-belief rituals.

Time and again, I go back to that invocation of Brigit.

*Come now, Brigit*
*Come now, Brigit*

When a particular Mysterious One is invoked in a ritual, I ask myself what I know about the attributes associated with them and the stories told about them, and I try to get a sense of what those characteristics might bring forth in myself. Apollo, for instance, is associated with *so many* things, but as someone whose life often feels chaotic and out of control, I feel most drawn to his aspect as the god of order. I have within me everything I need to get my act together—or, at least, I have within me the *keys* to everything I need to get my act together—but those keys, and the qualities they unlock, can be difficult to access, and sometimes an external metaphor can help me focus.

This is how I handle aspecting, of which we do a fair amount in Reclaiming. Aspecting is a ritual experience which allows participants to bring the energy of a Mysterious One, spirit, ancestor, or concept (like "Power" or "Community") into themselves. I've done it several times over the years, and, yes, even before I openly identified as an atheist, it felt like talking to imaginary friends. Amazing sensations of presence filled me, yet I always felt that that presence came from *within* me, rather than being a visitation by an external being. I used to struggle against that perception, but these days it feels like a gift.

If invoking a Mysterious One in ritual provides external focus for my personal and community work, then aspecting makes those qualities larger than life. It's "fake it till you make it": if I need to act more fiercely in a situation, wearing Freya's warrior face for a while may go a long way toward evoking and enhancing the warrior spirit within me.

People ask me why I bother with the symbols. If I need to be fierce, why not just either access what fierceness I already have or work on developing more, no Norse warrior goddess required? To which I say: if that works for you, then go for it, and good for you. But it's not that easy for everyone. Those of us who are taught that our opinions and voices are *lesser* because of our race, sex, gender alignment, sexual orientation, disability status, or other marginalized or oppressed identity, those of us who are called "uppity" and "bitch" every time we raise our voices, may find confidence and fierceness *very* difficult to access. We may need any help we can get to call forth those parts of ourselves. By the same token, those of us who grew up most immersed in, and therefore most damaged by, modern attitudes of toxic masculinity, white fragility, and resource scarcity may need help accessing vulnerability, humility, and generosity.

This approach to deity sometimes puts me at odds with both devotional polytheists who liken aspecting to an old-school possession experience and religious naturalists who don't understand why I bother with deity—or deistic Pagans—at all. My answer is community. Understanding what I believe about gods and goddesses and how I best interact with them allows me to participate more fully in group ritual, opening me to the possibilities of community and connection with my fellow Pagans. I am *always* eager to bring forth that aspect of myself.

* In my home Reclaiming community, we refer to the entire unknowable sacred as "Mystery." An individual piece of that sacredness may be referred to as "a Mystery" or "a Mysterious One." Athena, Inanna, and Tyr are Mysterious Ones, and so are the moon and the Mississippi River—and so are you and I.

## Myth and Meaning:
## A Non-Literal Pagan View of Deity
### by Ryan Cronin

"The phenomenon we call spirit depends on the existence of an autonomous primordial image which is universally present in the preconscious makeup of the human psyche."

— C. G. Jung, "The phenomenology of the spirit in fairytales"

"How can you be Pagan without believing in the gods?"

This is a question frequently asked of atheist, agnostic and other non-theistic Pagans. In some corners of the Pagan community, the words "Pagan" and "Polytheist" are synonymous, and the idea of atheistic Pagans is literally unthinkable (a position disproved by the sheer existence of non-theist Pagans).

However, the Pagan community is, and has always been, diverse in its beliefs. One of the first books on Paganism I read, *Paganism: An Introduction to Earth-Centered Religions*, by Joyce and River Higginbotham, says:

> "It's not difficult to find statements made by both Pagans and non-Pagans that Pagans are polytheistic. This can be true, but it isn't necessarily true. What is true for Paganism as a whole is that Pagans may believe anything they wish about Deity. Certain Pagan traditions may adopt specific beliefs, but those beliefs operate only within that tradition and do not carry over to Paganism as a whole."

The apparently simple question "do you believe the gods exist?" requires some unpacking of the terms "believe," "gods," and "exist." Every Pagan is likely to have different ideas of what those words mean, ranging from a strong, devout faith in supernatural spirits, to a non-literal and provisional understanding of gods as ideas or archetypes that exist within human minds.

One popular concept of deity within Paganism, which is at least as common as Polytheism, is that of Pantheism. Influenced by the 17th century philosopher Spinoza, Pantheists assert that the divine is nature itself and that there is no "supernatural" realm. For a Pantheist, the words "god" and "nature" are equivalents. Spinoza himself often wrote *"deus, sive natura"* ("God, or nature") to reinforce the idea that what we may call "God" is simply another word for the majestic, awe-inspiring universe of which we are a part.

It isn't a great leap to imagine a sort of Pagan-Pantheist synthesis, whereby each of the gods and goddesses worshipped by ancient and modern cultures can be seen as a personification of an aspect of nature, and/or of our human experience in relation to it. Evidence from archaeology and the emerging science of evolutionary psychology suggests that the earliest form of "religion" may have been animism, wherein natural forces are imbued with consciousness and intent. Early humans, facing an often hostile world where the powers of land, sea and sky held life and death in their hands, would no doubt have revered these powers, perhaps even worshipped them as gods.

Gradually, as stories were told and retold around the fire, these animistic forces began to take recognisable forms. Emma Restall Orr writes: "Slowly, the gods were coming to be represented in more human forms: nature, including human nature, with its storms and wars, its famine and flood, its lusts and jealousies, was depicted in the tales." Humans see the world through human eyes, and it is certainly easier to relate to a protective human-like god of thunder, such as Thor, than the wild power of the thunderstorm itself.

For some Pagans, however, Thor and the thunder are one. Rather than being literally a red-bearded hammer-wielding "god of thunder," Thor *is* the thunderstorm and the lightning and the rain in all its might and majesty. This view does not require us to believe, unscientifically, that thunder is really caused by Thor swinging his hammer, but it allows us to enter into the stories of Thor and, in some deep, intuitive way, *feel* his power expressed within, and as, the force of nature he represents.

This approach is espoused by some leading figures in modern Paganism. Hilmar örn Hilmarsson, Allsherjargoði (high priest) of the Icelandic Pagan organisation Ásatrúarfélagið, said, "I don't believe anyone [in Ásatrúarfélagið] believes in a one-eyed man who is riding about on a horse with eight feet. We see the stories as poetic metaphors and a manifestation of the forces of nature and human psychology."

Jung considered gods and spirits to be manifestations of *archetypes* in the collective unconscious: shared, primordial ideas from deep within the human psyche, concepts by which people think and understand themselves and the world around them. These archetypal concepts became embedded in stories as cultures and religions developed. In one sense, then, we can see the gods as characters in stories, from which we can draw important moral and practical lessons. This is not to relegate them to mere fiction, however. While we can learn from both the *Eddas* and *Harry Potter*, the difference between the two is that while the latter is fiction, the former is myth.

The word "myth" has unfortunate implications today, and there are some Polytheists who would be insulted and angry that their gods are "dismissed" as mere myths. In everyday language, myth has come to mean "false." Conspiracy theorists and so-called sceptics denounce everything from evolution to climate change to the moon landings as "myths," and new atheists use the term to mock religion as primitive superstition, but the word has a deeper and older meaning.

Myth is arguably *the* central feature of human culture. We are as much *pan narrans*, the storytelling ape, as we are *homo sapiens*, the wise man. Religious scholar Karen Armstrong writes: "In our scientific culture, we often have rather simplistic notions of the divine. In the ancient world, the 'gods' were rarely regarded as supernatural beings with discrete personalities, living a totally separate metaphysical existence. Mythology was not about theology, in the modern sense, but about human experience."

Myth reveals truths that "never happened but always are," to quote the 4$^{th}$ century Roman writer Sallustius. Myth is a sacred narrative that creates and expresses human relationship to the other-than-human world, the world of the wild, of gods and heroes, of Mother Earth and her creatures. When we as Pagans enter into the mythological landscape in meditation, ritual or magic, we weave that meaning into the fabric of our own lives.

"Truth" has been defined by Druid writer, John Beckett, as "that which is," and "meaning" as "that which makes life worth living." It is this meaning which is encoded in myth and embodied in the tales and archetypes of the gods and goddesses. In the never-ending and futile "science vs. religion" or "theist vs. atheist" arguments, people often swing to the extremes of either truth or meaning. Some religious people emphasise their particular faith's form of meaning at the expense of truth, and end up believing in absurdities like six-day creationism as a result. On the other side of the coin, some atheists advocate pure, rational truth at the expense of emotional, inner meaning.

For me, life is all about balancing those two: truth and meaning. I find truth in science, reason, and evidence. The scientific method is the single best tool we have for finding out what is real and how things work. In our current understanding of science, this rules out a lot of traditional religious or magical ideas. Yet I find meaning in Paganism, in spending time in nature, in doing ritual, in connecting with something sacred and greater than myself.

One intriguing psychological theory of mind suggests that our "central engine of meaning" is divided into a "propositional," rational system and an older "implicational" system, which understands the world in terms of symbol, correspondence, dream, and intuition. For a healthy balance, we need to "feed" both of these systems. Myth can be seen as working with the implicational system, allowing us to simultaneously disavow simplistic, literal ideas of supernatural, superhuman gods in the sky, and also experience a deep connection to the gods of nature, in this world here and now.

None of this is to say that Polytheists are necessarily wrong or misguided. In a universe as complex as ours, any one of us could be wrong, and most of us probably are at some point. Our ideas *about* the divine are not the divine itself. They are just ideas, opinions, models. Joanna Van Der Hoeven put it well: "In the true spirit of Druidry, one would never, ever, mock another's belief or lack of belief in deity, nor hold it in contempt or condemnation."

So what does Paganism informed by these ideas of the gods as non-literal, mythic representations of nature look like? Perhaps surprisingly, it can be almost indistinguishable from theistic Paganism. In my own Druid practice, I read the myths of ancient Europe, I draw ogham or runes for meditation, and I perform rituals to celebrate the Wheel of the Year. Within those rites, I may even invoke gods and goddesses. To an outside observer, there would be little difference between my practice and that of a Polytheist. The only difference is inside my head: rather than praying to the gods for supernatural aid, I am honouring and invoking their qualities, the virtues and powers they represent, in order to inspire my life and behaviour.

Paganism is often described as being about orthopraxy, rather than orthodoxy: the focus is on the practices, not the belief. I do the practices not because I think the gods command them, but because they work, and they help me to create a meaningful and wakeful life.

John Michael Greer, Archdruid of AODA, writes, "What are the gods? Again, ask any three Druids and you'll get at least six answers…Experience, not belief, is central to Druid spirituality, and so it doesn't actually matter that much to Druidry whether gods are objectively real individual divine beings, aspects or manifestations of some overarching unity, archetypal functions within the human mind, or something else entirely." What matters is not what we believe, but what we do.

All of which is to say that atheist, agnostic, naturalist and humanist Pagans *are* Pagan, and Paganism is big and broad enough to accommodate everyone on the belief map.

## References

Armstrong, K. *A Short History of Myth*. Canongate, 2005.

Beckett, J. "Truth and Meaning" from *Under the ancient oaks*, 2013. [online: retrieved from http://www.patheos.com/blogs/johnbeckett/2013/04/truth-and-meaning.html, 22/11/2015].

Carr-Gomm, P. *Druid Mysteries: Ancient Wisdom for the 21st Century*. Rider, 2002.

Greer, J.M. *The Druidry Handbook: Spiritual Practice Rooted in the Living Earth*. Weiser, 2006.

Higginbotham, J. and Higginbotham, R. *Paganism: An Introduction to Earth-Centered Religions*. Llewellyn, 2008.

Hilmarsson, H.O. quoted in "Iceland to build first temple to Norse gods since Viking age," *The Guardian*, 2015. [online: retrieved from http://www.theguardian.com/world/2015/feb/02/iceland-temple-norse-gods-1000-years, 22/11/2015].

Restall Orr, E. *The Wakeful World: Animism, Mind and the Self in Nature*. Moon Books, 2011.

Van Der Hoeven, J. *The Awen Alone: Walking the Path of the Solitary Druid*. Moon Books, 2014.

## Theism, or Down to the Sea (of Limitless Light)
### by Cat Chapin-Bishop

Sometimes, when I talk about my experiences in Quaker meeting, I throw around the word "God."

I do this not because I'm a monotheist or a Christian, but because I'm pretty sure the experiences of those who use that word in my Quaker meeting are consistent with my experiences in that context, and it was coming to feel precious—like a constant need to remind people of my specialness, my difference—never to use that commonly understood word when I discuss those shared experiences.

But then again…it doesn't quite fit.

Sometimes I use the vague, generic word "Spirit." I use it as a collective noun, meaning something like, "Ground of All Being," or, as I once put it in worship, "Big Fuzzy Warm Thing that Loves Us and Wants Us to Be Glad."

But then again…it doesn't quite fit.

I've sometimes thought about trying out other terms: "Elohim," for instance, that curious plural noun for the supposedly singular God of Israel, or "Great Spirit," which does convey at least a little of the sense of a spiritual presence *in* the world, woven through the world. But the one term implies a relationship to the Bible I don't have, and the other reeks of cultural appropriation.

In the end, all of the words just…don't quite fit.

Nor do names, in talking about the Pagan gods, when I talk about my life as a Pagan. All of it is subject to a false clarity, to distorting the direct light of spiritual encounter with a lens of human cognition.

I know there are Pagan polytheists out there who have the same clear, concrete sense of the boundaries of the named deities they worship that they might of the differences between one mineral and another. It's as if they've taken measurements somehow, and proved to their satisfaction that Thor has a different specific gravity than does Thunor, never mind Ares and Mars. Some Pagans are so clear and so definite about the identities and natures of the beings they worship.

But I am often left wondering about names entirely. (Who was that masked spiritual being? Cue my personal spiritual theme music.) And was that Being I was just listening to a god? A nature spirit? An aspect of my own deepest self?

I've never been terribly sure we know what we mean by the word "god," when you get right down to it. What is a god, and how are gods distinct from nymphs, ghosts, ancestors, or spirits of place? Where is the litmus paper that can let me measure these gradations of meaning?

Maybe somebody out there has that kind of clarity. They can speak with some authority about these things. I can't: When it comes to naming that spiritual experience, all I've got are the shifting sands of second-hand information and intellectual speculation. For myself, I've never seen a point in piecing together a purely intellectual theology for an experience as visceral, as immediate, as spiritual communion. I've never found a set of names that didn't invite more argument than it settled, didn't diminish more than it expressed what I encounter in worship.

While the disadvantages of this are obvious—I'm left without a language I can rely on—there are advantages, too. I find that I can hear and feel affinity for the language of polytheists and non-theists, animists and monotheists, whenever their words describe an experience I have personally had. I catch echoes of my own truths in the truths of others. And then I try to bounce words of my own back, to clothe my observations in language, not to define anyone else's religious life, but as a sort of spiritual sonar: words bouncing in the dark to help others, whose experiences echo mine, to also pick out those dim, underwater shapes of lived encounters with…something for which there are no words.

What kinds of experiences am I trying to describe?

Most of all, I am seeking words for those warm senses of presence, of Others, I have had at various times of my life. Sometimes, those encounters have been comforting; sometimes challenging. I have felt spiritual Presences within the boundaries of a cast circle, in the waters of a stream flowing through a dark wood, in certain trees, and within whole forests.

I have also felt another sort of Presence—not a person or like a person, and yet intensely personal. Sometimes my experience of that Presence comes in the company of certain people. Being with them, embracing them, makes me aware of That Other Being as well. It is like heat from a hearth, that thing that is coming through those people, a tenderness that is not only human, and not only about that one moment and that one relationship.

At other times, that tender Presence seems to fill all the world. It's vast, breathtaking, closer than my own skin and more personal than my own name. This is the experience I mean when I use the word "God." Or better, in an echo of the Kabbalah, let me name it the "Sea of Limitless Light."

That Spirit that is like the experience of water, and of light. I float in it; at times I am flooded by it; I am gently illuminated by it sometimes, and others, I am nearly blinded by it. My whole relationship with That Spirit is very much like a relationship with the sea. Large beyond my reckoning, with depths that are far beyond me. Overwhelming—but also centering.

Have you ever gone down to the ocean, on a break from your busy life? You get out of your car and leave the human world behind you. When you step out onto the sand and feel the salt breeze, there's a feeling of stepping outside time. How much older is the sea than our short history? How much more powerful than all our words and theories?

Seagulls' wild music washes over you...and then the soft, eternal, repeating breaths of the sea, the sound of waves curling over the shore. Those moments, when you feel the "too much with us," the "getting and spending" of life dissolve into the experience of simply *being with* the ocean…those moments are what I mean.

Is that "God"? Is there one Water, one Ocean? Should I even care?

Ancient Greek theatrical mask of Zeus

# Part 6: Just LARPing?
# Non-Theistic Pagan Practice

> "If we must play the theological game, let us never forget that it is a game. Religion, it seems to me, can survive only as a consciously accepted system of make-believe. People will accept certain theological statements of life and the world, will elect to perform certain rites and to follow certain rules of conduct, not because they imagine the statements to be true or the rules and rites to be divinely dictated, but because they have discovered experimentally that to live in a certain ritual rhythm, under certain ethical restraints, and as if certain metaphysical doctrines were true, is to live nobly, with style. Every art has its conventions which every artist must accept. The greatest, the most important of the arts is living."
>
> — Aldous Huxley, Conclusion to *Texts and Pretexts*

Contemporary Paganism has always included a wide array of beliefs. In contrast to the Abrahamic religions, there has never been a test of belief imposed for participation in Paganism. Non-theistic Pagans can easily practice alongside other kinds of Pagans, including theistic Pagans. In fact, the religious practices of some non-theistic Pagans may be outwardly indistinguishable from those of theistic Pagans. Some may use theistic symbolism in ritual, while others do not. Many observe some form of the Neo-Pagan Wheel of the Year. If you have participated in public Pagan events, it is likely that you have circled with a non-theistic Pagan already.

Ritual is an essential part of many Naturalistic Pagans' religious practice. Through ritual, Naturalistic Pagans seek to express their sense of wonder and reverence at the universe and to connect on a deeper level with that process of life. The ritual enactment of myth helps to transform our *understanding* of the natural world into a religious *experience*. Some Naturalistic Pagans may invoke deities, spirits, or ancestors as part of their rituals, but these are usually understood in poetic, allegorical, or psychological terms.

This is not the same thing as play-acting, though. The participation of non-theistic Pagans in public ritual has been referred to derisively by some as "LARPing" or "Live Action Role Playing." The truth is that most non-theistic Pagans approach ritual with a sincere and reverent attitude, and non-theistic Pagan ritual is not just "play acting."

Theistic Pagans might wonder why non-theistic Pagans would participate in Pagan ritual if they do not believe in gods. The answer is that ritual is known to have many psychological and social benefits, which are not affected by the absence of belief in supernatural gods, including:

- facilitation of group cohesion and cooperation,
- management of anxiety,
- cultivation of a sense of meaningfulness,
- fostering personal healing and transformation,
- deepening our awareness of our interconnectedness with the natural world,
- motivating socially and environmentally responsible behavior, and
- developing a sense of connection to something greater than ourselves.

The last one, "developing a sense of connection to something greater than ourselves," might seem a strange way to describe non-theistic ritual. But there are other things than gods that can be understood as transcending ourselves, including the natural world, the cosmos, the human community, the wider community of life, and our own deeper selves. These "transcendents" or "immensities" (to borrow Brendan Myers' term), share several common characteristics identified by B. T. Newberg:

- they are greater than us in both degree and kind,
- we participate in them even as they transcend us,
- they manifest not as problems that can be solved, but as mysteries to be accepted and integrated, and
- there is no avoiding or escaping them, since they are part of the human condition.

## Why I Pray to Isis
### by B. T. Newberg

If there is no Isis outside my mind, why do I pray to her? For me, there are two reasons that I'll highlight here, out of the many that could be said.

### Motivation to Act

First, motivation to act is not always at the beck and call of our rational decision-maker. Often we know what we "should" do, but can't get over the fear or laziness to do it. Prayer seems to help me focus my motivation, so that I can actually manifest intention into action. So focusing motivation is the first reason.

### Psychological Well-Being

The second reason I do prayer is for my own psychological well-being, which is indirectly related to the well-being of others with whom I interact. For whatever reason, I respond well to verbalizing aloud my thoughts and feelings to an image that embodies qualities I consider highest and best in humans. For me, that image is the goddess Isis. I sit before the statue of her, light a candle, chant to enter a relaxed and ever-so-slightly-altered mental state, then tell her what's bothering me. It's a kind of self-talk, but more effective than just sitting down and talking to myself, because the technique seems to get around certain blocks thrown up by the rational ego. Very frequently this kind of prayer leads to creative ideas, new insights, or just a sense of emotional release. I usually leave with a new sense of strength and clarity. So it is clearly therapeutic for me.

Then, when I go from there to interact with my wife, my friends, or anyone else, I am in a better emotional place to relate to them and give them what they need, since I'm no longer as muddled with my own unresolved emotional muck. I would like to think that whatever good behavior we achieve around others is also contagious, so that the influence of my better behavior spreads to those around me, which spreads to those around them, etc. So the second reason for prayer leads to direct benefit for me, and indirect benefit for others.

### It Just Works

There is no particular reason why prayer must specifically be engaged to achieve these same results, except that for me it has proven effective and I like it. It does seem to have certain powerful advantages as already alluded to (getting around ego blocks), but I can only speculate on the science of it. To make a long story short, it works for me. Other people coming from different experiences and contexts may not find it as effective as another means, but for me it has proven by straight-forward empirical results to be highly effective.

This is a case of "whatever works," as goes the common Neo-Pagan dictum. Often that phrase can be a smokescreen for lazy thinking, but if we are specific about what it means for something to "work," it is a powerful maxim to follow.

## The Three "Why's" of Ritual
### by NaturalPantheist

Is there any point to ritual for Naturalistic Pantheists? Can it bring value to our lives as Naturalistic Pantheists? Ritual is a major part of most religions, but the question is "Why?" I would like to suggest that there are three reasons why ritual is important, whether or not we believe in anything supernatural about it: it reminds us to stop and be aware of the world around us, it has an effect on us internally, and it helps us to connect to something bigger than ourselves.

### Awareness

How many of us think about all the plants and animals around us when we walk down the street? How many of us eat a meal without thinking about the fact that something had to die so that we could eat and live? Many of the spiritual practices of the world's religions have at their core, the practice of Mindfulness. They call to us to take time out, amidst the hustle and bustle of everyday life, to forget the baggage and distractions, and to stop, to be, to focus, to listen. They call us to be mindful and aware of the world around us, to be aware of other people and of nature. They put the important things in life at the centre of our attention—the sacred things—and give us the chance to focus on them.

### Change

Ritual is a powerful tool. It affects us in a way that mere intellectual thought and debate never can; it taps into our psyche in a very strong way because it allows us to experience something. Experience can have a very powerful influence on our thinking and behaviour and is a key factor in forming who we become. The ritual experience can change us at a deep level, it can help us to form and ingrain habits and to build character, so that we can become the type of people we wish to be.

## Connection

There is something "more" to life; there is something "bigger than ourselves." That thing is nature; it is the universe. Through ritual we can come to realise that—to realise there is more to life than our ego. Ritual helps to teach us to be humble, to be reverent and respectful and to celebrate life. It teaches us that we are just one part of a greater and awesome whole. And it can help us connect to that whole, to honour our relationship with it, in a way we couldn't do otherwise.

## Offerings to Mother Nature

If we don't believe in gods and spirits, then who are we giving offerings to? If there is no one there to receive them, then what's the point? My first answer to this would be that as Naturalistic Pantheists who see Nature as sacred, we are giving to Mother Nature. True, she is not a thinking, personal being who knows what we are doing, but nevertheless we are still offering to her. But why? There are two reasons. Firstly, as with all aspects of naturalistic ritual, it is about changing ourselves (or inner alchemy as the Taoists would say). It is about developing within ourselves greater reverence and respect for nature. It is about showing humility in the face of that which is so much greater than our individual selves and responding with gratefulness towards her. It is about connecting more deeply with nature and expressing our inner values. It is about learning the virtue of generosity. Secondly it is a way of helping Nature.

What should we use as offerings? There are many different options here and it really depends on what helps you connect best with nature. However, there are two guidelines from that can help us in choosing what offerings to make.

The first is that whatever we offer should be sustainable; it should be something that is environmentally friendly and helpful to Mother Nature. Imagining that Mother Nature was a conscious being with desires—what would she want us to give her? If we give her something harmful, not only would she reject it, but it would show us to be uncaring, destructive people (and humanity does enough of that already!) One of the worst and most harmful things we can do is buy something new to give as an offering. Our consumerist and materialistic culture is rapidly depleting resources around the world, and we should not contribute to it. There are plenty of offerings we can make without buying yet more "stuff" and taking from Mother Nature.

Secondly, the offerings should be meaningful to you. They should involve some kind of sacrifice. Without offerings, faith is all talk and no action. An offering should be something that involves you giving up something important to you. For example, when we work, we give up some of our time, i.e., our life, in order to earn money in return. If we then give some of that money in an offering, then we are in essence giving some of our own life to Mother Nature. If we spend time creating something like a poem for the specific purpose of giving it as an offering to Mother Nature, then we are giving up more of our life to her.

There are many possible ways to offer to Mother Nature. It can be biodegradeable foodstuffs put out for animals or it could be libations poured on the ground. It could be a prayer, song or poem you have composed specifically for the occasion as an offering. It could be some foodstuff you have made yourself—something you have put a lot of hard work and creativity into making. It could be something from Nature itself, something you've gathered, e.g., nuts for squirrels. It could be to actually do something like plant a seed and tend the plant for its life. You could choose to make a lifestyle change, e.g., to go vegetarian or to recycle more or to get rid of your car. Any lifestyle change that will benefit the environment and help you live more lightly on the land.

Finally, my favourite type of offering is to give coins. If you do ritual offerings daily this could be a few pennies, if it's less regular you could give bigger amounts. Put the coins in your offering bowl and then afterwards donate the money to a charity that helps the environment. In Christianity and Judaism there is a concept called tithing. It basically means you give 10% of your earnings to "God." I am not suggesting that we have to give this much, as many people cannot afford to; however, it is something to think about, to be challenged by, and doing it would certainly show our values.

## Why Modern Paganism Is Good for Today's Families
### by Debra Macleod

Let me ask you a question: How do you feel when you're sitting by a crackling fire? Whether it's a campfire under a starry sky or a fireplace in a book-lined living room, the feelings are the same. Warmth. Comfort. Well-being. Wonder and awe as you stare into the shifting, roaring orange flame, watching it snake around the wood and snap embers into the air. It almost feels...sacred.

People who lived before us—and not all that long before us—felt the same sense of reverence. Fire lit and warmed their homes, and served as the focus of family life. Fire was so important and inspirational that they gave it a name and an identity—Vesta, beloved goddess of the home, hearth and domestic life. Symbolized by a flame, she lived in the household fire.

It doesn't matter what year the calendar reads, people are people. The people who believed in Vesta had hopes and fears, just like we do. They loved their spouse and their children. In fact, many did a better job of this than we are doing, thanks to the ancient Roman virtue of pietas or sacred loyalty to one's family. Nothing came before your family—not your personal desires, not a deity, nothing. The simple rituals of Vesta worship reinforced this sense of family devotion and solidarity.

At that time, goddess worship wasn't a "girl thing." Men revered goddesses as much as women did, and it was in this pagan world that marriage was first conceived as a monogamous union. This was an early step toward improving the status of women. While women had few rights, they had respect and influence and nobody imaged the feminine as "less divine" than the masculine. From hard-working husbands to powerful emperors, men looked to goddesses for comfort, guidance and protection.

Even the great Julius Caesar was a goddess guy. He claimed to be descended from a goddess and bragged about it every chance he got. Many emperors, including Augustus, minted Vesta's image on their coins. Men wore Vesta seal rings. The Vestals, a venerated order of priestesses tasked with keeping Vesta's sacred fire going in the temple, was the only full-time, state-funded priesthood in Rome. They lived in luxury and led a privileged life. Statues of them still line the House of the Vestals in Rome. You weren't weird if you worshipped a goddess. You were weird if you *didn't* worship a goddess.

So imagine everyone's surprise when the new cult of Christianity hit town. One god. Oh, and the god's a man. Sort of. And this sort-of-man says there are no goddesses, and that women are divinely subordinate to men. He also says that, if your family doesn't accept him into their hearts, you should leave your family and follow him. He also says that the end is near and you have two choices: believe in him and live in a golden heaven, or don't believe in him and burn in a fiery pit.

Yikes. To a pagan man or woman who worshipped Vesta and who lived in a culture of religious co-existence, this message wasn't just bizarre; it was deeply offensive to their beliefs and values.

Today, many people believe that pagan traditions like Vesta naturally "died out" as people chose Christ. That is false. The truth is, Christianity only became the official religion of Rome after the rise of the first Christian emperors, at a time when most people were still devoutly pagan. These emperors instituted a brutal policy of Christianization.

They passed anti-pagan laws and ordered temples to be closed, pillaged and torn down. That included the Temple of Vesta. Christian vandals smashed the heads off the statues of the Vestals (which is why most of them are headless today) and defiled the ancient statues of beloved gods and goddesses by carving crosses into their foreheads.

Yet Vesta worship persisted. As their home goddess, Vesta had protected families for centuries and was a beloved symbol of everything

Romans held sacred—their history, traditions, values, way of life and especially their families. She was intertwined with their identity.

Stricter laws were passed that criminalized Vesta worship—even in the privacy of one's home—upon pain of death. It took years of forced Christianization before Vesta's great fire settled into embers. For most pagans, Christianity was not a choice. (Indeed, the "believe or die" approach persists in parts of our world.)

This Christianization continued as the Catholic church claimed elements of Vesta worship as its own. The goal was to make the androcentric, one god Christianity familiar enough that people would eventually forget the old ways. The powerful virgin goddess Vesta became the divinely subordinate Virgin Mary. As Vesta was depicted with her favourite animal, a donkey, Mary was depicted riding on a donkey.

The sacred flame of Vesta became the flame in Mary's immaculate heart. The privileged Vestal priestesses who served the great goddess, became the poverty-line Catholic nuns who served male priests and a male god. The salted-flour wafers prepared as offerings by the Vestals became the wafers of the Eucharist. The circular shape of Vesta's temple became the domes of Christian churches. And so on.

All of this incites the question: Why is modern Paganism seen as a fringe spirituality when, in truth, it is a natural form of spiritual expression? Indeed, the polytheism of Paganism allows people to explore their spirituality and personality, and to find the rituals and beliefs that are most relevant to their life. You know all those different saints in the Catholic church? They were established to serve the same purpose as the pantheon of gods and goddesses. You pick the one that fits you best, and you wear it.

Winston Churchill said it best: "History is written by the victors." How true. Once the Catholic church had sole power, it launched a smear campaign against paganism, one that persists to this day. In a recent Mass in Vatican City, Pope Francis warned people not to fall into the trap of paganism. According to the Pope—who spoke from the pulpit of the richest organization on the planet—pagans are too concerned with money and worldly desires. Another Catholic deacon attributed abortion and "toilet births" to "the return of ancient pagan practice."

Yet despite this kind of nonsense, paganism and the Vesta tradition persist. In fact, its popularity is on the rise, especially among people who have rejected religious doctrine on moral or intellectual grounds, or who have had negative experiences with organized religion. It's also on the rise among people who are re-embracing the virtue of pietas and Vesta's home rituals to strengthen marital and family bonds.

Vesta and modern Paganism is for women who long for a spirituality that resonates with them, and who refuse to be complicit in their own subordination. It is for men who long for a natural spirituality, who don't feel empowered by subordinating women, and who refuse to outsource their family's morality. It is for parents who refuse to teach their daughters they are "less" than men.

It's for people with humanist values such as gender equality and personal autonomy, who embrace science and reject the indoctrination of children into supernatural belief, and who don't believe that "mankind" has the "god-given right" to exploit the Earth or its life. It's for people who believe in co-existence and feel that spirituality, like life itself, should be dynamic and open to positive change.

We have this idea in the modern world that "we've arrived." We know best. The past is somehow less relevant than today, and we don't see those who lived before us as real people with important things to say. Their traditions are seen as mere stepping stones that got us where we are now. Their society's spirituality is seen as less sophisticated and valuable than our society's religions. A quick scroll through today's news headlines should be enough to shatter this kind of presumptuousness.

Despite spending most of my life as an atheist, I have come to realize that spirituality is part of the human condition. So is the ability to think for oneself, to follow one's own moral compass and to challenge stereotypes that others have created for their own purposes. If you agree, you might have a spark of Vesta's ancient fire in you after all.

## Four Devotional Practices for Naturalistic Pagans
### by Anna Walther

"Why is it so quiet?" my son asked. "I don't know," I replied in a whisper, without knowing why. My children and I were visiting Seiders Springs, limestone artesian springs that lie along Shoal Creek in Austin, Texas. They're framed by crowded city streets and two busy medical facilities, one on each bank of Shoal Creek, such that the quiet blanketing the path past the springs was arresting. Water babbled up through limestone to collect in shallow fern-framed pools. While we stood there listening, a couple of hospital workers walked by, chatting in hushed tones, enjoying the soft beauty and respite of natural springs in the heart of a bustling, rapidly-growing city.

My children stopped briefly to wonder at the improbability of water flowing from rock, then took off down the path, past the springs without me. I hastily gathered a handful of rocks and built a short tower on the ground beside one of the limestone pools. It was my way of saying, "I was here," "I care," and "Thank you."

Then I chased after my children down the path.

In my place-based Naturalistic Paganism, I relate most often to nature powers. Humans around the world share the old, great powers: the abundance of the Earth, the strength and direction of the Wind, the Sun's relentless fire. Other powers are younger and local: the bluebonnets that push up through the soil each spring, Central Texas's many limestone creeks and springs, and even the water that flows through the tap of my own kitchen sink. I am always in relationship with these powers, whether I will it or not. My goal as a Pagan is to cultivate mindful relationships with these nature powers. I do not believe that the springs in any sense needed or wanted my offering, but I was different for having made it.

Below are four ways in which I practice devotion to the powers of my place. These practices can be done quickly, discreetly, and economically; they require few materials other than what you find in your environment. None of the practices presupposes devotion to a personified deity; they require only simple wonder and worship of the world or nature itself.

1. **Offer collected rainwater.** Set a clean container outside when it rains. Use the rainwater you collect to offer libations to the land, whenever you're out experiencing the weather, woods, waters, and celebrated sites of your place.

2. **Make temporary art.** Humans make art. It's one of my favorite ways to offer conscious, human energy back to nature, and making temporary outdoor art can be a meditation on impermanence and change, too. Build rock towers or make mandalas from fallen leaves, while you're out experiencing the weather, woods, waters, and celebrated sites of your place. The elements will receive and reclaim your work after you leave.

3. **Pick up trash.** Take an extra bag (and gloves if needed), and pick up trash at the next neighborhood park you visit. Leave the woods, waters, and celebrated sites of your place a little cleaner than they were before your visit.

4. **Go outside,** and experience the weather, woods, waters, and celebrated sites of your place. What phase is the moon in? Go outside and look, instead of checking your moon phase calendar app. (Takes one to know one.) What birds sing at dawn in your neighborhood? Go outside, and listen. Try to learn a few of their names and songs. What plants are growing, blooming, and dying right now where you are? What

are the human persons around you doing? We're part of nature, too.

It isn't necessary to pray to an external entity in order to engage deeply with devotional practice. Acts of time, attention, and wonder are among the most precious gifts any of us mortals have to give. The practices above are just a few simple ways in which we can express *I am here, I care,* and *Thank you.*

## Pantheism, Archetype, and Deities in Ritual
### by Shauna Aura Knight

When I lead a ritual, I'm far less concerned with teaching and enforcing any given theology than I am with getting ritual participants to a place where they can commune with the divine. And, if they aren't theistic at all, perhaps that's more just getting people to a place where they can connect to their deep inner wisdom. I identify as a pantheist. I believe that the entirety of the world, of the universe, is divine, So I'm usually going to refer to that "something" that I'm helping people connect to as the divine, as deity, as archetype, as mystery.

I see it as divine communion, but not with something external or "above." I see it as connecting to the divine within us that always was. We just can't stay in a constant state of perceiving that divine. If the ritual is working for my participants, that's all that matters to me. I'm not concerned with their specific theological beliefs.

In the rituals I do in Chicago, or at festivals, I try to make space for many different theologies and traditions. I often use that typical ritual template of grounding/centering, casting a circle, inviting in the elements and other allies, but for me, it's less about theology and more about ritual as a pattern. It's more about the process of moving into the deep within. While I'm coming at it as a pantheist, I know that many are coming in as duotheists or polytheists or henotheists or humanists or atheists or animists. I try to make space for that as much as possible, though I'm aware that people with a pantheistic or archetypal leaning will probably resonate more with the work I do.

Ultimately, I just want everyone to be able to have that experience of the divine, in whatever way they experience that, in whatever form, by whatever name they call it. That something sacred that is always there for us, but sometimes we just have such a hard time finding it.

## My Own Beliefs

I approach deity in a somewhat agnostic way, in the sense that I have my own beliefs about the divine, but I don't pretend to have all the answers. I could be completely wrong about how deity works.

I'm a Gnostic in the sense that I have had direct experience of the divine in a way that transformed me. Many people use the word "mystic" and "mysticism" without understanding its core definition; it's often a word that is used to mean "magical" or "woo-woo." A mystic is one who has had direct connection and apprehension of the divine.

I stumbled into a class years ago called "Mysticism in the Third Millennium." I was a Pagan looking for a community at the time, but I took this class as I figured it would be an easy college credit while I was working full time. Instead, the class completely transformed me and my understanding of theology and spirituality. It was offered by Wayne Teasdale, an interreligious monk and Sannyasa (renunciate).

In his book, *The Mystic Heart* (1999), he addresses "mysticism, or primary religious experience, whether it be revelation or a personal mystical state of consciousness…direct contact with the divine, or ultimate mystery…" He offers several qualities of mystic communion with the divine including "practical, experiential, ineffable or nonconceptual, unitive or nondual, noetic, integrative, sapiential, giving certitude, and in possession of transcendent knowledge from direct experience." The class he offered, and his book, helped me to frame my own mystical experiences and understand that they fell in line with the mystic experiences that others have had (and tried to write about) over the millennia. But I also began to call into question my own theology and spirituality and how I view the divine.

## How Theistic Am I?

I'm a pantheist, but I hold onto the "theism" part with the bare edges of my fingernails. I don't really believe in a divine being that looks over us and makes plans for us. Just over a year ago when I was in a car accident, I posted about it on my Facebook and people were commenting, "The Goddess was looking out for you," and "The gods were protecting you," and—though I appreciate the sentiment—that's not what I believe. If I believed that, then I would need to believe that all the other people who died in car accidents that night around the world were somehow less deserving of life, less deserving of the blessings of the gods. I don't believe the gods/deities/the divine take any kind of direct hand in my life, or in anyone else's. Not like that, anyways.

When I first started working with the idea of the Goddess, I was eleven or twelve. My mom was into some woo-woo New-Agey stuff, and I was introduced to the idea of the Goddess and also to angels. I was severely bullied in middle school by my peers, and I can honestly say that talking to the Moon/Water Goddess/Angel at night was a big part of what kept me alive through that. I thought that she was looking out for me, that I was important, *that I was meant for something*.

Later, I came to understand that children who are bullied and abused often survive through such psychological coping strategies. In fact, the children who sustain the belief that they are special and meant for something more are the ones who tend to have a stronger, healthier ego later in life when they are no longer being abused. The kids who go the other way and believe they somehow deserved the abuse suffer different (and usually more severe) wounds to the ego.

As an adult wrestling with my own theology, I had to ask myself the question: What was the Goddess I talked to in my teen years? Was she just a mirror, a reflection, a psychological phantom I'd conjured up to survive? That didn't seem right to me. I'd felt this luminescence, that transcendent, moving, permeating *connectedness*. It had felt holy, complete, right. I'd had visions, real ones. I'd had dreams that were nothing short of connecting to the face of the divine and feeling that energy pour through me.

## Abandoned By the Divine

However, there was a stretch of years where that divine connection seemed gone. In fact, the irony was that this began around the time I started Pagan leadership training at Diana's Grove. Though I was learning the skills to do this work that had called to me, it was like *the juice that had called me onto that path was suddenly gone.*

Years later, I recovered that juice in fits and starts, and then in a series of raptures. Weeping, whole-body, connected-to-the-universe raptures. Feeling myself held and cradled by the mother that was the universe whispering to me, "You're not alone. You were never alone." Feeling that water of life pouring into my chest, hollowing me out and filling me with starlight and universes and love. Things I can't capture in words but, having felt them, I now understand Rumi's poetry far better and what he was trying to put into paltry language.

So, in essence, I do believe in the larger divine, in that something else, in that energy beneath the surface. I just don't believe that it takes much of a direct hand in our lives. It's just love…energy…something that doesn't fit well into words.

## Deities or Archetypes?

In general, but specifically in ritual, I tend to work with deities as archetypes, as stories. I'm a mystic, but I also have a scientific bent. I think about the various stories of the gods, and culture and sociology and how cultures form around their stories, and around their environment. And I think about how deities change over time just as language changes over time. The Greek word Zeus and Latin Deus and Norse Tiw (Tyr) all come from a Proto-Indo-European root word *deiwos*. I believe that gods changed over time just as cultures spread and changed and became unique from one another.

An example of how gods change over time can be seen in how Egyptian Isis took on aspects of the previous goddess Hathor. And the story of Isis and Osiris changed depending on the time frame, as well as where one lived along the Nile.

For me, the fact that the stories of these gods changed over time *doesn't make the stories any less potent*. The fact that the Proto-Indo-European gods became more specific cultural gods as the various tribes spread out and changed over time doesn't take away the power of those stories. At the core, I believe that mythology and story tells us a lot about ourselves; it speaks to the storyteller, and the culture of the storyteller. Myths tell us a lot about a culture and what that culture considers to be important.

But stories also change us. And when we rewrite a story, we are claiming our own power and what we find to be important for ourselves.

Personally, I believe that the various deities and spirits from different cultures are energies that are an intermingling of collective thought and natural energy. They may have a consciousness, but it's not the same kind of consciousness that humans have.

### Where Do Gods Begin?

Imagine, our clan has just moved to the foot of the mountain by the sea. Over the years, we come to fear the storms that come from the sea, the way they part around the mountain, the lightning that threatens our village during the spring storms. We come to fear the seasonal waves that steal away the fisherfolk. We tell stories about the lightning, about the waves. We revere the return of the sun and the warm weather it brings after the storms, and the fruits that grow in the warm part of the year.

I can easily see how, over generations, these natural forces became known by names, and those names and stories grew in power as they were told. They had energy inherently as nature, and human consciousness gave them names, forms, stories. And perhaps those stories begin to take on a life and consciousness of their own. Perhaps not.

Given that our own human brains are a couple of pounds of meat and electrical signals that form a consciousness, it's certainly possible that there are different types of consciousness out there formed out of the interconnected ecosystem of our planet, or a specific place, a forest of trees and plants and interconnected roots. *But certainly it's not a conscious-*

*ness that operates in the same way as a human brain does.* I believe the entire planet may have a consciousness of a sort, but a gender? Probably not. For that matter, the entire idea of gods that have human-like form, and are gendered the way humans are, is part of why I'm an archetypist instead of a polytheist. It means to me that we humans are the ones who shaped the forms and stories of those gods to look like us.

I don't think it serves to say that we're somehow "bad" for anthropomorphizing these energies, these stories, in this way. I believe that we cannot encompass the whole of the divine, and our story-loving minds not only want to tell stories about what we see and make meaning out of it, we also tend to work better with concepts we can wrap our brains around. When we think of gods and spirits that look like us, perhaps that's just a way that we can more easily connect to that larger divine. Perhaps we need that mirror, that gateway. Perhaps the larger divine around us is just too huge to encompass, so we shape it into a face we know well—our own.

This doesn't necessarily mean that those gods/archetypes/spirits don't have a consciousness, or an energy. And, as I said earlier, I'm willing to be wrong. Talking about these nuances of my own beliefs is where I'm the most likely to offend a devout hard polytheist, and that's not my intention. This is just to offer some of my own theological beliefs, and my general approach to public ritual.

I tend to work with deities as facets, as masks, as pieces. They are larger than a human, vast amounts of energy and thought, vast amounts of story. And those stories have power. There may be an individual consciousness there, but it's not a consciousness that directly impacts the physical plane. And it's not a consciousness that requires worship or offerings, or commands us to act in certain ways.

Even if these consciousnesses are just stories, I strongly feel that the power of story is not to be brushed off lightly. Archetype—original story—is some of the most powerful magic there is.

## Archetype and Deity in Ritual

Often in ritual, I'll work with a particular deity or mythological story. Sometimes I'll use a particular culture's story, such as the myth of King Arthur, tales of Brigid, Inanna's Descent, or Isis and Osiris, or fairytales and other stories. In those instances, I refer to the deities by name to tell the story.

Other times, I'll use the archetypal role to tell the story. Instead of telling the story of going to the cave at the mouth of the Underworld and the Horned One is there, guiding us into the below, I might refer to the Gatekeeper. Or instead of working with Brigid or Hephaestus, I might call the Worker at the Forge. This has the advantage of not excluding people who don't identify with a particular pantheon, and also has the advantage of being gender inclusive. "Gatekeeper" is inclusive to all genders and allows the participants to use the image/concept/deity that works for them.

However, this is also the place where some polytheists can't always theologically fit into the rituals I offer. This is why I feel like I'm walking a tightrope as a ritual planner, particularly given most of the rituals I offer are public or large festival rituals, so my goal is to be as inclusive as I can be.

There are times when it makes sense to me to work with a particular deity or myth, and there are times when it makes more sense to work with the archetypes and roles. If I want to explore the story of Arthur pulling the Sword from the Stone, it would be distracting to not refer to Arthur, as it's a popular story. Similarly, if I'm working with the tale of Isis and Osiris and Horus, it makes sense to use the names.

Some archetypal stories are more flexible, though. I can work with Inanna's Descent in ritual and work with the Sumerian myth from the ancient text…or I can make it more archetypal and just focus on the descent, on moving down, on passing challengers and gates as we move into the depth of the down below. I can leave the names and the challengers and the mysteries up to the participant to determine. And given that Inanna's Descent is replicated in a number of different pantheons, it's easy to make this one more universal. Persephone's story is another descent, and there are Welsh stories of visiting the Otherworld…Odin sacrifices himself in different ways to gain Otherworldly wisdom…in other words, many pantheons have their own story of a character who goes through a road of trials to gain a particular magic, power, or strength.

Or I can just entirely leave it up to the ritual participant to create the experience for themselves in the way that works best for them.

For that matter, one of the reasons I use open-language trance (meaning, I ask questions instead of making statements about what they see) is that when I ask someone, "What stands before you? What challenges you? What tells you that you cannot pass?", what they come up with will be far worse, far more intimidating or challenging—and far more ultimately empowering—than anything I could envision for them.

### "But Those Gods Hate Each Other!"

I've heard a Pagan urban legend. "I was at this one ritual," people tell me, "where the priest/ess told everyone to call whatever deity they'd like. I saw the thunderstorm rolling in and I ran! I got to my car right before the storm hit. Lightning struck a tree right near the ritual!"

Yeah, tell me that one again?!

Because I've heard the same story from a dozen people, *as if they were there*. They never mention the group or the tradition. It's an urban legend with a little dose of overdramatization. A variant is, "She called Freyja and Loki and I just ran!" or "Hephaestus and Aries and Aphrodite were called, those gods were pissed!"

I facilitate rituals like that all the time. If I'm working with archetypes (like the Gatekeeper or the Weaver of Fate or the Guardian of the Well), I'll often invite the participants to invite in any ally, spirit, ancestor, or deity to be present for them in the ritual, to guide them or support them in their work. Or, if I'm calling in the archetype of the Gatekeeper or Guardian of the Crossroads, I'll invite people to call out their own deity in their pantheon. People have called Hecate, Legba, Cernunnos, Eshu, Ganesh, and many others.

And I never have had any thunderstorms or other crazy phenomena happen. I can't speak to gods being pissed off at each other because it doesn't really function that way in my theology. Though, perhaps this is also related to the kind of agreements I set up before I offer a ritual, and the pantheistic "container," if you will.

It's not that I haven't had ritual disasters. I have set a few things on fire, but I call that user error, not gods. I admit I'm a bit of a ritual pyro sometimes.

The point is, I'm working with stories, I'm not worshiping gods or making offerings to them. I don't do divination on rituals on whether or not things worked. I don't believe that if you're trying to light a candle in ritual to symbolize your devotion to ABC or your wish for DEF and it keeps blowing out that this is the divine's way of sending you an omen. I absolutely do not believe that a thunderstorm raining out a ritual or a flood ending a festival or anything else like that is somehow the gods' way of sending a bad portent.

If I believed that, I'd have to believe those fundamentalists who believe that earthquakes and tornadoes are because God is mad about gay marriage being legalized.

That's not to say I don't believe in prophetic visions. I've dreamed the future myself before it came to pass. But hearing/seeing/sensing echoes from the future doesn't require the intervention of gods or spirits.

## Divine Communion and Ritual Goals

What strikes me as a bit of a paradox is that one of the core pieces of any of the rituals I do is trying to help people get to divine communion. I'm trying to get ritual participants in real connection with the divine. With their own gods and spirits, if that's their theology, even if I don't share their theological views.

I'm doing that through ecstatic trance techniques with chanting, dancing, singing, drumming, movement…with open-language and multi-voice trance journeys…with the structure of the ritual itself.

The rituals I facilitate generally have three goals. To help people connect together as a community, to help people connect to their deep selves and/or connect to the divine, and to help people engage in personal and spiritual transformation, to help each person step into their best selves.

Ritual is, for me, a way to help each of us—myself included—explore our shadows, our fears, our joys and loves and griefs, our hopes and yearnings. It's to achieve the axiom, "Know Thyself." It's to become better human beings so that we can better serve our families and friends and broader communities, and the world around us.

In rituals with ecstatic energy raising, some groups and traditions will send the energy to a specific magical task, or to a specific deity in other cases. In my rituals, the energy is a cauldron. It's there for us to drink of it. Instead of a "cone," I see it as a "bowl." The energy of the ritual fuels us, fuels our divine communion, fuels our personal transformation. And the actions we take when we leave that ritual are far more potent—and far more impactful—than any energy we could send "out" to something.

## Ritual Techniques:
## Gods, Aspecting and Trance Possession

Sometimes in the rituals I lead I have people speaking in the voice of the gods. When we're telling stories and working with gods in rituals, there's sort of a spectrum of how the deity is being worked with. This falls under the category of "ritual tech" since we're talking about facilitation techniques and choices around ritual planning.

There's telling the story of Isis and Osiris in the third person: "Isis wept tears into the Nile." Then there's performing the story as a mystery play, where you have someone in the role of Isis: "I wept tears into the Nile!" Or, you might have someone speaking in the first person as Isis, embodying that role, but not aspecting or getting trance possessed. I've often used this technique to take a storytelling piece and turn it into a trance journey.

> *Storytelling:* "My love was dead. I wept, I wept tears into the Nile. The Nile flooded over…"
>
> *Trance Journey:* "When have you lost something you loved? When have you wept? When have you grieved? How did it feel?"

Then we move into the spectrum of embodying, aspecting, and trance possession. It's also referred to as drawing down, but each definition has its own connotations depending on the Pagan tradition you're talking about. Here's a rough overview of where the concepts fit on a spectrum.

*Embodying* is generally just speaking in the first person as the deity. *Aspecting* tends to be a spectrum of light to medium drawing down. The deity may be partly within you (like, 10%) or you may be approaching a full trance possession (80%) but you're still in charge of what your body is doing. Typically, *trance possession* refers to a total 100% possession by the deity or spirit. Often the vessel (the human person drawing the deity/spirit in) will have no memory of the experience.

Similar to this is oracular work, where the vessel/dedicant is asking the deity questions, and relaying them to people. This isn't typically a trance possession; it's more like the deity is whispering in their ear, to use a metaphor. Though, oracular work can sometimes shift into a trance possession.

## Pantheistic Trance Possession

A ritual participant who is on the more atheistic side of the theism spectrum is probably going to have some issues getting into a ritual that is using aspecting, drawing down, and trance possession. If someone's storytelling about a myth, that's cool. Or play-acting the myth, that's cool. Or even speaking in first person as a storytelling/trance technique, that's cool. But once you ask someone who is an atheist to believe that an actual god is being drawn down into a human vessel, then the suspension of disbelief can start to disappear. And, at the same time, when I have someone aspect an archetype, like the Water Bearer or the Worker at the Forge, I lose the polytheists who work with very specific gods vs. archetypes.

Here's how I approach it. Because I believe in these archetypes as part of the larger divine, and because I believe in the power of story, I believe that it's possible that we can be not just inspired by that larger story, but *we can fill ourselves up with it.* And this works whether we're working with a particular god or goddess (like Hephaestus or Brigid) or the archetype (Worker at the Forge). When I look at the Water Bearer archetype, there are goddesses that fit this role (Isis), but also astrological signs (Aquarius), Tarot cards (the Star Card) and characters from the Grail myths.

I've done rituals where I and others aspected the astrological signs or Tarot cards, and I've worked with characters in stories that aren't gods such as King Arthur, Merlin, and the Lady of the Lake.

I believe it's possible to not only aspect these stories, characters, archetypes, and gods—meaning, take the story into ourselves partway—but I also believe it's possible to be trance possessed by them. And going further, I don't believe that it's "fake" to be trance possessed by an archetype. I believe it serves a particular ritual function. And again, I'm agnostic enough to believe that it might be an archetype. It might be a god It might all be a figment of our imaginations.

For me the question is, "Does it serve?" Does it serve a purpose in the ritual for the ritual participants? Does it transform us? Does it have that quality of divine communion? Does it serve the three goals of the ritual work I'm doing, particularly the personal transformation or divine communion functions?

### Is it Real?

I've talked to atheistic Pagans who just can't get into any ritual where someone is invoking/drawing down/possessed by a deity. They just feel that it's fake, because deities don't exist for them. And if they were going to do a ritual with any deities, they'd have to make sure that they didn't refer to them as deities, to the point of saying they would clarify during rituals, "And here we have Aphrodite, who isn't really Aphrodite."

Here's the thing. A lot of ritual is about engaging the trance state. It's about a light suspension of disbelief. Storytelling in ritual, and ecstatic trance techniques, only really work if people are allowed to go with the flow. In the rituals I facilitate, I'm trying to get people comfortable with singing, dancing, chanting, moving…I'm trying to get people willing to explore their shadow sides, willing to connect to their deep selves or commune with the divine if that's in their theology.

There's an axiom of ritual that every time you do something that takes people out of trance, people will remind everyone that we're just a bunch of people in a room doing something ridiculous. Then people remember to be conscious of how they appear socially, and then you have to start all over. A simpler axiom is, every time you say, "This is what we're doing now," or "And now we're gonna…", you can just watch everyone come right back up out of trance. That's entirely what I'm trying to prevent in a ritual.

The reason I use ancient archetypes and stories…the reason I use inclusive trance language…the reason I use chanting and movement…the reason I decorate the space with candles…the reason I use drumming…the reason I encourage ritualists to wear timeless clothing and to not wear t-shirts or other clothing that is very modern…*is all to help get people into that deeper trance state.*

Trancework is theologically independent. It's going to work whether you're a polytheist, pantheist, or atheist. It's the kind of magic that is about our brains and chemistry. Whether you believe someone is possessed by a deity, or whether you believe that they are in a heightened trance state inspired by an intense and archetypal story, there's value to this practice in ritual.

Stories have power in and of themselves. We humans have been carving and painting stories in stone since we figured out how…Story works whether you're an atheist or a polytheist.

Again, stories—especially old stories—have power in and of themselves. We humans are pretty obsessed with story. We've marked our battles in cave walls with paint and later wedged them into clay and scribbled them onto papyrus. Stories inspire us; it's how we're wired.

Story works whether you're an atheist or a polytheist. And story is one of the most potent tools I leverage as a ritualist, whether I'm telling an ancient story of Isis or Freyja or Inanna…or I'm helping someone to tell their own story, their own journey, the struggles they have endured, the challengers they have faced, the treasures they have won. I'd say that the core of the rituals I offer—indeed, of the workshops I teach—is helping people to become the heroes of their own journey.

## Creating a Container Through Agreements

When I facilitate a ritual, I work to first address my approach to ritual with the attendees. That helps create the container, and I believe it's a big help in setting the tone for the ritual. I explain that I'm coming at things as a pantheist, and that people can approach this ritual in whatever way works for them. They don't have to believe in gods; they can just experience the story as a useful model for our work. Or, they can work with gods, deities, and spirits. I encourage people to be self-responsible in a number of ways before the ritual even begins.

When I facilitate a ritual where I'm going to have people to invite in any deity, spirit, or other ally they'd like to have present, I make sure to offer that same self-responsibility. I might say something like, "You can invite any deity, spirit, or ally you'd like to have present here for this work, and they are here for you as your ally. We may all come from different pantheons and traditions, but we can connect to our own gods in our own ways without any concern about interfering with one another's work." Maybe someone's inviting Loki and someone else's deity hates Loki. There doesn't need to be a conflict there at all. It's people inviting in deities for their own work, so long as every person takes responsibility for themselves and doesn't try to make a big dramatic conflict out of it.

For that matter, I make it clear that extreme drama isn't going to gain my time and attention. I know of a number of folks in the Reclaiming tradition (where I take a number of my ritual techniques from) who refer to rituals focused on personal growth and shadow work as "puking cauldron" rituals. What can happen with shadow/mirror work rituals is that some people are drawn to rituals like that because they'll get worked up into a sobbing fit and need to be "tended" and cared for. *They aren't there to actually do personal work—they're there to derail the ritual by getting lots of attention.*

As part of my "self-responsibility" talk at the beginning, I often say, "This ritual work is challenging work. We're going into the Underworld to confront our shadows. If you are making sounds of grief or joy, if you're crying, if you're on the floor, I'm going to leave you be. I'm going to let you have your emotion and I'm not going to come over and try to fix you. I'm going to trust that if you need something you'll ask for help. If you have trouble coming back after the ritual, I, or these three folks over here, are on hand to help. But I'm going to give you the opportunity to handle things on your own without my interference. Often when we try to comfort someone, we're trying to fix them, so I'm going to ask everyone else here to not go hug someone unasked. Don't try to fix anyone, let them have their process." I get everyone's buy-in on that, and that creates part of the container for the ritual.

### Paradox

A lot of the ritual work I do requires me to hold paradox. Are they gods? Are they archetypes? Is someone actually trance possessed? At a certain point, I leave the theological wrestling behind. I focus on technique and what works. Singing works, drumming works, chanting works, dancing works. Trance language works. And story works, every time. Whether I believe they are gods or just old stories, it doesn't really matter. The stories themselves drive us and inspire us; always have, probably always will.

## "As the Gods Pour, So Do Mortals":
## An Alternative Conception of Divine Reciprocity
### by John Halstead

I've always been uncomfortable with the idea of divine reciprocity, even when I was a Christian. Divine reciprocity is the idea that the gods will grant worshipers blessings in exchange for something, like worship or offerings or oaths. This is a foundational idea for many theists, both Christian monotheists and Pagan polytheists. For Christians, the reciprocity often takes the form of promises of good behavior or refraining from other enjoyable behaviors (i.e., fasting), offered in exchange for blessings. For Pagan polytheists, the reciprocity often takes the form of material offerings to the gods, like food and drink, in conjunction with a request for a blessing—sometimes a blessing of a material or practical nature. As a Religious Naturalist, I don't believe in this kind of divine reciprocity.

But there is another conception of divine reciprocity that makes sense to my naturalistic sensibilities. It is rooted in the notion of the interdependence of all things—where "all things" includes the gods (whatever they are). It contrasts with the conception of a god who is transcendent and independent of creation. This kind of reciprocity has nothing to do with the granting of wishes for material blessings. Instead, it is about the idea of our being "in relation" to every other thing and to the world itself.

As a pantheist, my divine "Other" is the Universe itself, and especially the Earth. We are dependent on the material world in every way, for sustenance and for resources. Our very bodies are made of matter, and our ability to think depends on a material brain.

But it goes even deeper than that. As the theologian Martin Buber and the philosopher Emmanuel Levinas have explained, our very sense of self is constituted by the encounter with that which we call "other." David Abram, the author of *Spell of the Sensuous* (1996), explains one way in which we experience this reciprocity with the world itself:

> "Caught up in a mass of abstractions, our attention hypnotized by a host of human-made technologies that only reflect us back to ourselves, it is all too easy for us to forget our carnal inherence in a more-than-human matrix of sensations and sensibilities. Our bodies have formed themselves in delicate reciprocity with the manifold textures, sounds, and shapes of an animate earth—our eyes have evolved in subtle interaction with other eyes, as our ears are attuned by their very structure to the howling of wolves and the honking of geese…
>
> "Our most immediate experience of things is necessarily an experience of reciprocal encounter—of tension, communication, and commingling. From within the depths of this encounter, we know the thing or phenomenon only as our interlocutor—as a dynamic presence that that confronts us and draws us into relation…
>
> "There is an intimate reciprocity to the senses; as we touch the bark of a tree, we feel the tree touching us; as we lend our ears to the local sounds and ally our nose to the seasonal scents, the terrain gradually tunes us in turn."

We can try to mentally remove ourselves from our picture of the world or we can describe the world as consisting solely of inert or passive things. But this objectivity is an illusion. Our immediate experience of the world is one of sensuous reciprocity. In this sense, *reciprocity is not something we do*; it is, rather, *something we realize*. It is a condition of the possibility of our being in the world.

226 | Godless Paganism

Zeus (left) pouring a libation with the assistance of Ares (right)

Apollo pouring a libation

Divine (left) and mortal (right) libation scenes on the same krater

When reciprocity is understood in this way, as something which *already is*, rather than something we create, then ritualized offerings take on a different meaning. Offerings, usually the pouring of libations, have always been a part of my Humanistic Pagan practice. (Aesthetically, I prefer liquid libations because of how they are absorbed by the earth.) Theists and atheists alike would probably find this hypocritical. "Who am I pouring libations to?" they must wonder.

To answer this question, consider the numerous images on ancient vases and pottery which depict Classical gods and goddesses pouring libations and making sacrifices. These scenes would undoubtedly strike a theist and an atheist equally as strange. Who, after all, are the gods making offerings to? Kimberly Christin Patton observes in her book, *Religion of the Gods: Ritual, Paradox, and Reflexivity* (2009), that the gods' worship in these scenes "seems to both parallel and respond to human cultic observance." "This is why mortal libation scenes appear on the opposite side of the vases," Patton writes, "*As the gods pour, so do mortals. As mortals pour, so do the gods*" (emphasis added).

This may or may not be a historically accurate explanation of these scenes, but this image—of gods and mortals pouring libations in one continuous circle—expresses one meaning which ritualized offerings might have for a Religious Naturalist like me.

While I pour libations, I don't imagine that I am making an offering *to someone* or even to some*thing*. Such a conception presumes a separateness which is precisely what I am trying to overcome through ritual. I do not pour libations out to gods, who I wouldn't imagine would need them if they did exist. Nor do I make offerings to the Earth or to Nature (unless you count my compost box), which would inevitably receive the matter I am offering in some other way. Nor am I making offerings to myself. Instead, these offerings are a way of remembering, a way of restoring the experience of connection—*of reciprocity*—with the world, a reciprocity which is always already present, but which we human beings have the ability to (intentionally or unintentionally) make ourselves blind to.

228 | Godless Paganism

Dionysos (right) pouring a libation
(Pennsylvania Museum of Anthropology and Archaeology)

As I pour out the water, wine, honey, or vegetable oil on the earth, I create, in the form of the stream of liquid, a living connection between myself and the Earth. It is a visual and visceral representation of my connection to the Earth. And in so doing, I experience both an "emptying," what the Greeks called *kenosis* (κένωσις), and also simultaneously a "filling," what the Greeks called *pleroma* (πλήρωμα). It is as if I am both emptying the vessel of myself and filling myself at the same time, as if I am both the cup that pours and the Earth which receives—emptying because I am giving up substance which I might take into my body as sustenance, and filling because my body is already connected with the Earth so intimately that I cannot give to the earth without sustaining myself.

In this act, I restore in a small measure that sense of sensual connection which I have to the world. Especially if the libation is water, I am reminded how this water long ago traveled across the cosmos in comets, how it was part of ancient oceans, and how it has traveled from the bottom of the ocean to the highest mountains. I am reminded how this water at one time was part of great glaciers and tiny snowflakes, how it has flowed through the bodies of great dinosaurs, tiny amoeba, and the bodies of my ancestors. I am reminded that this is the water I am made of, the water that sustains me, the water that I was formed in, and the water that I will return to.

I don't just *think* it; the ritual helps me *feel* it. As I pour the libation, I watch the stream of liquid flowing onto the Earth and being absorbed by the soil, and this connection moves from the conceptual to the visceral, from my mind to my flesh and bones. This, for me, is the true meaning of divine reciprocity.

## Our Gender-Neutral Atheistic Pagan Wedding Ceremony Script
### by Irene Hilldale

My partner and I are decidedly non-traditional people. On the outside, we look like a (stereo)typical heterosexual couple. On the inside, we are anything but. So when we decided to get married, we knew that our wedding needed to reflect us as a couple, and not our parents' or anyone else's vision of what was supposedly correct.

With a bit of help from the internet, a few books, and my personal experience writing atheistic Pagan sabbat rituals, we wrote our ceremony script ourselves. It was an undertaking, but ultimately we came up with something that we absolutely loved.

Much of the symbolism here is highly personal, and can easily be changed to suit your own needs and vision. For example, our elemental representation for earth was a potted plant surrounded with symbolic stones; some people may feel that a better representation would be a bowl of salt, a seed, a crystal, or something else they associate with earth, and that is perfectly okay.

*A few clarifying notes regarding the ceremony:* We and our wedding party processed into the ceremony from the sides, and exited up a center aisle, in a 'T' shape. This allowed my partner and I to walk toward each other while carrying our lanterns, symbolizing our coming together as equals. Our exit up the center aisle symbolized our unification into that partnership. See the diagram below for an illustration of how this worked:

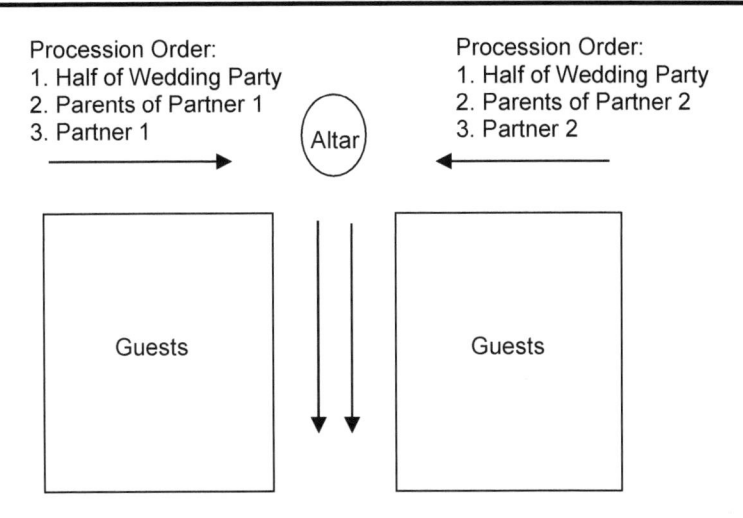

```
Procession Order:                    Procession Order:
1. Half of Wedding Party             1. Half of Wedding Party
2. Parents of Partner 1              2. Parents of Partner 2
3. Partner 1          (Altar)        3. Partner 2
   ─────────►                           ◄─────────

   ┌─────────┐                       ┌─────────┐
   │         │         │ │           │         │
   │  Guests │         │ │           │  Guests │
   │         │         ▼ ▼           │         │
   └─────────┘                       └─────────┘
```

## Ceremony Materials

Altar table

Altar cloth

Earth: Plant with stones

Air: Incense

Fire: Candle

Water: Goblet of water

Handfasting cord

Wedding rings

Lanterns and shepherd's hook

Personal Letters of Love & Commitment (written in advance by each partner)

### I. Introduction and Statement of Intent

**Officiant:** Love is the energy that binds our universe together, makes us whole, and human. While we may all be young in consciousness, and our lives fleeting, the matter of which we are made is as old as the universe itself. This brief but beautiful organization of matter into individuals and the intertwining of our lives have been celebrated for much of human history, in many different ways and across cultures.

And so today, we are gathered here to witness the formal, public, and legal declaration of love and commitment between [Partner 1] and [Partner 2].

[Partner 1] and [Partner 2], do you come into this marriage of your own free will, and with full conscious intent?

**[Partner 1] and [Partner 2]:** We do.

**Officiant:** Then please place your lanterns, your individual lights, on the hook behind me to signify your intent to continue to build your future together as a lawfully wedded couple.

*[Partner 1] and [Partner 2] move to either side of the officiant, and hang lanterns from the shepherd's hook, then return to original place.*

## II. Readings

**Officiant:** With this marriage, you not only bring your own lives together, but those of your friends, your family, your communities. A supportive community is a cornerstone for loving and lasting relationships. And so, in acknowledgement of the role of community, of friends and family, we will now hear readings from [your wedding party/parents/whomever you choose to read].

**Reading:** *The Couple's Tao Te Ching*: "Transforming Power" & "A Sacred Space" by Lao Tzu, interpreted by William Martin

> "Your love contains the power
> of a thousand suns.
> It unfolds as naturally and effortlessly
> as does a flower,
> and graces the world with its blooming.
> Its beauty radiates a transforming energy
> that enlivens all who see it.
> Because of you, compassion and joy
> are added to the world.

That is why the stars sing together
because of your love."

"Your love requires space in which to grow.
This space must be safe enough
to allow your hearts to be revealed.
It must offer refreshment for your spirits
and renewal for your minds.
It must be a space made sacred
by the quality of your honesty,
attention, love, and compassion.
It may be anywhere,
inside or out,
but it must exist."

**Reading:** Excerpts from *Obergefell et al. v. Hodges, Director, Ohio Department of Health, et al.*

> "The nature of injustice is that we may not always see it in our own times. The generations that wrote and ratified the Bill of Rights and the Fourteenth Amendment did not presume to know the extent of freedom in all of its dimensions, and so they entrusted to future generations a charter protecting the right of all persons to enjoy liberty as we learn its meaning. When new insight reveals discord between the Constitution's central protections and a received legal stricture, a claim to liberty must be addressed.
>
> "If rights were defined by who exercised them in the past, then received practices could serve as their own continued justification and new groups could not invoke rights once denied. This Court has rejected that approach, both with respect to the right to marry and the rights of gays and lesbians.
>
> "The right to marry is fundamental as a matter of history and tradition, but rights come not from ancient sources alone. They

rise, too, from a better-informed understanding of how constitutional imperatives define a liberty that remains urgent in our own era.

"Choices about marriage shape an individual's destiny. As the Supreme Judicial Court of Massachusetts has explained, because 'it fulfills yearnings for security, safe haven, and connection that express our common humanity, civil marriage is an esteemed institution, and the decision whether and whom to marry is among life's momentous acts of self-definition.'

"Marriage is a coming together for better or for worse, hopefully enduring, and intimate to the degree of being sacred. It is an association that promotes a way of life, not causes; a harmony in living, not political faiths; a bilateral loyalty, not commercial or social projects.

"The nature of marriage is that, through its enduring bond, two persons together can find other freedoms, such as expression, intimacy, and spirituality. This is true for all persons, whatever their sexual orientation."

**Reading:** "To Love is Not to Possess," by James Kavanaugh

"To love is not to possess,
To own or imprison,
Nor to lose one's self in another.
Love is to join and separate,
To walk alone and together,
To find a laughing freedom
That lonely isolation does not permit.
It is finally to be able
To be who we really are
No longer clinging in childish dependency
Nor docilely living separate lives in silence,
It is to be perfectly one's self

And perfectly joined in permanent commitment
To another—and to one's inner self.
Love only endures when it moves like waves,
Receding and returning gently or passionately,
Or moving lovingly like the tide
In the moon's own predictable harmony,
Because finally, despite a child's scars
Or an adult's deepest wounds,
They are openly free to be
Who they really are—and always secretly were,
In the very core of their being
Where true and lasting love can alone abide."

**Reading:** "Epithalamium" by Liz Lochhead

"For marriage, love and love alone's the argument.
Sweet ceremony, then hand in hand we go
Taking to our changed, still dangerous days, our complement.
We think we know ourselves, but all we know
Is: love surprises us. It's like when sunlight flings
A sudden shaft that lights up glamorous the rain
Across a Glasgow street—or when Botanic Spring's
First crisp, dry breath turns February air champagne.
Delight's infectious—your friends
Put on, with glad rag finery today, your joy,
Renew in themselves the right true ends
They won't let old griefs, old lives, destroy.
When at our lover's feet our opened selves we've laid
We find ourselves, and all the world, remade."

## III. Declaration of Love and Commitment

**Officiant:** Thank you all for your kind and profound words on love, partnership, and marriage.

[Partner 1] and [Partner 2], as you proceed into your future, happy and difficult times will come as surely as the sun rises and sets, as surely as the seasons cycle and change. As life partners, you promise to weather the changes and difficult times, take solace and support in one another, and share equally your burdens and your joys. At this time, with the blessing of your community here today, as well as those who could not be in attendance, you will make your declarations of love and commitment. To determine who will go first, you will partake in the ancient and sacred ritual of rock-paper-scissors.

*[Partner 1] and [Partner 2] read their letters of love and commitment to each other, in the order determined by rock-paper-scissors. The person who "wins" the game reads first.*

## IV. Handfasting and Vows

**Officiant:** [Partner 1] and [Partner 2] have chosen a handfasting ceremony to formalize their union. This type of ceremony, in which the partners' hands are bound as a sign of their commitment to one another, is the source of the phrase, to "Tie the Knot." Today, they will incorporate four knots, each representing one of the four classical elements as well as a corresponding pillar of their relationship. [Partner 1] and [Partner 2], please join your hands.

*They join hands. Officiant lays the cord across their hands.*

**Officiant:** These cords will now be tied around your hands as a physical representation of the decision you make to bind together your lives. As I make each knot, each party member will approach and place the elemental symbols of your love upon the altar.

And so we begin.

*[Party Member 1] approaches the altar and places the potted plant on the altar.*

**[Party Member 1]:** Like Earth, let your trust in one another be steadfast, a rich ground where love can grow stronger and flourish.

*Officiant makes the first knot.*

**[Partner 1] and [Partner 2]:** We will.

*[Party Member 2] approaches the altar and places the incense on the altar.*

**[Party Member 2]:** Like Air, take joy in your flights of fancy, and feed one another's interests, curiosities, and intellect.

*Officiant makes the second knot.*

**[Partner 1] and [Partner 2]:** We will.

*[Party Member 3] approaches the altar and places the candle on the altar.*

**[Party Member 3]:** Like Fire, let love and compassion for each other burn brightly, lighting your way forward and warming your spirits.

*Officiant makes the third knot.*

**[Partner 1] and [Partner 2]:** We will.

*[Party Member 4] approaches the altar and places the goblet on the altar.*

**[Party Member 4]:** Like Water, be gentle enough to follow the natural paths of the earth and strong enough to rise up and reshape the world together.*

*Officiant makes the fourth knot.*

**[Partner 1] and [Partner 2]:** We will.

**Officiant:** These cords and the knots formed around your hands represent the commitments you make here today. They are strong enough to hold you together through times of struggle, yet flexible enough to allow for individuality and personal growth.

[Partner 1] and [Partner 2], do you promise to treat each other with compassion, to actively listen, and communicate without judgment? If so, please say, "We do."

**[Partner 1] and [Partner 2]:** We do.

**Officiant:** Do you promise to honor and respect one another in your mutual humanity, accepting each other fully in your flaws and strengths? If so, please say, "We do."

**[Partner 1] and [Partner 2]:** We do.

**Officiant:** Do you promise to support each other through good times and bad, and grow together in your love and life experiences? If so, please say, "We do."

**[Partner 1] and [Partner 2]:** We do.

**Officiant:** Do you promise to care for one another, in sickness and in health, physically and emotionally? If so, please say, "We do."

**[Partner 1] and [Partner 2]:** We do.

**Officiant:** Do you promise to laugh together, make terrible puns, crack plenty of jokes, and otherwise be equal partners in crime? If so, please say, "We doo-doo."

**[Partner 1] and [Partner 2]:** We doo-doo.

**Officiant:** Do you promise to love one another always, cook and eat dinner together as much as possible, and make time to spend together even when schedules are full and time is scarce? If so, please say, "We do."

**[Partner 1] and [Partner 2]:** We do.

**Officiant:** Above all, do you choose each other as life partners? If so, please say, "We do."

**[Partner 1] and [Partner 2]:** We do.

**Officiant:** You may now release your hands and place the cord on the altar. Like your lives and your love, the cord remains knotted in a circle, a continuous, infinite loop.

*[Partner 1] and [Partner 2] place the cord on the altar and return to position.*

## V. Exchange of rings

*Officiant picks up rings from altar.*

**Officiant:** As a reminder of that infinity, and to seal the promises you have made to each other here today, you will exchange rings and mark the transition from engagement to marriage.

The precious metal in these rings came from the ground as a rough ore and was heated and purified, shaped and polished. Something beautiful was made from raw elements. Love is like that. It comes from humble beginnings, made by imperfect beings.

*Officiant hands a ring to whoever "won" rock-paper-scissors.*

**Officiant:** Please repeat after me: With this ring, I seal my love and my promises to you.

**[Partner 1] or [Partner 2]:** With this ring, I seal my love and my promises to you.

**Officiant:** Please repeat after me: Let this ring remind you that I chose you, and will always choose you, to be my partner.

**[Partner 1] or [Partner 2]:** Let this ring remind you that I chose you, and will always choose you, to be my partner.

*[Partner 1] or [Partner 2] slides the ring onto the other's finger. Officiant then repeats these lines with the other partner.*

## VI. Pronouncement

**Officiant:** I now pronounce you partners in life. You may proceed to gross everyone out with your first spousal snog.

*[Partner 1] and [Partner 2] kiss, then turn towards the audience, holding hands.*

**Officiant:** I present to you all, [Partner 1] and [Partner 2]. May you two live long and prosper.

## References

Dreizen, Genevieve. "Sample Wedding Ceremony: Non-Traditional, With A Handfasting." *A Practical Wedding Blog Ideas for the Modern Wedding Plus Marriage Sample Wedding Ceremony NonTraditional With A Handfasting Comments*. Practical Media Inc., 19 Aug. 2013. Web. 1 Sep. 2015. <http://apracticalwedding.com/2013/08/sample-handfasting-ceremony/>.

Kaldera, Raven, and Tannin Schwartzstein. *Handfasting and Wedding Rituals: Welcoming Hera's Blessing*. St Paul, MN: Llewellyn Publications, 2003.

\* Brenda Peterson

## Minimalist Religion
### by Brendan Myers

In my spiritual life, I think of myself as a philosopher first, and everything else second. The pursuit of knowledge is a deeply important value for me. In that respect, my spirituality can be called humanist, rather than theist. In fact, much to the chagrin of many friends, I've reported why I think the worship of the gods is not what matters. [See Part 1.] The discovery of this proposition was one of the most intellectually liberating moments in my life.

*And yet I still have a shrine to Herself in my house.* And I find myself very reluctant to part with it. Lately, I've been wondering why that is.

Perhaps I keep it as a show of commitment to my friends and community. Perhaps it's because I live alone, so the shrine to Herself offers me the feeling that I'm not alone—this feeling might be an illusion, but it seems a comforting one. Perhaps it's a small concession to Pascal's Wager: If She does exist, and I ignore her, she'd probably be quite pissed. Or, perhaps I keep it there out of mere nostalgia.

But here's a thought: *Perhaps I have accidentally discovered what might be called "minimalist religion."* This might be comparable to "minimalist music" of composers like John Adams or Philip Glass, whose music strips away everything down to the point where, if anything else was taken away, it would no longer be music. Similarly, minimalist religion might be the level of religious practice such that, if anything else was taken away, it would no longer be religion.

In what does minimalist religion consist?

1. *Some image which represents or symbolizes a spiritual principle.*
   The spiritual principle might be a god, but could also be

something to do with one's own spiritual being, like the Atman, or something outside yourself but impersonal, like the Tao. So the object could be a statue of the god, or a geometric diagram representing the Tao, or a quotation from a sacred text written in elegant calligraphy, or even a building or a whole landscape to which one undertakes a pilgrimage (the Masjid al-Haram, perhaps? or the Hill of Tara?)

2. *A receptacle with which you address yourself to the spiritual principle,* or in some way enact your relationship with it. (Notice that I do not say "worship.") This receptacle could be an offering bowl for libations, or a candle which can be lit, or a holder for a burning wick of incense, or a sound-maker of some kind (a small bell, a wind chime, etc.).

3. *A written or spoken statement* which expresses the significance of the spiritual principle. It might be an expression of gratitude, a request for further blessings, a promise or an oath, a recitation from a sacred text, some poetry or storytelling, a formal or informal prayer, or even simply the uttering of a deity's name with some show of "faith" or sincerity.

Actually, even as I think of it, this third element might be disposable, too. For one could pour wine to Herself, or light a candle to the ancestors, or whatever, without *saying* anything. You can acknowledge your relationship to the divine with a searching gaze, and a listening ear. The act of laying out the offering, and of being present and attentive before the deity, becomes one's statement. But somewhere, somehow, a spoken or written expression has to be part of the event: for if you cannot put your beliefs into words, it is possible to doubt that you believe anything at all. Hence why all religions have a text. (And modern Paganism has many texts!)

I'm not the only, nor the first, person to consider whether there is a minimalist religion. Immanuel Kant, in typical Protestant zeal, thought that the core of a religion is its moral teachings, and so one could dispose of all the ritual elements and still be religious. Thus he would have kept the statement of "faith," but dropped the representational image and the offering-receptacle. He started with a similar question as myself, but reached a different conclusion!

Perhaps minimalist religion can go even more minimalist, by choosing any two of those three criteria and merging them into one. In Hinduism, for instance, the uttering of certain mantras serves as the statement of the significance of the spiritual principle, and at the same time the image of the spiritual principle itself. In Islam, the Kaaba is both the image representing one's relationship to God and at the same time the receptacle to which one enacts that relationship through prayer. Exactly *which* two you see as really one may depend on which of these two propositions you prefer: that religion is something you *do* because of what you experience and/or believe, or that religion is something you *experience and/or believe* because of what you do.

Here is what my minimalist religion involves:

A three-pronged candlestick to which I have affixed some oak leaves, holly leaves, raven feathers, and a triskele carved from African rosewood (the latter was a gift from my first lover, almost 20 years ago). These are the three candles which illuminate every darkness: I'm sure the druids reading this text will understand me.

A copper cauldron, which is set before the candle stick, in which I sometimes pour a shot of wine or beer, although just as frequently I will go into the forest and make an offering of apples into a nearby lake. In that case, the lake serves as my "representational object," and as my "receptacle of communication," at the same time. The lake is important to me, for reasons I might describe some other day.

For a statement, I often turn to the Charge of the Goddess, various proverbs and kennings from Celtic mythology, and this prayer which I composed many years ago:

"A spell to charm the life!
For a life well worth living,

Truths well worth knowing,
Love well worth feeling,
Success in my endeavours,
Protection from harm,
Guidance against harming others,
And may my name and story be spoken with pride by good people, after I die."

### An Atheopagan Prayer
### by Mark Green

Praise to the wide spinning world
Unfolding each of all the destined tales compressed
In the moment of your catastrophic birth
Wide to the fluid expanse, blowing outward
Kindling in stars and galaxies, in bright pools
Of Christmas-colored gas; cohering in marbles hot
And cold, ringed, round, gray and red and gold and dun
And blue
Pure blue, the eye of a child, spinning in a veil of air,
Warm island, home to us, kind beyond measure: the stones
And trees, the round river flowing sky to deepest chasm, salt
And sweet.
Praise to Time, enormous and precious,
And we with so little, seeing our world go as it will
Ruing, cheering, the treasured fading, precious arriving,
Fear and wonder,
Fear and wonder always.
Praise O black expanse of mostly nothing
Though you do not hear, you have no ear nor mind to hear
Praise O inevitable, O mysterious, praise
Praise and thanks be a wave
Expanding from this tiny temporary mouth this tiny dot
Of world a bubble
Going out forever meeting everything as it goes
All the great and infinitesimal

Gracious and terrible
All the works of blessed Being.
May it be so.
May it be so.
May our hearts sing to say it is so.

Earthrise
(December 24, 1968, NASA)

## Part 7: Bringing It Down to Earth: Non-Theistic Paganism and Wild Nature

"I believe in the cosmos. All of us are linked to the cosmos. So nature is my god. To me, nature is sacred. Trees are my temples and forests are my cathedrals. Being at one with nature."

— Mikhail Gorbachev

"God does not die on that day when we cease to believe in a personal deity, but we die when our lives cease to be illuminated by the steady radiance, renewed daily, of a wonder, the source of which is beyond all reasoning…When the sense of the earth unites with the sense of one's body, one becomes earth of the earth, a plant among plants, an animal born from the soil and fertilizing it. In this union, the body is confirmed in its pantheism."

— Dag Hammarskjöld, *Markings*

Nature, the earth, the cosmos: for many Naturalistic Pagans, these are the gateway to transcendence—not transcendence in the sense of an escape to another world or another metaphysical condition, but something more akin to Luce Irigaray's "sensible transcendental" or what Dietrich Bonhoeffer called "the beyond which is found in the midst of life."

In common parlance, "transcendence" is understood as a movement beyond the human condition, beyond our embodiment, and beyond our connections to the world around us. But there is another kind of transcendence which interests Naturalistic Pagans, what Phil Hine (enfolding.org) calls "lateral" or horizontal transcendence. Hine draws on the work of Ursula Goodenough, Vaclav Havel, and Merleau-Ponty to describe a relational transcendence which, rather than leaving behind the world of nature and other people, is a kind of "reaching out" *toward* the world. Hine explains:

> "Transcendence, in these terms, is not some unknowable absence, but a feature of phenomena as they announce themselves within a horizon. Transcendence means that what is perceived 'always contains more than what is actually given'—that any phenomenon has the capacity to surprise us, to broaden or even explode our horizons. Lateral transcendence can be thought of as a reaching-beyond the boundaries of isolated selfhood towards the web of relationships, and perhaps, an openness to novelty, surprise, the unexpected."

In nature, especially wild nature, the experience of "otherness" is common. We experience this when contemplating the vastness of the cosmos and the infinitesimal complexity of life. When this experience reaches a certain intensity, we call it "numinous" or "transcendent." For example, B. T. Newberg has explained how the experience of transcendence can arise out of an encounter with a mountain:

> "…stand at the foot of a mountain and you may be impressed by how much greater it is than you in degree, how alien it is from you in kind. Climb that mountain and confront limits of endurance beyond which you thought yourself incapable, feel the relation between yourself and the mountain's flora and fauna as part of one interdependent ecosystem, and discover how the experience of the mountain becomes part of you and changes who you are—then you may draw close to something like transcendence."

While we tend to find this experience in unfamiliar natural settings, like wild nature or unreachable places in the cosmos, it is possible to find it in familiar settings as well, like our own backyard. As George Orwell wrote, "To see what is in front of one's nose needs a constant struggle." We don't really see the familiar. Instead we see our projections. So, oftentimes, we need to escape the familiar and go into the wild to experience nature as "other" once again.

Paradoxically, this experience of "otherness" or "transcendence" can give rise to a mystical experience of connectedness or oneness with nature. Neil deGrasse Tyson explains how he experiences this connectedness:

> "So that when I look up at the night sky and I know that yes, we are part of this universe, we are in this universe, but perhaps more important than both of those facts is that the Universe is in us. When I reflect on that fact, I look up—many people feel small because they're small and the Universe is big—but I feel big, because my atoms came from those stars. There's a level of connectivity. That's really what you want in life, you want to feel connected, you want to feel relevant you want to feel like a participant in the goings on of activities and events around you. That's precisely what we are, just by being alive."

## Salt Marsh Goddess
### by Michelle Joers

You may need
a super-human
   super-hero
   super-natural god/dess,
hammer or harp in hand,
horse-bodied or jackal-headed,
Lady of the Lake or Lord of the Seas.*

But I have the deep, deep ocean
and strong winds driving waves upon the shore
        driving me to my knees for absolution
        driving me to oblivion;
I have a sun that warms tender shoots,
crooning them from the loamy body of a Living Earth;
The caress of the Willow branch as I lie beneath her roots,
book in hand, and squirmy child in lap.

The Salt Marsh Goddess speaks to me in ringing tones,
as clear as any god of myth does for you
& she speaks in a thousand tongues—
*Spartina, Juniperus, Myrica, Sesarma,*
*Uca, Littorina, Malaclemys, Ardea, Alligator*
...just to name a few.

I have prayed at her temple as the tide pours into my boots
And divined my future with her bones

I have bled for her | I have tasted her flesh
And drank of her blood | And given her mine

While you argue
over how to resurrect
gods of long passed cultures,
I'll be the one covered in mud and dancing with the rushes,
celebrating a goddess born of glaciers.

*And that's okay for you.
But it's not enough for me.

## Gods Like Mountains, Gods Like Mist
### by Alison Leigh Lilly

My gods are not tame. They do not always come when they are called. This is not a failure of ritual or a weakness of belief. It is the nature of my gods. I would no more expect a god to "show up" in my ritual space than I would expect to be able to call a mountain into my living room. That is simply not the nature of mountains. If I want to meet a mountain, I am the one who must move.

Because I do not believe that humans are the only beings with agency in the world, I do not expect my gods to express their agency in the same ways that human beings do. There are gods who forever remain elusive, whose identities shift with the landscape, the seasons and the stars. And there are gods so intimate that they are never really absent at all, and meeting them is not a matter of inviting their presence but rather of quieting my own expectations and learning how to listen. There are gods whose presence looms like a mountain range on the horizon, and gods with(in) whom I walk with grace, my footsteps just one more melody in the great pattern of their being. What does hospitality look like to a mountain? How does a forest speak its mind? What does it mean to invoke a god of mist and sea on a mist-strewn shore?

My gods are not always like human beings. Sometimes my gods are like mountains, sometimes they are like mist. Sometimes I seek my gods in the forests, sometimes in ritual space or the beat of the drum. Sometimes my gods are inscrutable or apophatic, and my relationship with them is one of longing and seeking rather than invocation and offering. And sometimes it is the mountains themselves who are gods, and the rivers and trees who speak.

## The Forgotten Gods of Nature
### by Lupa

When you think of the gods of nature, who do you think of? Do you think of the Wiccan Lord and Lady (also beloved of many non-Wiccan Pagans), she a long-haired woman wrapped in vines and fruits and grain, he a man hirsute and burly and surrounded by large, wild mammals? Do you imagine Artemis or Diana, huntresses and maidens and carriers of the moon? Or perhaps Gaea, her swelling belly the Earth itself? I wager that nine times out of ten, the deity you first thought of took the form of a human, female or male or otherwise, but almost certainly formed in our own image.

But I want to tell you about the forgotten gods of nature, the ones whose stories were never written down because their devoted ones never wrote a word in their lives. I want to tell you about the gods who refused to give up their own shapes and vowed never to bow to the hubristic human ape. I want to tell you about the gods underfoot, hidden in the trees, nestled in the rocks among swift-running currents and riding breezes higher than the cirrus clouds that never once soil themselves with the earth. Let me tell you a few tales of nameless divinities, all but obliterated by the rise of woman and man and the deities they brought with them.

I sing to you of the goddess and god of the family of Salmon, whose children hurl themselves upon stone and flood each year so that the family may go on. I sing to you of the divine twin faces, he with the strongest, boldest coloring of the spawning male, she the skeletal maw that waits to slay all who mate in the birthing pool. She it is who beckons the salmon on in their madness, even as they plunge to their own deaths;

he it is who urges them onward and fills their muscles with strength pulled from every last fiber of being. For years, the young salmon hear tales of the gods' irresistible pull, but even the most vehement naysayers among them are helpless the moment they hear divine fate's song in their bones.

I sing to you of the wind god of the family of Pine, whose generations may be furthered by the swift breeze, but who may be laid low to the ground in the fearsome storm. I sing to you of prayers whispered through clasped needles and released into gentle eddies of air, that the god may be merciful in spring storms and in winter blizzards, in the chill autumn night and the sudden summer squall. For it is the god who decides which line of trees will go forth into the future, and a capricious wind it is that carries the pollen safely to the cone—or onto barren stone to die. And it is the god who carries the trees away in his terrible anger, leaving one standing but snatching a root-mate away in an instant.

I sing to you of the deities of the Dictyostelidal slime molds, sexless and strange, at once a thousand voices and one song united. I sing to you of hard times when the wood has rotted away and the sun bakes the earth, and while as individuals we die, together we thrive. The divinities ask for sacrifice, the thousand voices demand it. Those who die to give life to the others, who raise up the new generation so that they may spread far and wide—these become a part of that sacred host, their voices immortalized not in cells but in spirit.

I sing to you of the duotheism of the female fig wasp, the Great Tree Mother whose fruits shelter tender wasp eggs, and the Nematode Demon that strikes down the tired egg-layers to feed its own spawn. I sing to you of the duotheism of the male fig wasp, the Dark Goddess from whose confining spheres few male wasps ever escape, and the Seductress who calls upon the males to mate and send their issue forth into the world, promising the closest thing to freedom they will ever know in their brief lives. The Tree and the Nematode, the Fig and the Wasp—their tales are whispered to the young as their mother lays their eggs in the cradle, all they will ever know of her.

I sing to you of the Creator of clownfish, who in the morning is a god, who at noon shines brightly from above, who in the afternoon is a goddess, who in the evening lays her eggs, and who at night dies, only to be reborn as a god again at the next dawning. I sing to you of those pisceans who hold vigil each night, awaiting the return of the Creator with the light, and quieting the troubled who huddle in darkness and quaking faith.

I sing to you of the pantheon of the earthworms, every single one female and male together, all brought into one, who reside deep in the ground below. I sing to you of their devils, flawed gods split apart into male or female, hungry beings that devour all in search of their missing halves and forever cursed to roam the surface, denied the safety of cool, dark soil. When the ground trembles, the earthworms say the gods and the devils are fighting, and they tell their young to take shelter. When the soil cracks open above them and lets in the burning fire, the earthworms squirm and flee lest they be split asunder and join the hellish ranks of the skies.

I sing to you of the countless, endless divine host of the ants. I sing to you of courageous warrior goddesses, and tales of lowly trickster males that sought to take their power. All ants know the story of the greatest Queen Goddess of all, who stole away her mate's wings when he dared to usurp her throne, and cast him down to the earth to die, and so she reigned alone.

I sing to you of the One and Many of the bamboo family, who is all bamboo and each bamboo. I sing to you of the dance of the One and Many, who grows and grows and always becomes more and never becomes more. Only once a century, when the stars are in their right places, does the One and Many become the Flower Which Kills, and it is said all shall die when this happens, for who is alive yet today who remembers any differently? But from the remains of the dead the One and Many grows again, and brings back the dead to life, relieved of the memories of their previous lives so they may begin fresh and new.

I sing to you the sad song of the pale, ghostly gods of the dodo and the aurochs, the Tyrannosaurs and the Callistophytales, of the gods of Wiwaxia and Prototaxites and Cooksonia. I sing to you the victory-songs of the gods that surpassed them and reign today, the gods of the wolves and the morels, the oaks and the bees, and of the brave single goddess of the coelacanths. I leave it to others who shall come after me to sing the songs of those gods yet to be born into this world, long may they reign and watch over their own.

I sing to you of many more gods, gods of wind and water, gods of each mineral and the events that created them. I sing to you of the gods of protons, of quarks, of atomic forces binding and holding. I sing to you of the god of the dust that flies off the ice-burned comet, and the god of the spaces in between. I sing to you of the god that twists like a serpent at the center of every sun and is found again coiled within every electron, shared by both and worshiped by each in its own way. I sing to you of the god that collects asteroids together in mockeries of his sister's solar systems, jealous of his elder sibling's power. I sing to you of all these, and many, many more.

These, then, are the unnamed gods, the forgotten gods, those who lay in the shadows of the many pantheons of humans. When you speak of the gods of nature, do not neglect them. When you speak of the gods of nature, remember that nature is not only in human form—nor is the Divine. For there are gods far beyond those ever committed to paper or stone, whose names were never uttered by human throat nor drummed upon human ear.

## I Lost My Religion, and Gained the World
### by Lupa

When I was young, I very quickly discovered the Great Outdoors. In fact, it was sometimes pretty hard to get me to go back inside! And even when I was under a human-made roof, I was usually reading books about nature, or playing with toy animals, or watching wildlife shows on TV. In short, the natural world was my first true love, and it's a relationship that's never ended.

However, it was about more than just the physical trees and grass and rabbits and snakes. Even at a young age I felt there was vivacity to the world beyond the basic science of it. People had been writing myths about nature spirits for millennia all around the world. Shouldn't there be something to that, at least? And so I began talking to the bushes and the birds, and while they never spoke back to me in so many words, I sometimes felt that I was at least acknowledged.

These feelings came more fully into focus when, as a teenager, I discovered Neo-Paganism. Here was a group of people for whom the moon was more than a rock in the sky orbiting the earth, and for whom magic was a possibility. I dove in headfirst, and for half my life now I've identified as some variant of Pagan.

But what of the spirits themselves? Almost immediately I latched onto animal totemism; for years that was the center of everything I practiced. I explored generic Wicca-flavored Neo-Paganism, chaos magic, and other paths, but the critters were always a part of it. In 2007, I began to formulate Therioshamanism, a more formalized neoshamanic path dedicated to their service.

It was here that my animism began to really take shape. Not that I didn't acknowledge spirits before. But I hadn't really considered their nature all that much, nor the nature of my relationships with them. Formalizing my path caused me to take a step back and really consider the mechanics of my beliefs, not just practice them, but explore them more deeply and my reasons for them.

And then a peculiar thing happened. Instead of becoming more formal, with set devotional acts and greater structure and taboos and so forth, I found myself moving away from overt rituals and "thou shalts." I struggled against this for a while. I was supposed to be honoring the spirits with rituals and journeys and offerings, like so many other devotional Pagans I knew! So why did I grate against these things? Why did I feel less enthused about what I thought I was supposed to be doing? Why did the spirits themselves even seem tired of the rites and prayers and gestures of faith?

The answer lay in my childhood. Back then, my relationship with nature and its denizens was uncomplicated. I simply went out into the thick of it, and was a part of it, and that was where the connection lay. I had wanted to find that again so much that I tried entirely too hard, using other people's solutions. But the spirits knew better. They kept calling me further away from ritual tools and altar setups and a set schedule of holy days, and invited me into the forests and deserts and along the coast of the mighty Pacific and down the banks of the rolling Columbia River. They coaxed me away from my drum and the journeys I did in the spirit world, and enticed me to follow them further on the trails I loved to hike.

It was there that I finally found what I'd lost so many years ago—that deep, abiding link to the nonhuman world, as well as my place as a human animal. Once I shed the religious trappings and artificial rituals, the barriers fell away, and it was just me and what was most sacred to me. I was called to learn and discover more and more, and like my childhood self, I devoured books and watched documentaries whenever I couldn't get outside. I found Carl Sagan and David Attenborough and Jane Goodall and so many other classic teachers of the wilderness, and I adhered to ecopsychology as a practice to deepen my cognitive understanding of the human connection to nature even more.

What I had thought I wanted was more structure and piety, sharing nature through an evangelism of orthopraxy. What I needed, in fact, was to toss the entire artifice away and simply immerse myself in the world of awe and wonder I'd rediscovered. As for the spirits? I no longer needed to try to keep convincing myself that their presence was a literal reality despite all my doubts and inconsistencies. I didn't need "belief," I didn't need to use speculation and pseudoscience to "prove" that the spirits are "real," and I ceased caring whether they even existed outside of my own deeply rooted imagination or not, because I only needed them to be important to me. I had the twin flames of science and creativity, the one creating a structure of general objective understanding, and the other adding wholly personal, subjective color that didn't have to be "true" for anyone but me.

And that is where I am today. I still honor my totems and other spirits, but as a personal pantheon carried inside of me. They are what gives added vitality to the world around me; they embody my wonder and awe, my imagination and creativity, the things that I as a human being bring to the relationships I have to everything else in this world. Science is important in that it tells me how the moon was formed, what the dust on it is made of, and how it affects the tides, but there is a spirit inside of me that loves the beautiful silver of the moonlight and all the stories we've told about Mama Luna. In balance and complement, science and spirits both become my animism today.

## Place-Based Paganism
## by Anna Walther

My place-based Pagan practice is grounded in the land around Austin, Texas. Learning how to be in respectful relationship with the land beneath my feet and the other beings with whom I share it is my goal. Here on the southeastern edge of the Edwards Plateau we have short, mild winters and long, hot, humid summers. Where the city has not encroached, the limestone hills are covered with juniper and oak scrub woodland and crisscrossed by creeks that rush with the rains of spring and fall and parch dry in the summer. A thin layer of topsoil over limestone layers composes our rocky soil. To the east lies the Blackland Prairie, with its heavy, black clay soil and Austin's iconic, gnarled southern liveoaks. Being Pagan in place is about getting outside, putting foot to ground, and doing my holy work directly, at the closest creek, at my neighborhood park, at the community garden, and in my own backyard.

Central Texas is home to both human and other-than-human beings: junipers and oaks, mockingbirds and grackles, snakes and coyotes, wildflowers and bees, limestones and springs. I strive to build conscious relationship with these and other neighbors via meditation, walking outside, ritual, journaling, storytelling, and acts of social and environmental justice. I learn to identify birds by their songs: the screeching bluejays, the whinnying screech owls, chirping cardinals, yodeling Carolina wrens, and trilling red-bellied woodpeckers. I collect and retell folktales about the many wildflowers that blanket our hills and prairies in the spring. In summer, I note the time of day when cicadas begin beating their strident songs, and I watch cumulus clouds evaporate under the searing noon sun. I walk in the woods, and I listen. This, as much as anything else, is the heart of my practice. I make space, I connect, I play. I honor the land beneath my feet and the air and waters that sustain me. I observe the way wind and trees dance, and I listen to the way water talks to stone in this particular place.

Numina loci
(Austin)

> Let us begin our song
> with ocean, earth, and sky;
> the Sun: fuel, fire, and light;
> and the Moon: three-fold mirror and mistress of tides;
> Their great and holy dance gives rise to
> El Niño y La Niña, bickering twins;
> and Polar Vortex, a trickster;
> North Wind, a winter hag, blue and wild;
> Green Rising, a spring maiden mild, and
> the wildflowers that rise up where she sings,
> beloved by the Lady of the Lake.
> From earth rise the Liveoak Kings, attended by grackles;
> in sky fly bats who birth under the Bridge,
> in sight of Lady Liberty, an immigrant,
> great-granddaughter of Pallas Athena,
> who holds the five-pointed Star of Texas
> over where river, prairie, and plateau meet.
> White Buffalo and Gray Wolf, ghosts, roam
> limestone hills and drink from
> springs that babble at their feet;
> From this very land they rise,
> gates to memory and myth:
> the clear creek, this green tree, that gray stone,
> rough bark, cold water, smooth bone:
> numina loci.
> *Hic sunt enim spiritus.*

## A Daily Heron
### by Sara Amis

I've been musing upon the question of "why nature religion anyway?" I will say first that I don't consider humanity and all our works to be essentially separate from nature; quite the opposite. I do think we ignore the non-human world at our peril and to our impoverishment. It's a kind of narcissism to attend only to the doings of our own species, fascinating as they are. Looking outside of ourselves calls us to a deeper understanding of existence, on all levels, one that easily outstrips our capacity to comprehend in an ordinary sense. "Nature mysticism" might be a better phrase for what I mean. But to reach that kind of understanding, first you start with where you are.

> "I come to Hollins Pond not so much to learn how to live as, frankly, to forget about it. That is, I don't think I can learn from a wild animal how to live in particular—shall I suck warm blood, hold my tail high, walk with my footprints precisely over the prints of my hands?—but I might learn something of mindlessness, something of the purity of living in the physical sense and the dignity of living without bias or motive." —"Living Like Weasels" by Annie Dillard

I love me some Annie Dillard, most particularly her essay, "Living Like Weasels," which I am prone to give as assigned reading to my university students and my witchcraft students alike. It is that kind of work. I love her lithe and ferocious prose, her oblique but unmistakable allusions to Thoreau, her juxtapositions. I love Thoreau too, though he is a little pompous. His curmudgeon saves him in my eyes; he says cranky and outrageous things about newspapers and post offices and the stupidity of people and makes me laugh. How he would loathe the internet, while finding a way to make use of it; Thoreau, who lived a short stroll from town in Concord and made it sound like the edge of the wild. This in the mid-1800s, when people knew from wilderness and frontiers.

I bring all this up because I am now living next to a pond, or a lake if you believe what it says about itself. It is the eponymous body of water belonging to Pine Lake, Georgia. Pine Lake is a tiny hamlet, once a resort where people would go in order to escape the hustle and bustle of Atlanta by building funky little cottages and fishing. Atlanta was *the city* then and Pine Lake was *the country*. That was in the 1930s. Now we are just past I-285, "outside the Perimeter" in Atlanta's parlance. Inside the Perimeter is city-cool; beyond that, in the outer darkness, the suburbs.

> "This is, mind you, suburbia. It is a five-minute walk in three directions to rows of houses, though none is visible here. There's a 55-mph highway at one end of the pond, and a nesting pair of wood ducks at the other. Under every bush is a muskrat hole or a beer can." —Annie Dillard, "Living Like Weasels"

Pine Lake isn't quite like that; the houses gather near the lake like hunters warming their hands around a bonfire in winter, and while the Interstate is within shouting distance it is neither visible nor audible. Pine Lake wasn't planned as suburban and is no development with cookie-cutter houses; rather it is resolutely individual, not to say quirky. There is also more than one pair of ducks. At either end of the lake is constructed wetlands, built with Federal grant money to help improve the water quality of Snapfinger Creek, and both the wetlands and the lake are full of life.

There are no weasels, that I am aware of. There are fish (mostly bream), turtles, and assorted frogs. There is a sinister troupe of Canada geese, the presence of which is a source of some consternation, many jokes, and quite a bit of goose poop. There is a possible fox, and definite beavers. There is a great blue heron.

The heron! It sometimes sits out on a half-submerged log, looking for dinner. It favors the marsh at the west end of town, where the creek flows away from the lake and passes out of the city limits. Once it sat on a tree limb outside our dining room window, preening.

I haven't lived here very long, but I know the heron's habits. At any time of day, more or less, I could catch a glimpse of it if I wanted to; all it requires is the time and willingness to walk along the trails to its favorite haunts, patience, and an observant eye. Some days, I don't have the time to go heron-stalking; other days, I can see it from my window, and go walking just for exercise. Still others, I decide I want to see what's going on at the other end of the lake where the mallards like to hang out, and don't think about the heron at all unless it shows up unexpectedly. Whenever I see it, though, it draws my attention: regal, nearly silent, graceful, predatory, and singular.

The heron must be used to people, and yet it never lets you get too close. Draw parallel to it with the width of one of the marsh's holding ponds between you, and it will duck its head, eyeing you with suspicion, then fly. I cannot approach the heron, certainly could never touch it; I can only look for it, entranced.

This is how I understand the divine, and why I continue to seek it in the resolutely non-human world, with which we nonetheless recognize a numinous kinship. Sometimes, it will turn and lock eyes with you, lifting you out of yourself, changing everything. Other times, it will give you the side-eye and swoop away, leaving you longing for retreating beauty. You might not see it every single time you go looking, or where you expect to find it. No matter how common the experience, every time you stumble across mystery, or independent wild being, it is a surprise and a miracle. And every day, you can look.

## The Voice of God
### by Nimue Brown

I wanted to be a polytheist. It's not an easy confession to make, because despite my best efforts at various times in my life, I have never had any coherent experience of deity. Only shadows and suggestions, and odd moments in dreams. I've read enough words from true polytheists to know that personal gnosis is a big part of how they experience the world. My failure to have any kind of serious firsthand experience of deities informed a lot of writing *When a Pagan Prays*. It's not a book for people who have comfortable exchanges with their deities—it's more for anyone else out there who does not get what they went looking for, or who is not comfortable with believing.

I had a bit of a light bulb moment last week. I realised that I've been so busy angsting over my failure to experience deity, that I really haven't given enough thought or attention to what I *do* experience. There are other things in my life. They're subtle and they seldom come with a side-order of words (although I talk to everything). And it occurs to me that this is, for me at least, the most important stuff.

Here's an example: My computer is at the window. If I raise my gaze, I can see trees and sky. On any given day, I will at some point raise my head at just the right moment to see buzzards, a heron, woodpeckers, nuthatches, flocks of little birds, comedy squirrel activity, rainbow light, tiny whirlwinds…It's the same when I go walking—I always see something. If I walk the hills, I'll find fossils or limestone quartz. It's easy to ignore, because it is normal for me. I've always been very open to what's around me, and I have got into the habit of considering it all fairly mundane.

On the Five Valley's Walk, we saw a lizard and a deer. 1700 people walking the 21 mile route—hardly an invitation to wild things to show up. I watched half a dozen other people walk right past the lizard, not seeing it. But I was drawn to it at once. I knew it was there. I see kingfishers and little grebes. I hear owls. I do not experience these as messages from the divine or the otherworld, just nature doing its thing and me noticing. I do not read what I see for omens or symbols, but I do feel blessed.

Even as I try to square the idea that this could be something really precious and important, I am conscious of my own reluctance to put any big names on it. Knowing when to turn my head to see the deer is just being present. It's not the voice of gods or the voice of spirit. It's just me in a wood and everything else in the wood. Would someone else construct a different narrative? Would someone else feel the need to turn, and in turning, see something beautiful, and understand that as the presence of deity?

I've spent about twenty years stumbling around, feeling lost, and feeling on a very fundamental level that I wasn't a very good Pagan at all. It may be that I just do not default to the language of deity when making sense of experience. I don't see the horned god in the deer. I don't see goddess in the flash of kingfisher wings. I see the deer and the kingfisher. Perhaps that isn't a failing. Perhaps I am not as shut out of mystery, as incapable of experiencing it, as I had feared myself to be. Maybe I've been so busy being enchanted by one tree at a time that I did not grasp that I'd been in the forest all along.

## What Being an Animist Means To Me
### by Traci Laird

I rarely speak publicly about my spiritual practice. This is mainly due to the intimate nature of relationship. You see, my worldview is animistic, and for me, this means I view the universe as a community of living persons, of which humans are a part. I perceive everything within the universe, including the Universe herself, as possessing unique worldview, culture, and language (method of communication), e.g., the Ash tree near my front door is a living person, who possesses a worldview, culture, and language distinct from my own. Because I live within such a vital world, I try my best to "live respectfully as a member of the diverse community of living persons" (Graham Harvey).

### How animism informs my spirituality

All living persons have an agenda. We also all have an impact on others, for good or for ill: no person is an island. Without trying, my footsteps have a profound effect on ant-persons, grass-persons, worm-persons, and so on. This also applies to persons smaller (hello, bacteria and microbes) and larger than myself, such as the various Oceans, Moon, Sun, other Stars, Dark Matter, and the countless other persons residing in the cosmos. By simply living their lives, and expressing their unique culture and worldview, they impact me—sometimes positively, sometimes negatively. Red, in tooth and claw.

The cacophony of life, and chaos of existence, that emerges experientially with this view, is not something I am afraid of, or seek to propitiate (though, hearing it does overload my system); rather, I am curious. I want to understand the boundless universe I live within. I do not worship other persons. I do not engage in adoration of, or devotion to, other persons. *I do have relationships, both with human and other-than-human persons, and I nurture and cherish those connections.*

## How I "do" animism

I also practice witchcraft, which I am equally discrete about, owing to the tradition's focus on silence. My affinity for the Craft is due, in large part, to its long history of shamanic practice and my own extrasensory leanings—that, and my Grandma teaching me so much folklore!

For me, there is no distinction between "spirit" world and "material" world—they are of a kind. Therefore, there is no mundane experience. Yes, there are other-persons living in the universe who are so alien, so different from myself that encountering them feels like I have stepped into another realm, but they are still part of my everyday world—the one I wake-up in, the one where I live my work-a-day life.

Since I am a witch who views everything she sees (and doesn't see) as sentient and existing within a cosmos of living persons, *relationship is vital*. In community, whether familial or something broader, relationship building is foundational—it's how we get our needs met, and it is psycho-logically nourishing. In my working life, relationship building is a primary focus. Again, it's how I get my needs met. It's also how we organically interact with friends, family, and acquaintances: we build relationships. I am interested in building relationship with the persons, both human and other-than-human, I interact with daily. We may not be best friends, but, hopefully, we can foster a mutually satisfying connection. *It's also simple good manners*. Like I learned from my human neighbors here in Ireland, the first thing to be done is to invite a newcomer over for tea, and then greet each other whenever you meet.

## A day in the life of an animist

I'm fortunate. My current life circumstance affords me the opportunity to live away from alarm clocks and deadlines. I wake with the sun, and the first thing I do upon waking is notice the quality of the light, and how it feels. Light is different in Ireland, and special—so special the indigenous inhabitants exerted great effort constructing monuments that enabled them sensual interaction with the Sun (Brú na Bóinne). The low angle with which the sun's electromagnetic waves enter the atmosphere produces a dramatic effect indicative of the earth's tilt (the season) — the morning light at Lughnasadh is vastly different from the light of a winter morning. By paying attention to the light, my body communes with the Sun and my day begins with intimacy. The Sun, as a Great Power, is someone I want to develop relationship with. By attending to the presence of the Sun, and actively communing, I forge connection.

The very next thing I attend to is the birdsong. Many different voices are heard here in east Cork, and the timing of their song tells me a lot: Raven sits in the Pine and talks in her low voices only in summer, Robin chatters early in spring, and blackbird talks to us late in autumn. I may not live here long enough to understand their patterns, but I have noticed. So, I greet the birds, both vocally and extrasensorially, in order to build relationship with them — my neighbors. *Think about how isolating and cold the lack of acknowledgment and greeting feels when sitting on the metro, or the bus.* I certainly don't want that atmosphere cultivated around my home.

Once I'm up, and dressed, I wash-up any dishes from the night before. My house, made from the same star dust I am, is alive, too. By tending to the orderliness and cleanliness of it, I show respect and affection, thus building relationship. Do I imagine my house has an unseen "soul" or incorporeal entity residing within its "body"? No. I'm not a fan of the soul/body divide. I perceive consciousness as inhabiting all of the universe. How that Mind moves through and within all things is a Great Mystery.

The act of relationship building, with and within my environment, influences my sense of a dynamic Place — one which includes my physical location and my role within it.

## Awakening to Gaia
### by Bart Everson

Can I share a secret with you? It's my own personal vision statement, formulated as part of a visioning workshop I facilitated. I was amazed that I could boil it down to three words:

> "Awakening to Gaia."

There's a bit more. It continues thusly: "a transformation of consciousness in myself and others, toward an ecocentric perspective and a sense of divine possibility in life." But those first three words really encapsulate it all for me.

That was eight months ago, and so far I've kept it mostly to myself, a secret. It's a personal statement, after all, so that's highly appropriate. It's something on which I reflect, which provides guidance on setting priorities, goals, and plans. It helps me stay focused.

It means something to me, and that's probably sufficient for a personal vision statement. But as a rule, I'm not interested in keeping secrets. I'm a communicator by nature.

I'm curious to know if I can articulate what this phrase means to me, such that other people might understand and not think me a crazy person. What does it mean, awakening to Gaia? Sounds straight loony — at least, some people would think so.

I understand Gaia to be a metaphor for the co-evolutionary, interconnected, planetary ecosystem. Stronger formulations of Gaia theory are more controversial, so these distinctions become important. The science behind co-evolutionary Gaia seems pretty solid, though there is hardly a consensus on the value of the metaphor; in other words, scientists support the concept, even if they don't like the name. The value of the metaphor is aesthetic and affective. Picturing the Earth as mother goddess fosters biophilia (an instinctive bond between human beings and other living systems), and the name lends itself to poetic expressions.

Awakening to Gaia means awakening to the reality behind this metaphor. To awaken to Gaia is to recognize our interconnectedness, our radical interdependence, our participation in the web of life. To awaken to Gaia is to recognize other animals and plants as our distant cousins, to recognize that our kinship extends even to rocks, to the sea, to the atmosphere. To awaken to Gaia is to recognize these realities, to become more fully alive, alert, aware, involved, and mindful. To awaken to Gaia is to wake up from the zombified slumber of American-style consumerism, to come alive to what it means to be a social primate in the 21st century. Awakening to Gaia means awakening to oneself, to one's own potential, to one's own responsibilities.

This awakening is no abstract exercise but a transformation with profound consequences. The dominant narrative of Western-style industrial growth society has been predicated on a view of the Earth as inert matter for human exploitation. In light of the fact that we are now living through the sixth great extinction, on the brink of global ecological catastrophe, awakening to Gaia is crucially important, as it provides a basis and an impetus for right action.

It's not a one-time deal. It's more of an ongoing process. I'm not preaching from some sort of purified pinnacle of imagined perfection here. Far from it. Awakening to Gaia is something I aim to accomplish more fully every day.

Though I've experienced this awakening in glimmers and fits my whole life, it was only a few years ago that I was able to put a name to it. There's a power in names, and in the metaphor of Gaia, and that power gives me pause. There's danger here, of sloppy thinking, of complacency, of becoming fixated on the metaphor and losing sight of the underlying reality it represents. And yet, on balance, and after years of consideration, I think the value of the metaphor may well be worth the risks.

On this autumnal equinox, I found my intentions coalescing into form, both symbolic and actual. I found myself giving voice (in ritual, with my circle) to my commitment and dedication to this vision. I also found myself convening a meeting of people interested in working together for social justice, grassroots democracy, ecological wisdom and peace.

So, too, with this essay I rededicate myself to this vision: Awakening to Gaia.

Join me if you will.

## Lost Gods of the Witches:
## A User's Guide to Post-Ragnarok Paganism
### by Steven Posch

The late summer thunderstorm was bearing down on us fast. In unearthly silence—the thunder still too far away to hear—the livid northwestern sky juddered with lightning.

But in the circle around the bonfire, no one was thinking about the storm. The business at hand was the evening ritual: something to do with (I kid you not) community, popcorn, and the festival organizer's most recent art project.

Thoroughly bored, I watched the storm approach. "A god is coming," I thought, "and we're too busy doing a ritual even to notice."

In his book *On Being a Pagan*, philosopher Alain de Benoist notes that the new paganism cannot simply be the old paganism revivified. The truth of this observation is sadly apparent in the state of the contemporary pagan revival, which may broadly be characterized as a "paradigm of pretense": a Society for Creative Spiritual Anachronism whose efforts, while on occasion aesthetically pleasing, have only rarely managed to achieve any notable authenticity.

To date, the theology of this pagan revival has taken three main forms: Wiccan bitheism, catch-as-catch-can eclecticism, and ethnic reconstructionism. I would contend that none of these overarching conceptual frameworks is equal to providing us with a genuinely contemporary articulation of pagan experience.

Classic Wiccan bitheism has ultimately proved itself a dead-end, its cast of characters too constricted to adequately articulate the vast drama of existence. Sometimes referred to as "soft polytheism," bitheism is in reality no sort of polytheism at all. To paraphrase Violet Firth: "A bitheistic religion is half-way to monotheism." At best, a two-deity system is useful as a halfway house between monotheism and something more authentically the pagan. For the post-modern witch, the Lord and Lady must be a point of departure, not a terminus.

We know how many gods are too few. How many, then, are too many?

The eclectic neo-pagan "Chinese restaurant" approach ("One from pantheon A, one from pantheon B") must always be incapable of authenticity because it will never constitute actual polytheism. Too often it functions as, in effect, serial monotheism: Brigid today, Ganesha next Tuesday, Chango next time we feel like it. Once we have learned to think polytheistically, as the old pagans did, we will come to understand that genuine paganism must of necessity inhere in relationships.

To say "pantheon" implies lateral interaction within the pantheon itself, not merely between the worshiper and whichever god she deigns to "summon" today. The eclectic surrounded by her gods who don't speak with one another together constitute a rimless wheel made up of hub and spokes only, unable to move or withstand pressure: a wheel so incomplete as to be no wheel at all. At the last, eclecticism offers the insights and correctives of comparativism, but can take us no farther.

This brings us to the reconstructionisms. I would contend that all attempts to resurrect the historic pantheons, any of them, are ultimately doomed to inconsequence. The old pantheons are dead languages, which we can study, but no longer speak. Even if, through diligent study, we do learn to speak them fluently, they will never be anything more than idiosyncratic curios, lacking modern vocabulary and forever incomprehensible to our contemporaries. Necessarily ungrounded in our own real-world experience, they will always be second languages, never mother tongues.

While the ethnic paganisms have important things to teach us concerning the necessity of cultural authenticity, at their worst they become purist ghettos of nostalgia-driven re-enactors. We must never forget our Received Tradition or fail to learn from it; without it, we have no solid basis by which to evaluate our own experience. But ultimately the ways of our ancestors cannot teach us what we most need to know: how to be honestly pagan for our own time and place. That understanding can come only from our own encounter with the very sources that inspired these ethnic traditions in the first place. We must drink from the original wellspring itself.

A thousand years ago and more, the younger gods fell in valiant battle, and a world fell with them. In a very real sense, it was the end of tens of thousands of years of human history.

Who are these failed gods, why did they fail, and why are they not the gods our post-Ragnarok era requires? The younger gods are the imaginal powers, nothing more and nothing less than products of the human imagination, their existence verifiable by subjective means only. Most named gods of the historic pantheons belong to this category. These gods neither pre-existed humanity, nor will they continue after us; they have no power apart from what we give them. But because they are the makings of our own minds, we love them for their human faces.

Our tendency to divinize our own ideas is rooted in the nature of language. Because Love, Justice, and War are (grammatically speaking) nouns, we tend to think of them as solids, as tangible things or beings which occupy real space. But of course in reality they have no active existence outside the sphere of human thought and action. We must always be wary of deifying ideas, a collective hubris of the most destructive sort. Abstractions, fictional characters, and personifications of functions, simply put, cannot; they are gods only be courtesy. The products of our own minds can never have the power to save us from ourselves because they are, at the last, nothing more than the human brain chattering to itself. Until we make the courageous, radical leap out of our own internal dialogue and into actual relationship with real, non-human others, we will ultimately continue as we are now, locked inside our own heads.

In the end, the younger gods failed because they departed from what must always be the touchstone for the best and truest human spirituality: the interaction of the human mind with the natural world. Gods cannot be said to have real, ontological existence except insofar as they correlate with the natural world.

In our day humanity must return to the primal source, the great archaic powers that truly exist and always have: what we may call the elder gods. These first beings existed long before homo became sapiens, and they will continue long after we are gone. There are gods ontologically real, their existence objectively verifiable.

*Twelve*

*Each of us knows them intimately already,*
*being the ground of every birth:*
*Earth, mighty mother of us all;*
*Sun, splendid in royal self-immolation;*
*Moon, queen of witches, threefold mistress of fate;*
*Storm, called Thunder by the ancestors;*
*Sea, the fish-tailed lady of the deep;*
*the winged Winds, wide-faring;*
*Fire, youngest elder, fallen from heaven;*
*the Horned One, master of animals—*
*ourselves among them—*
*and the Green his firstborn brother, lord of leaf and tendril.*
*These themselves are they, themselves themselves.*

I have cited here a few among many, but in this matter poet and critic Ezra Pound has sage counsel to offer. "Do we know the number of the gods?" he asks, and answers his own question: "It would be rash to say that we do. [One] should be content with a reasonable number" (Pound).

For reasons that should be abundantly obvious, these gods make their appearance in culture after culture. (While the younger gods, by their very nature, vary widely from pantheon to pantheon, the elder gods are generally more or less the same.) Pleniscient, plenipresent, and plenipotent, they constitute our oldest known pantheon; they are also the most modern, no belief required. Though long eclipsed by younger, more human gods, in their enduring power, presence, and majesty they have never ceased to speak to us. Neither allegories nor symbols, they are real beings, with whom we, at every moment of our lives, cannot help but engage. They are as near eternity as we may hope to touch, ontologically permanent, oldest and most young.

It is wholly due to them, quite literally, that I exist to write this and you to read it: without which, not. This is polytheism of the "hardest" sort. They are Themselves, non-identifiable with one another: to say, after all, that Earth is Sun is Moon is a nonsense. Their interactions are real relationships, both with one another and with us. Polytheism has never been a matter of mere plurality, but rather of pantheon, of gods in community. To rearticulate these relationships in the language of myth is to begin the process of humanity's return to spiritual intimacy with the non-human world.

Some will wish to distinguish, to take just one example, Earth the goddess from Earth the planet. In my opinion, this is a distinction without a difference. To borrow a term from Hindu theology, they are "non-different." Goddess Earth is co-extensive with planet Earth.

We are, and cannot help but be, citizens of our own century. We know irrevocably about physics, evolution, and depth psychology. Try as we might (and some have tried mightily), we can never return to a pre-scientific worldview premised on "belief." In what sense, after all, may one be said to "believe" in Earth or Sun? Belief, so prominent in the monotheisms, recedes into deserved irrelevance when we embrace instead what Anthony Scott has called (in a rather different context) a "glorious sacred materialism."

Moreover, the resurgence of the elder gods breaks down the wall of separation between religion and science that has partitioned Western thought since the Enlightenment. The rise of science has taught us things about the Earth, Sun, and Storm that the ancients would have marveled to know. We are in the enviable, irresistible, position of being able to learn, through science, about the very gods themselves.

"Glorious sacred materialism" indeed.

The elder gods have always been the special province of the witch.

Pace Wicca, witchery is not and has never been a religion per se; it is, rather, a magical technology. That said, no magical technology exists independent of a cultural matrix, and the first and truest matrices of the Craft are the old polytheist worldviews of ancient Europe. When others turned their faces towards younger gods, the witch continued to treat with the untamed elder powers in the making of her magic. This is one reason why even in antiquity people held the witch and her powers in fear and suspicion.

This being so, how then did the Horned One and the Lady of the Moon come to be regarded as the witch's only gods?

It is as if, high in the Greek mountains, a village of goat-herding magic-workers had continued in the old ways long after the advent of the new religion. In time, due to pressures both internal and external, all the other gods, younger and elder alike—Zeus, Athena, even Dionysus (perish the thought)—have come to be forgotten. The sole survivors of this leveraged divine attrition—as one might expect—are the preeminent gods of herding and magic: Pan and Hekate.

This is the contemporary Craft as we find it. The Lord and Lady are the witch-gods par excellence because in ages of ages it was they who first learned the magic arts and taught them to their children, and so to this day we their children honor them first among all other gods.

And they're a wonderful couple, really they are. But now it's time to meet the rest of the family.

With the return of the elder gods, exciting new panoramas of possibility open before us. Wicca's bitheism has stifled the emergence of new mythology precisely because its divine population was too small to create a compelling narrative. But once we come to understand that the Horned

One is not the Sun, is not Thunder, is not the Green God, the new myths begin spontaneously to tell themselves.

If we view the Horns and the Green, not as different faces of the same god, but rather as distinct beings, who then are they and what are they to one another? To pose the question is to begin to answer it: they are twin sons of Earth, born at one birth, lovers and rivals, and the Green the elder of the two.

The new mythologies are waiting, posed on the threshold of articulation.

When we redefine "god" in such a way as to encompass this old-new understanding of the world, the burning question becomes, not "Do the gods exist?", but rather, "Do they know that we are here?" Are the elder gods sentient, self-aware beings who, for instance, act with conscious intent and hear us when we speak to them?

The ancestors would certainly seem, for the most part, to have thought so. If, indeed, they are sentient, we should realistically expect to find among them a sentience very different from our own. At the very least we may say that, whether the old gods are sentient or not, they are real, their gifts to us are real, and their relationships with us are real.

We know for certain that self-awareness does exist in the world of nature: it is we ourselves. In humanity the universe achieves the ability to perceive and reflect upon itself, and to reflect upon that process of reflection. This is what makes us the wise. This is the proper work of the witch: to be the eyes through which the world understands itself. Let us not expect the gods to do our work for us; they are busy enough with their own.

If Sun and Storm do not hear us when we praise them, or receive the offerings that we make, why then offer or praise at all? Our relationships with them are real enough; so long as we acknowledge this, what does it matter whether we ritualize those relationships or not?

I would contend that we do so out of a sense of identity, of solidarity with our past (and future): this is what our people do and have always done. We converse with the gods through symbols. Myth and ritual are the language by which the mind articulates to itself realities that cannot be directly expressed in other ways; prayer and offerings are metaphors that express very real relationships. It is the spiritual technology of the ancestors; how else shall we do it?

In our day we continue to make offerings because at the heart of pagan social ethic stands the principle *Do ut des*: a gift for a gift. Since everything that we have has, in effect, been given to us, it behooves us to give in return. Only infants take heedlessly without giving back. Our entire social worldview revolves around this principle. From the elder gods, ultimately, comes everything that we have, love, and are; from them comes life itself. For this, the best of gifts, do we not owe them, at the very least, our thanks, our respect, our praise, regardless of whether they hear us or not? Or do we, like spoiled children, continue to take and take without the least obligation of thanks, gratitude, or even recognition?

In this old-new world of the Many, we should expect that the gods will show us multiple faces; as we know, they have always been shifters of shape. Old Hornie is wont to wear the form—or at least the horns—of whichever animal figures largest in the local economy. In forest country he tends to be antlered. (This is true across much of the eastern US, where the white-tailed deer is the primary game animal.) On the Great Plains of North America he often sports, as one might expect, bison horns. Among cattle-herders, he is bull-horned; in the Mediterranean hills, his horns are often a goat's or a ram's. In Australia, where there are no native horned animals, he typically shows himself as the Kangaroo Man.

That the Sun, to take another example, should be seen differently by different people in different places should surprise no one. All the Sun gods of humanity point to the same underlying reality: for us all, there is only one Sun, call him what you will. That you in your valley know him (or her) by a different name than I in mine only adds to the interest. One story is never enough.

We must become once again the people of the Many, our goal nothing less than the repolytheization of the West. In polytheist society, it is understood that we benefit by cultivating our relationship with the gods, just as any intimate relationship requires ongoing maintenance. Since there are too many gods for anyone to properly befriend them all, it only stands to benefit us when others honor different gods than we do; in that way, all the gods receive their due, and everyone comes out ahead.

Above all, we new pagans must learn to know and honor the Many as they manifest in our own time and place. While the ways of the ancestors—the Received Tradition—must always inform our thought and action, we are truest to our heritage when we think and act as natives of here and now. Our mandate is to be the pagans for our own time, our own place, our own post-modern, science-driven Western culture. This is the only kind of pagan that we can honestly be; anything else is pretense.

The elder gods were the gods of my ancestors and yours. In our own day, it is for us to enter once again into right relationship with them.

We live, as John Michael Greer has said, in a world full of gods. The Earth upon whom we live and die, the Sun rising in splendor, worthy of worship, as is the Moon by night, the Winds that grant us breath, the Fire that burns at the heart of history, Him of the Horns who has haunted humanity's dreams from the very beginning: these are our lost-found pantheon, our once and future gods.

Somewhere a god with a voice of thunder, speaking the primal word, is even now moving in beauty and terror towards us.

My friends, let us rise and go and meet him.

### References

de Benoist, Alain. *On Being a Pagan* (tr. Jon Graham) (2004). Atlanta: Ultra.

Greer, John Michael. *A World Full of Gods: An Inquiry into Polytheism* (2005), Tucson: ADF Publishing.

Lincoln, Bruce. *Death, War, and Sacrifice: Studies in Ideology and Practice* (1991), Chicago: University of Chicago Press.

Pound, Ezra. "Religio, or The Child's Guide to Knowledge," in *Pavannes and Divisions* (1918). New York: Alfred P. Knopf.

Scott, Anthony. "Pilgrimage to Freedom" in *Journeys to Orthodoxy* (ed. Thomas Doulis). (1986) Minneapolis: Light and Life Publishing.

The Creation of Adam
Sistine Chapel (edited)

## Part 8: Origin Stories: Becoming a Non-Theistic Pagan:

Fredrick Buechner said that "all theology is biography." We never talk about religion in a vacuum. We come to every religious discussion enmeshed in a history—a story which we (consciously or unconsciously) tell about ourselves and our place in the world. This is true of both theists and non-theists. We can't talk about God or gods without talking about that story; likewise, we also can't talk about *their absence* without revealing our story as well. We do ourselves and others a disservice when we pretend otherwise, claiming some imaginary objectivity. The historically and culturally contingent nature of our beliefs does not invalidate them— *in fact, it is what gives them their meaning.*

Sharing one's personal religious journeys is an important part of any religion, especially one which seeks to distinguish itself from mainstream culture. As members of a countercultural religion, this is especially important for Pagans, including non-theistic Pagans. Many non-theistic Pagans come to this place from Christianity or another mainstream religion. Others were theistic Pagans before becoming atheists. Still others came to non-theistic Paganism by way of secular atheism or another form of religious naturalism like Buddhism.

## Godlessness and the Sacred Universe
### by Kathleen Cole

When I was first introduced to Paganism, I was 16. I had been, in a sense, taken in by a Pagan family. Their Paganism was eclectic—influenced by Wicca, Feri, and the Reclaiming tradition, as well as B.'s Native American heritage and spirituality. The Paganism I first learned was an Earth-based spirituality, but one in which the primary myth through which to connect to the Earth was the Wiccan myth of the lifecycle progression of the Goddess and God.

Since I came to Paganism primarily through that myth, I naturally assumed that belief in the Goddess and the God was a necessary component of Pagan practice. As I began to participate in ritual with their circle, I witnessed the goddesses and gods of various pantheons called out and invoked. Eventually, I came to think that being properly Pagan required belief in at least some gods and goddesses. And so I set out in search of a pantheon to which I could connect myself.

My great-grandparents on both sides were immigrants. On my father's side, they came from Ireland. On my mother's, from Sweden. And so I naïvely assumed that I would feel some kind of deep connection to the Celtic and/or Norse gods and they would play a central role in my Paganism going forward. I did what I could at 16 or 17 to learn about the spiritual practices of my ancestors, and recover what I could about their gods, goddesses, myths, and rituals. Where information was lacking, I tried intuitive connection. I tried to call out to them, and I heard no answer. I tried to visualize them, and could see nothing. After trying my hardest, no matter what I did, I felt nothing.

## The Loss of the Gods

What I came to realize about myself is that it is simply not in my constitution to believe in gods and goddesses as actual beings with personalities and narratives of battles and romances and petty squabbles among them. I can appreciate them as cultural symbols, as mythological characters that speak to the experience of a people located in a particular time and place. But I cannot honestly see gods and goddesses as anything other than products of the imagination of humans. We made them; they did not make us.

My realization that I could not believe in goddesses and gods put an end to my burgeoning Paganism. Since I associated Paganism with belief in deities, I felt I could no longer be at home in the Pagan community. And this was a great loss for me. In the Pagan community I had found the first examples of adult womanhood that spoke to me. In B., my mentor, I had found a woman who was fierce, intelligent, creative, sexual, loving, exuberant, and deep. I had found married couples—heterosexual and other—that were truly egalitarian and celebrated each other's unique powers. I had found a circle of open and artistic people, who practiced together even though they served different gods and believed different myths. I had found a deep experience of beauty and wonder in the ritual practices and warmth in the togetherness that came from being in the circle.

I mourned the loss of Pagan community. I felt a deep absence in my life. But I was also unwilling to fake belief in goddesses and gods. I could not be inauthentic in that way.

After leaving the Pagan community, I spent a few years studying meditation. I read Buddhist and Hindu texts. I started learning what I could about physics. And it was through this combination of meditation and physics that I found my way back home to the Pagan community. Instead of goddesses and gods, I found sacredness in the structure and process of the universe. It is this sense of the sacred that grounds my Pagan practice.

## The Sacred Universe Regained

Contemporary physics tells us that the universe began denser, hotter, and smaller than most humans are capable of even imagining. All matter/energy in the universe at that moment was together and relatively uniform. It was the pure potential out of which all objects and beings would be born.

As the universe expanded, it also became less and less uniform. What began out of only two elements became increasingly diverse. New elements were formed out of the life and death of stars. Eventually, stars were joined by planets. Over billions of years, the universe that was once characterized by its uniformity, heat, and small size grew and changed. Diversity had begun to emerge alongside development.

The Earth was formed. It too went through periods of tremendous transformations. Meteorites rained down on the earth. Continents broke apart and collided. In the oceans, eventually, life formed. As life progressed, it too became increasingly diverse. Life took on multiple forms that would eventually either evolve or die off.

My sense of the sacred comes from the fact that, with sentience in humans and perhaps other animals, the universe has evolved to be able to recognize itself. As physical beings, we are made from the elements birthed in the stars. We are part of the Earth. Life emerged out of the chemicals on her surface. We exist because of the long chain of evolution and life's generous diversity with respect to forms. So, not only are we connected in deep and meaningful ways to all things in the universe and in the world. It is also in us (and potentially in other beings) that the universe, through our sentience, is able to gaze upon herself. Our sentience allows us to witness the majesty from which we come. And this witnessing, this recognition of our interconnectedness and embeddedness, grounds my sense of the sacred.

Biologists and other life scientists speak of a common ancestor for all life, LUCA. But our commonality, the oneness that grounds our existence goes back much further. All the way back. All the way back to the mysterious, dense, hot beginnings of the universe. Our story begins at that moment. Together. With everything that has ever been and everything that ever will be. That knowledge is awe inspiring to me. It fills me with deep wonder and gratitude. The oneness of all things, our eventual emergence, our dependence and interconnection with the Earth. To me, this is the Sacred. To me, this is divine.

For some, this sense of the sacred might not seem particularly Pagan, since my experience of the divine is not grounded in some external personality or authority. But the values I came to hold in Pagan community and the energy states I experienced in Pagan practice thoroughly pervade my spiritual experiences. In their eclectic circle, I learned reverence for the earth and the interconnectedness of all beings, and a deep love for the wisdom and beauty of the life cycle—of birth, growth, death, and decay. In circle and in meditations guided by my mentor, I felt the warm peace and ecstasy that comes from the experience of union with the universe. I may have given up on finding the goddesses and gods, but I have reclaimed and rediscovered those values and experiences that I think most importantly capture the spirit of Paganism through a naturalistic, Earth-based practice.

All of this is perhaps only a very long winded way of saying what Neil deGrasse Tyson may have said best: "Not only are we in the universe, the universe is in us. I don't know of any deeper spiritual feeling than what that brings upon me."

## The Sacred
### by Dr. Jon Cleland Host

I was raised Catholic. The religion one is raised in often gives a set of deeply held views and perspectives—most of them subconscious. My family and I were very involved in our church—missing Sunday Mass was nearly unthinkable, I was an altar boy, had a big first communion and later confirmation, etc. In Sunday school, I learned that we lived in a fallen world, and that our church was a rare patch of sacred ground, where the Holy Spirit came down to us. As a teenager, while still Christian, I began to learn about our fallen world—through biology, geology, and the other sciences. What an incredible Universe! From the tiny biological machines in our cells to the slow crawl of the continents, everywhere I looked, I found more and more stunning examples of God's creative power. This invigorated my spirituality, and gave me an insatiable desire to learn more and more.

As my love of learning blossomed, I seem to have forgotten that this was supposed to be a corrupted world, literally far below the glory of God. Separately, but at the same time, I began to question Christianity for other reasons (logical questions), and eventually left Christianity—but that's a whole story for another time. With less time and energy devoted to worship and focus on some afterlife, my mind was free to drink in the majesty around me. I learned about many forms of vastness, such as the vastness of galaxies light years across, the tininess of cells and molecules, the vast stretches of billions of years behind us, and the ages ahead of us.

When I had been examining my Christianity, I had discovered that the stories about God's glory, God's gleaming throne, God's majestic white hair, God's power, and so on, were stories made up by a few people—all in a small patch of land in Palestine, long ago. These stories were good—after all, we humans are very creative—but even these stories described glories which didn't quite measure up to those found around us. How could they, being made when so much less was known, when we couldn't see supernovae by X-rays nor DNA with microscopes and the writers thought we lived under a hard dome? It wasn't their fault. But that did explain why the dichotomy of the "perfect and wonderful" divine realm set against the "fallen, mundane and debased" world around us made no sense anymore. My world had grown far beyond the world of the ancient biblical writers.

And what a world I now saw! My journey of learning had given me gifts of seeing the wonder around me. Looking across a landscape here in Michigan, I could ~~imagine~~, no, <u>see</u> the past—seeing the lake dwindle to a river, with an Anishinaabe village butchering a mastodon long before the Europeans arrived, and earlier still, the land buried under a mile of glacial ice. Earlier, a lush cretaceous jungle, and an evaporating Devonian sea, bare rocks before that, bubbling lava, and the formation of elements in supernovae! Behind my mom and dad, I see a concurrent image of their great grandparents, of thousands of generations of human love, of earlier immigrants, of my French Les Voyageur Ancestors portaging canoes, of feudal peasants and hardworking hunter-gatherers. I see an overlayed image of brave pioneers leaving Africa, of a prehensile tail steadying a young mother nursing her baby, of a tiny, furry creature looking for food amid a barren, snowy landscape after the cretaceous asteroid impact, and so on back through deep-time eyes. Looking forward, I see the world we will create for future generations with our actions. In this light, my choices are more than important; they are sacred.

More wonders opened to me through atomic and cosmic eyes. I see the bent water molecules jostling for position in my glass of pop, the rigid rows and columns of metal atoms in a fork, the speeding pairs of nitrogen atoms around me. Even in my office during the day, I'm aware of the yawning void of space starting 8,000 miles under my chair, the unblinking black hole in the galactic center, like the eye of Sauron, and of the distances that make the speed of light become a crawl. All of these and so many more connect me to the rest of existence, of which I'm only one small part.

It was a joyful discovery to find Paganism and celebrate the Wheel of the Year. Paganism contains spiritual traditions that don't see our world as lesser or devalued—traditions that celebrated our glorious world! Paganism includes so many different ways to see divinity. Pantheistic Pagans see all of the Universe as deity. Hard theists sometimes see their deity or deities as separate from our Universe, or related to it in different ways. Theists of other types see their deities as expressions of the Universe or of psychological archetypes. Naturalistic Pagans like me don't believe in anything without objective evidence, while we sometimes connect with deities as psychological archetypes or personifications of natural forces. Though there are many different ways to see the divine within Paganism, a common thread among many of us Pagans is the sacrality of our world—the overwhelming feeling of being in love with our Universe, our Earth, and our family of all life on Earth. Pagan sacred places and rituals—both those I lead as well as those led by others—so often touch me deeply, bringing me powerful spiritual experiences that I hadn't known as a Christian.

Now the sacred is all around me, touching me every day, always available if only looked for. I can't imagine trying to live in that sad, fallen world I lived in, back when I still thought that the Christian god held the keys to the sacred. Finding our Pagan community has helped me see how many people our sacred world now touches.

## The Death of God and the Rebirth of the Gods
### by John Halstead

"God is dead. God remains dead. And we have killed him. How shall we comfort ourselves, the murderers of all murderers? What was holiest and mightiest of all that the world has yet owned has bled to death under our knives: who will wipe this blood off us? What water is there for us to clean ourselves? What festivals of atonement, what sacred games shall we have to invent? Is not the greatness of this deed too great for us? Must we ourselves not become gods simply to appear worthy of it?"

— Nietzsche, *The Gay Science* (1882)

In 1882, Friedrich Nietzsche declared those fateful words:

"God is dead."

Almost 100 years later, David Miller declared, in *The New Polytheism* (1974), "The death of God gives birth to the rebirth of the Gods." Sometimes the gods have to die in order for us to rediscover them. At least this was true for me.

One of the defining moments in my religious evolution was the moment God died for me. It was the year 2000. I don't recall where I was, but I do recall what it felt like. It was the culmination of years of difficult struggle to make sense of the Mormon faith I had been raised with. And when it happened, I felt both terrible fear and exhilarating joy.

This was the moment I realized that I had unconsciously created God in my own image—or rather I had created God in the image of a part of me: the stern, cold, judgmental part of me. I realized that this Being whose disapproval I had felt breathing hot and heavy down upon me for 25 years was actually…me. It was like looking at someone who you had known and feared your whole life and realizing all of a sudden that you were looking at a mirror.

What happened next is the story of the rebirth of the gods for me. Carl Jung wrote: "Only an unparalleled impoverishment of symbolism could enable us to rediscover the gods as psychological factors, which is to say, as archetypes of the unconscious." Jung was describing a society-wide impoverishment of symbolism which he was witnessing, but I experienced this on a personal scale—an unparalleled impoverishment of my personal symbolism, in the form of the death of God, and the rediscovery of the gods, this time as psychological archetypes.

### "Must we ourselves not become gods?"

Jung wrote that, when the image of God loses its significance, the psychological energy which had previously been projected outward onto God comes back to us, giving rise to a feeling of intense vitality, a new potential. That is precisely what I felt. All that energy I had been projecting outward onto God came back home to me. I felt like I had been reborn.

At that point, it is common for a person's ego to take the place of God in the psyche. Jung explains that we make the "materialistic error" of inferring that, since the throne of God could not be discovered among the galactic systems, God never existed. When this happens, we in our hubris, "make the ego, in all its ridiculous paltriness, lord of the universe." Jung explained:

> "The gods at first lived in superhuman power and beauty on the top of snow-clad mountains or in the darkness of caves, woods, and seas. Later they drew together into one god, and then that god became man. But in our day even the God-man seems to have descended from his throne and to be dissolving himself in the common man…the common man suffers from a hubris of consciousness that borders on the pathological."

This is what happened in Nietzsche's case. "Must we ourselves not become gods?" asks Nietzsche. Jung wrote that Nietzsche's tragedy was that, "because his God died, Nietzsche himself became a god…It seems dangerous for such a man to assert that 'God is dead': he instantly becomes a victim of inflation." "Inflation" refers to the confusion of one's conscious ego with the much larger wholeness of the psyche.

"It suits our hypertrophied and hubristic modern consciousness not to be mindful of the dangerous autonomy of the unconscious and to treat it negatively as an [mere] absence of consciousness," wrote Jung. In this "hubris of consciousness," we imagine that we know who we are; we think that we are merely our conscious minds. "When one speaks of man, everyone means his own ego-personality—that is, his personality so far as he is conscious of it." But, according to Jung, our individual consciousness is surrounded by a practically unbounded unconscious psyche—like a vast ocean encircling a tiny island. "Whereas the island is small and narrow, the ocean is immensely wide and deep and contains a life infinitely surpassing, in kind and degree, anything known on the island."

### "An Olympus full of deities"

According to Jung, when we look into the "water" of this ocean, standing on our little island of consciousness, at first all we see is our own image—our egos—reflected back in the water. We think we are all the life there is. But then other images loom up, fishes and…nixies? And we discover that the waters are full of life which had previously been invisible to us. "Since the stars have fallen from heaven and our highest symbols have paled, a secret life holds sway in the unconscious," wrote Jung. These other forms of life are the "gods" of the unconscious:

> "We think we can congratulate ourselves on having already reached such a pinnacle of clarity, imagining that we have left all the phantasmal gods far behind. But what we have left behind are only verbal spectres, not the psychological facts that were responsible for the birth of the gods. We are still as much pos-

sessed by autonomous psychological contents as if they were Olympians."

"[We are] influenced and indeed dominated by desires, habits, impulses, prejudices, resentments, and by every conceivable kind of complex. All these natural facts function exactly like an Olympus full of deities who want to be propitiated, served, feared and worshiped, not only by the individual owner of this assorted pantheon, but by everybody in his vicinity."

We do not *have* desires, habits, prejudices, etc., said Jung—*they have us*. These "gods" have the power to quite literally possess us.

### "Called or not..."

Over the door of his home in Switzerland, Jung had carved a Latin phrase: "VOCATUS ATQUE NON VOCATUS DEUS ADERIT," translated "Called or not called, the god will be there." Jung warned that, when we discover that we have created God in our own image, it is easy to draw the false conclusion that we have a choice whether or not to create gods for ourselves.

I thought this myself at one time. If I had created God in my own image, why not create better gods for myself? And Neo-Paganism offered many interesting gods to choose from. But this, warns David Tacey in *Jung and the New Age* (2001), "is consumer capitalism disguising itself as spiritual technology." He explains, "If modern man does not consciously sacrifice to the Gods, he finds himself unconsciously sacrificed to the many pathologies and diseases that assailed him."

We cannot consciously create our gods; we can only discover them. Just as we do not create our dreams, so the gods cannot be created. Like our dreams, the gods arise from not our conscious mind, but from our unconscious. "Psychologically speaking, the domain of 'gods' begins where consciousness leaves off," wrote Jung. And so, the gods are something that happens to us, not something we cause to happen. But while we cannot create our gods, Jung says we *can* choose which ones to serve—in the hope that the service of one or more may safeguard us against being mastered by others.

### "Storming the citadel of the ego"

The shift from theism to atheism is a treacherous one, Jung explained, because as we withdraw our metaphysical projections, we become even less conscious of the power of the "gods" over us:

> "The truth is that we do not enjoy masterless freedom; we are continually threatened by psychological factors which…may take possession of us at any moment. The withdrawal of metaphysical projections leaves us almost defenseless in the face of this happening, for we immediately identify with every impulse instead of giving it the name of the 'other,' which would at least hold it at arm's length and prevent it from storming the citadel of the ego."

The gods do not cease to exist when we stop believing in them. They merely slip out of the image we had made for them, and "go on working as before, like an unknown quantity in the depths of the psyche." And so long as we remain unconscious of them, they run amok in our lives.

I experienced this personally as I internalized all the judgmentalness that I had previously projected onto God. After I stopped believing in God, I could not forgive myself for having been "duped" into believing, and this made me judgmental of all those who continued to believe. The same "God" who I had felt judging me from "without" was now judging me (and everyone else) from "within." Only now I had even less power over it because I identified with that judgmentalness, whereas before I had the option of rejecting God's judgment (at least theoretically).

### Who hardened Pharaoh's heart?

"But why call them gods?" you may ask. Why use religious language? Why not just use words like "desires," "habits," "prejudices," etc. One reason is that these psychological forces exercise the same power over us that a god might. Humans "cannot grasp, comprehend, dominate them; nor can they free themselves or escape from them," wrote Jung, "and therefore feels them as overpowering. Recognizing that they do not spring from their conscious personality, they call them mana, daimon, or God."

Consider this curious line from the book of the Exodus in Judeo-Christian scripture: "But the Lord hardened Pharaoh's heart and he would not listen to Moses…" This comes from the story of the seven plagues of Egypt, which were sent from God as a warning to the Pharaoh to release the Hebrew people from bondage. But why would God send warnings and then harden Pharaoh's heart? In *The Origins of Consciousness in the Breakdown of the Bicameral Mind* (1976), Julian Jaynes points out that, in parts of the Old Testament and in the Homeric *Iliad*, there are no words for mental acts like introspection and no evidence of consciousness or free will in the actors. It is always a god who moves the action: a god causes Agamemnon to steal the mistress of Achilles, a god rouses Achilles to fight,, a god causes the Trojans to panic at the sound of Achilles' scream. In these ancient texts, the gods function like "little personalities" (Jung's term) in the human psyche.

I know I feel like this myself sometimes. Jung explains that the unity of the human psyche is an illusion. "We like to think that we are one; but we are not, most decidedly not. We are not really masters in our house." Have you ever done something, perhaps in anger, and later regretted it? Perhaps you said something like, "That wasn't me." Sometimes, in retrospect, our actions don't make sense to us. We feel as though we had been possessed by something alien. In Jungian terms, these are archetypes and complexes; but in religious or mythic terms they are gods and daimons. "Anything despotic and inescapable is in this sense [a] God," explained Jung. "That psychological fact that wields the greatest power in your system functions as a god."

## A god by any other name...

Using the mythic language of "gods" has a *practical* advantage which is often not appreciated by those who favor more precise language: It helps us objectify the psychological forces which would otherwise dominate us. So long as we use the "objective" language of psychology to describe these dominating forces, we identify with them and confuse them with our conscious ego. But by personifying them, we render them "other," distancing them from our conscious egos, holding them "at arm's length" (as Jung says), giving us psychological space to breathe and the opportunity to take back possession of our lives from them.

In addition, theistic language is laden with emotional resonance and has unique potential to evoke powerful emotions of a special character, which more objective language lacks. We may call these psychological powers by any number of words, like "mana," a "daimon," a "god," or the "unconscious." For Jung, these terms were synonymous, but he said that "the first three terms have the great merit of including and evoking the emotional quality of numinosity [a mysterious otherness], whereas the latter 'the unconscious' is banal and therefor closer to reality...The 'unconscious' is too neutral and rational a term to give much impetus to the imagination."

Using the word "god," instead of "archetype," encourages us to engage with these powers with our whole being. Anthropomorphic language stimulates different parts of the brain than non-anthropomorphic language, the regions of the brain associated with sociality and relationship, in contrast to the parts of the brain that process objects and abstractions, and so we have a different experience in response to words like "god" or "goddess" than we do to more abstract or impersonal words like "archetype" or "complex." As a result, we become open to a kind of relationship that would have been impossible had we used more objective language, and we become more susceptible to the life-transforming experiences that flow from that relationship.

> "The great advantage of the concepts 'daimon' and 'God' lies in making possible a much better objectification...a *personification* of it. Their emotional quality confers life and effectuality upon them. Hate and love, fear and reverence, enter the scene of the confrontation and raise it to a drama. What has merely been 'displayed' becomes 'acted.' The whole person is challenged and enters the fray with their total reality. Only then can they become whole..."

In other words, so long as we treat the gods as "mere" psychological archetypes, we tend to engage them only with our minds. But when we see them as "gods," we engage them with our whole being: heart and mind and body.

### "Dionysus versus the crucified"

This is how the death of God led to the rebirth of the gods within me. Yahweh, the god of my youth, "died" when I realized that he did not exist independently of me. At first I thought he was gone from my life when I stopped believing in him. But he was still there, imperiously working in the background of my consciousness. I had no choice as to whether or not he existed; he was a part of me. I could only choose whether to remain conscious of him or to repress him again. As a character in Hermann Hesse's novel *Demian* explains, rather than trying to drive away or exorcising parts of ourselves, we should treat all of our drives and so-called temptations with respect and love, and then they will reveal their meaning to us. When I realized this, I decided to reclaim Yahweh. I had to find a time and a place to honor him, and integrate him into my life in a healthy way. To do so, I turned to myth.

In the Judeo-Christian scripture, Yahweh is the creator God who brought order to the universe by dividing light from darkness, land from sea, and so on. The Yahweh of my youth was the god who brought order to my personal universe. He was the power of *logos*, the power of judgment, the power of dividing one thing from another. Left unchecked, though, this god killed all spontaneity, vitality, and feeling of connection for me. He made it impossible for me to let go mentally so I could immerse myself in the experience of life.

The problem was not Yahweh's existence, but the lack of balance. As Jung said, "Without the experience of opposites, there is no experience of wholeness." To borrow a Nietzschean concept, Yahweh was the Apollonian pole of my psyche, which needed to be balanced with the Dionysian pole—the power of *eros*, of connection and union with the "other." (Not coincidentally, Dionysus was also Nietzsche's new god, which he invoked to replace the crucified Christian god.) I needed to balance reason and structure with instinct and spontaneity, *logos* with *eros*, Apollo with Dionysus.

Paganism has given me opportunities to engage with Dionysus, the wild god of ecstasy and abandon. Paganism is a religion of drums, moonlight, feasting, dancing, masks, flowers, divine possession. But I still need Yahweh—or "Apollo" as he has been reborn for me. To use Jung's metaphor of the island in the ocean above, I need a lifeline of Apollonian rationality connecting me to the shore, so that I can feel safe plunging into the depths of ecstatic religious experience which is represented by Dionysos. In my religious devotions, then, I pay homage to both gods, Apollo and Dionysos. And thereby I find the balance that I need.

## How Persephone Killed the Gods for Me
## by B. T. Newberg

Persephone killed the gods for me.

That slender-ankled goddess, mistress of the underworld—she *killed* them. And, in that strange way that only gods can do, they came to life again.

Whatever I believed about deities before her, it all changed one summer solstice. This is the story of how Persephone turned me into a Humanistic Pagan.

### The gods are dead

For me it was not Nietzsche but Persephone who proclaimed "God is dead." It is appropriate, for she is a goddess of death after all, a being who dies and rises with the seasons.

According to myth, the young maiden Persephone was picking flowers in a meadow one day when suddenly the earth opened and out came Hades, god of death. He swept her into his chariot and plunged back down to the underworld. There, she was to be his bride. Meanwhile, her mother, Demeter, goddess of grain and fertility, searched frantically for her missing daughter. So distraught was she that nothing on earth would grow, no plant nor animal would bear life. At last, Zeus, ruler of the gods, had to step in. The human race was withering, and without them the gods would receive no offerings. Without offerings, the gods too would wither. So a deal was brokered: Persephone would spend most of the year with her mother, but a third of the year she must return to the land of the dead. Thus began the seasons.[1]

So, Persephone knew about dying. If any had authority to declare the demise of the gods, it was her—this lady of life and death, this woman of both worlds.

Let me back up a little. It was the summer of 2009, and I was standing over a small altar built beside the river. In my hand was a copy of Sargent's *Homeric Hymns*, and around my neck was a special pendant. I had worn it for nine months, from the season of her last rising to the present moment of her imminent descent. It was to be an offering for Persephone. Just as she would go below, so I would bury it in the earth. What I didn't realize was that I would bury the gods too.

For years I had been experimenting with polytheism. I had joined an organization of Pagans, gone through its rigorous training program, and emerged fully proficient in myth and ritual. Demeter and Persephone had been with me through it all. Through them I felt a kinship with the cycles of nature; through them the changing of the seasons came alive. The year felt enchanted, full of meaning. And that experience was very real. But the gods were not—I knew that, and could bear it no longer. As I poured a libation of barley tea, read aloud the "Hymn to Demeter," and called out to the Two Goddesses, Demeter and Persephone, a dull frustration was in the air. The words rang empty.

Then, as my fingers dug into the dirt and deposited the pendant into the ground, a rush came over me. Through my mind flashed a voice:

"Let them die."

It was one of those moments, the ones you remember long after other memories have faded. I was left ruminating over what it meant, and where to go from there.

One thing was certain: I could no longer pretend, neither in public nor in the privacy of my own mind, that the gods were real. For me, the gods were dead.

## The gods live again

Yet that was not the end of the story. Persephone had still more mysteries to unveil.

How could it be that the goddess herself wanted me to disbelieve in gods? Didn't they need human offerings, as told in the myth? Without us, wouldn't they wither away?

I began to ask myself what it was that had persuaded me to "believe" in the gods in the first place. In truth, I had carried an agnostic attitude through it all—intellectually. But emotionally, I had developed a deep relationship with the gods. In some sense, the gods had been real to me.

When I sensed their presence, it was an intensification of emotion that tipped me off. Likewise, a successful ritual was a ritual that was moving, that felt powerful. These were the experiences that "proved" the gods, as it were.

Not all polytheists rely so exclusively on feeling. Others point to more objective phenomena, like strange coincidences or perceptual visions. I experienced some things like that too, but nothing that could not be explained by a naturalistic interpretation. Nor did I ever hear others tell of more convincing happenings. Some had inexplicable experiences, like one friend who saw phantom smoke wisps during ritual. But it is a long leap from seeing something to concluding that gods are real. Better to admit the unknown than to leap to an explanation, theistic or otherwise.[2] Ultimately, it is an act of faith. And my faith was based on emotion, it seemed. Yet it was not insignificant.

Real or not, the gods did provoke powerful and beautiful experiences. I am a better person for having them. I feel more in tune with my world, and more alive as a person. This is no small thing in an era when alienation and apathy run rampant. To find connection to the world is to find meaning.

So maybe, in a sense, the gods are real after all. They may not be literal, independently existing entities. They may not be causal agents with the power to influence events, save through the actions of my own two hands. They may not send messages, save for what pops to mind through the power of imagination. Yet in some meaningful sense, they are real.

As presences in the imagination, they are real. As cultural and psychological forms, they are real. As sources of meaning and beauty, they are real.

The gods live again.

### Thank you, Persephone

Persephone killed the gods for me. And she brought them back to life.

She showed me that gods don't have to be real in order to be *real*. You can develop wonderful relationships with them. They can enhance quality of life, and motivate responsible action. Through their power, your world can grow vibrant.

In that fateful way that makes sense only in myth, the gods had to die in order to bring life back to the world. Inside me, it had been the barren season. Like Demeter searching for her daughter, I was searching for my truth. So long as I had not found it, no living thing could grow. But by letting the gods die, life returned. They were reborn as beings of the mind.

Ultimately, I had to be honest with myself. I simply didn't believe literally in the gods. Yet that was no reason to foreswear them. On the contrary, it was reason to embrace them all the more.

Since that fateful summer ritual, where I buried the pendant and the gods too, my world has come alive again. No longer do I feel that dull frustration in ritual, that sense of empty words. Now I speak with full knowledge and confidence in what I'm saying. Now I see gods in the human, and the human in the gods.

I became a Humanistic Pagan.

And that's why I say to you, Persephone, beautiful goddess in my head: "Thank you."

### Notes

1. The timing of the barren season is debated. Since *Bulfinch's Mythology*, many have assumed it to be winter. But Nilsson challenged this in his book, *Greek*

*Folk Religion*, arguing that in Athens it is the summer when crops cease to grow due to the oppressive heat.

2. My friend did in fact admit the unknown. He himself offered a number of alternative, brain-based explanations for the wisps. He prefers to believe in the gods, but claims no conclusive evidence.

## The Impossible Atheist
### by Bart Everson

I've identified myself as an atheist for many years, but now I'm reconsidering this label. It's not that my worldview has changed. It's a matter of intellectual honesty.

I started rethinking this after reading an essay on Religion Dispatches in 2010. A key point: The atheisms of most committed, principled atheists are often not more than mirror images—inversions—of the theisms they negate.

That rang true.

### Teenage hubris

I was raised in a doctrinally conservative Protestant Christian denomination. It's that particular conception of the divine with which I am most familiar. It's that particular set of beliefs and values that I rejected some quarter-century ago, when I realized my Christianity was an accident of birth. I recall a very specific moment of epiphany in the autumn of my senior year in high school, as I sat in the church balcony during an evening service. I thought to myself: *If I'd been born in India, perhaps I would have followed some form of Hinduism.* That led me to question, and ultimately reject, the received wisdom of the church.

I visited other churches in my hometown, but they were all Christian churches, mostly Protestant. Not a great deal of variation. There's some irony there. I knew there was a bigger world, but I had no access to it. The idea of Hinduism was central to my apostasy, yet I knew nothing of it. But that didn't stop me. If there was no Jehovah, there was also no Shiva, no Kali, no Sitala.

Having no real knowledge of those gods, knowing nothing of Hindu conceptions of divinity, my dismissal was an act of teenage hubris. At most, it might be said that I rejected mainstream Christian ideas about God. Anything more was overreaching.

It wasn't until a few years later, at college, that I learned a bit more about other conceptions of divinity. I was drawn to study the philosophy of religion. Process theology, in particular, struck me as viable and intellectually coherent. Though some of these ideas seemed internally consistent, even plausible, they did not seem *necessary*. I could not see any compelling reason to actually accept them as true descriptions of reality.

So I considered myself an atheist, in the strong or positive sense. I'd considered theism and rejected it. I went through a long process of self-editing, as it were, eliminating the theistic basis for my morality and worldview, building a new, humanistic self.

## And yet...

My thoughts on the subject now seem woefully contradictory. Consider a reflection I composed just a few years ago:

> *America also has many people of other religions, and if you consider the entire world and the whole history of humanity, these other religions loom even larger: Islam, Hinduism, Zoroastrianism, Judaism—to name only a few. These many diverse religions have at least one thing in common: They are all theistic. They all believe in God, or in some cases, in multiple gods. I don't. In my heart of hearts I do not believe that there is a God. Certainly I do not believe in a personal creator god of the sort envisioned by these religions. So I am not a theist, by definition.*

I speak of "many diverse religions" and then assert that they are all centered on a "personal creator god."

## Well, are they?

I now realize that my collegiate exposure to these ideas was fairly limited and very academic. Even though I nurtured a burgeoning interest in folklore, I never looked much at folk religion. Consider this definition from *Spiritual Direction in Paganism* (Master's thesis, 1999) by Saraswati Rain.

"Just as Christianity is the path following the teachings of Jesus, Judaism is the path following the teachings of the Torah or Talmud, and Buddhism is the path following the teachings of Buddha; Paganism is the path following the teachings of the people, the common folk, and the ways of the Earth. The word Pagan is often interpreted as "not religious" or "not believing in a Judeo-Christian God." But the word "Pagan" harks back to the Latin "paganus," which is literally, "peasant" referring to a rural country-dweller (Random House Webster's Unabridged Dictionary). Neo-Paganism, specifically, is the modern version of Pagan ways, the practices of the common folk, the traditional beliefs of the ancestors, adapted and re-constructed by contemporary people, pieced together from ancient lore, from traditional practices, and from the practitioners' creative imaginings, speculations and inclinations."

It wasn't until I encountered the broad diversity of ideas in contemporary Paganism that I found myself and my assumptions truly challenged. Here, at last, were conceptions of divinity which I could not so easily dismiss.

### Beauty and truth

I attended a discussion of "Existential Paganism," sponsored by a group called Lamplight Circle here in New Orleans. We talked about the notion of gods as *metaphors* or *archetypes*. I can hear committed atheists objecting: "Metaphors? But that's not really belief at all is it?" No, certainly not according to the Christian paradigm in which I was raised. But there are other ways of looking at the world.

The equation of beauty and truth is an ancient and familiar one. Consider it seriously for a moment, as a thought experiment. If beauty is truth, then how do we react to the beautiful mythologies of the ancient world? If we say they are beautiful but false, then we are making very narrow definitions indeed, and our aesthetics are crippled. If we can understand them as metaphor, then we're no longer concerned with a binary distinction between truth and falsity. One doesn't ask if a metaphor is true. The relevant questions shift. How does it resonate? What does it mean?

## Accuracy in reporting

When it comes to accurately reporting my atheism, the only coherent statement I feel qualified to make is that I reject most mainstream monotheistic Abrahamic theologies, insofar as I understand them. As far as many of my fellow Americans are concerned, then, the atheist label is an accurate description.

(When questioned on the subject of atheism, Joseph Campbell supposedly said, "If you are, I'm not; if you're not, I am." I'm beginning to understand how he felt.)

However, this definition neglects substantial minority religious perspectives. It neglects the true diversity of ideas in this sphere. It privileges the center and neglects the periphery—a position I find politically obnoxious. In short, strong atheism in the broadest sense has come to seem like an impossibility. (Weak atheism is another matter.) To reject what one does not know is merely ignorant. To reject all theisms one would have to know them all, and who has done that?

In and through Paganism I've discovered that my ideas about divinity were really too narrow. My worldview remains humanistic and naturalistic, but I have now encountered naturalistic conceptions of the divine. It's a most unexpected development, and it's left me scratching my head.

I'm not ready to call myself a theist, but I'm no longer quite comfortable calling myself an atheist. Perhaps it's more accurate to say I'm simply not theocentric. I'd describe my values as more ecocentric. Better yet, perhaps I should say I'm a work in progress. Conceptions previously held in separate mental compartments are running together and mixing. Rather than rushing to an answer, I'm following Rilke's advice and learning to "love the questions."

## Adventures of a Non-Deist, or Why I Don't "Believe" in the Gods
### by Peg Aloi

I was raised Catholic. Not very strictly, but enough to carry away a profound sense of discomfort with anything remotely connected to religion. I did kind of enjoy the music and chanting and stories and pageantry of mass, but of course in later life I understood it was a love of ritual, not a love of Catholic liturgy. I was also raised in a family fairly in touch with nature: we hunted and fished and grew and gathered much of our own food. So when I discovered neo-paganism in graduate school, I mainly related to the environmental activism and the nature worship components. In fact, until I found out there were witches and pagans in the contemporary world, I basically considered myself an atheist. As I moved in circles of pagans and encountered more and more witches, "Wiccans," and others who followed some form of nature spirituality, I understood that many of them worshipped the gods, or, in some cases, mainly the Goddess.

I played along, you know. But none of this ever really felt right to me.

Over the years, as I began to identify as a neo-pagan witch, I met other witches who worshipped god and goddess, but also, I met a number of folks in these circles who were not primarily god- and goddess-worshippers, some of whom called themselves "non-deists": a clunky word, but one that seems to sum up how I feel. Gods help me, I even referred to myself for years as a "non-deist shamanic witch" (shamanic being a term used to loosely refer to using slightly altered states of consciousness brought on by various activities like drumming or dancing to encounter visions and insights).

Nowadays, I just call myself a witch. Yeah, no upper case letters for me, people. The only reason I use a capital "w" for "Wicca" or "Wiccan" is that these words were kind of invented by Gardner to refer to what a lot of us do now, which, for all intents and purposes, is kind of a religion. Or, at least, a fairly organized and solidified set of beliefs and practices.

I call on various gods and goddesses in ritual. I invoke them in the four quarters. I have statues of them on my altars and images of them on my walls. But, and this is a bit hard to explain, I don't actually worship them. I find them to be useful archetypes (ah, there's that word you were waiting for me to use) and forms of inspiration. I like to focus on their characteristics and narratives to try to bring about change in my life: identifying with Pomona to bring abundance, for example, or Artemis to find peace in solitude, or Herne to connect with the wilder unspoken aspects of nature. I give them places of honor and look at them and think about them. But I do not worship them.

So what do I do? I spend time in orchards and meadows and beneath the stars and moon, breathing in the perfumes of the woods, looking for fairy lights in the twilight mist, and delighting in birdsong and finding peace in the sound of rain dripping from the trees. I open myself to the awesome power of the sun and the wind and the trees and the stars, the lessons of the hummingbird and the horse and the horned owl. All of these experiences and a myriad others make me think of the worldviews of my ancestors (for mainly I identify with western European lore and myth, Greco-Roman and Celtic), the emotions they felt encountering the beauty and mystery of the natural world. I know they saw these things as gods, or as embodiments or dwelling places of gods. And this understanding comforts and intrigues me. But I do not share this belief.

Even as I write rituals, crafting them from poetry I gather from a plethora of writers or that I create myself, even as I describe the attributes of these deities and write passionate paeans to them, I do not think of what I do as worshipping these figures. I think the most accurate way to describe it is to say that I engage with the energy and imagery of these deities: I take part in their mythology, their ancient story, which has been reborn around the world.

I was talking with friends once about a time in my life when I was having unsettling thoughts about death. One of them said he didn't even think about it, that when you die you "lie in the arms of the Goddess." I understand this to be a deeply comforting thought for some, and certainly a powerfully beautiful image. But I simply don't believe it, and can't really envision it on any sort of imaginative or cognitive level. Maybe it is simply too close to my experiences as a child and adolescent, when I was asked to believe in a god I thought cruel, capricious and bigoted. (Of course I later understood the Church was the problem, not God.) Maybe my inability to conceive of worshipping godforms makes it impossible for me to find any abiding comfort in what awaits me after death. Returning to the earth is as much comfort as I am willing to allow myself, immersing myself in the Eternal Return, and I am okay with that. I still fear death, but not eternity. Because it seems to me that all life is somehow eternal and cyclical; even as we watch what humans have wrought in our short time on the Earth, we see that this great organism is enormously adaptable and reliably predictable.

The question, I suppose, is: Am I a "real" pagan if I do not worship the gods? Or am I just some sad dreamy neo-hippie who enjoys gardening and fantasy literature?

I deeply respect those who follow earth-based paths that encourage a deep connection to deity. And I don't question their devotion or beliefs, nor do I think my path is superior to theirs in any way. If anything, I feel a tinge of envy for those who can give this part of themselves freely, whose hearts and souls are open to mysteries I only seem to experience in my mind and body. But I also feel that my imaginative entanglement with the world of nature and spirit is as close to religion as I am likely to come in this life, and that it has been enormously rewarding, and that, on my saddest and most wearying days, my commitment to this path keeps me balanced and content.

## Paganism at Home: For the Love of Ritual
### by Debra Macleod

I grew up in an atheist home. It was a happy, kind-hearted and good-humoured one, with parents who loved each other as much as they loved their kids (and who still do). We had our own traditions: summer trips to the cabin, car wash blitzes on the driveway, and sledding in the winter. Suckers for a hard-luck story, we fostered stray animals—abused pups, orphaned ducklings, one-legged pigeons, you name it.

My dad—a self-proclaimed redneck—was a man ahead of his time. Despite living in Canada's Evangelical Bible belt, he had the guts to speak up for gay rights at a time in our province when not many voices were. He was unflinching in his pro-choice stance and raised two daughters who never believed that a woman should "obey" a husband. Love and respect, absolutely. But obey? Fat chance.

My mom was the same way. I remember her getting mad because evolution wasn't being taught in our public school, the instruction having been opposed by religious lobby groups. Despite this, my family wasn't anti-religious. We were just indifferent-religious. Even looking back, there was nothing that religion could have added to my family life. We were good without god.

My husband grew up in a Pentecostal home. The churches he attended were hardcore: talking in tongues, faith healings, the Rapture, river baptisms, trembling hands raised to the sky, the works. As a child he experienced more than one "End of Times" countdown where he would stare up in terror, waiting for the sky to open up. He had recurring nightmares of being sawn in half by atheists, who he was taught were agents of the devil.

He was also taught by the church that dinosaur bones were put there by god to "test" people's faith, and that gay people were an abomination. He spent most of his childhood at church functions, and his parents divorced when he was a teenager. By the time we met as adults, he had become a fierce atheist. In fact, our mutual non-belief was something that attracted us to each other.

While my husband and I believe that Christianity and today's other dominant religions are a positive part of many people's lives, we don't believe these faiths have a monopoly on creating the foundation for a strong family unit or creating "moral" children. In addition to my husband, I have known many people, clients and friends alike, who feel that organized religion has been a divisive force in their family.

Some resent, as did my husband, that much of the family's "down time" was devoted to church going. When he was young, church was held on Sunday mornings and evenings. The problem was, *Battlestar Galactica* aired on Sunday nights. As a kid, he wanted nothing more than to hang out with his family, watching Starbuck and Apollo battle the Cylons. I have to laugh when he talks about the various "illnesses" that would strike him around six o'clock every Sunday night. It's funny, but also sad. To me, an hour of sci-fi spent with family is worth more than a thousand sermons from a stranger.

Others have experienced religious-based ostracism or shunning from the family unit because of their sexual orientation or choice to leave the faith. Still others cannot reconcile their personal values with religious doctrine that, indirectly or directly, supports sexism, misogyny, violence and which acts like a lead weight on the advancement of science and medicine. Some simply resent the fact that they missed the magic of believing in Santa or going trick-or-treating with friends. The reasons are many and varied.

Even though I grew up in an atheist home, I was always drawn to religious places and rituals. Churches, ceremonies and customs—I loved them all. I was the kid who peeked through the church window to watch people take the Eucharist. I was the kid who, when she got a box of Smarties, ate the red ones last.

There are many people like me. People who love ritual and long for spiritual expression, but who can't get on board with Abrahamic religious dogma or scripture. There are many people like my husband, too. People who were indoctrinated into religious belief as a child, but who have rejected that belief as an adult. And these are the folks who are increasingly turning to modern Paganism.

I was several years into my couples meditation practice when I found myself—and many of my non-religious clients—longing for a spiritual focus for their homes. Some romanticized the vogue journey of self-discovery in Elizabeth's Gilbert's *Eat Pray Love*. I had more than one client say she was ready to leave her family and head to Bali where she would scale a mountain and find her own guru or Yoda (or at least someone wearing a robe) who could tell her what life was all about.

I just turned kind of bitchy. Despite having a happy marriage and family life, I longed for a sense of meaning and ritual. I found it, too, by revisiting an experience in my past. When I was 20 years old, I had visited Rome where I was briefly schooled in the ancient gods and goddesses, and even met a Pagan priestess who was keeping the "old ways" alive. It was the first time I was exposed to a spirituality beyond the monotheistic, androcentric variety. And I liked it. It meant something to me.

The experience sparked a lifelong interest in Roman classics and mythology; however, it wasn't until midlife that I found myself embracing modern Paganism—specifically the New Vesta tradition—as a form of personal spirituality, one that resonated with me and reflected my humanist values. Cliché? Midlife crisis? Maybe. But a real experience nonetheless.

In antiquity, Vesta was the goddess of the home, hearth and domestic life. Residing in the household fireplace and symbolized by a flame, she warmed and lit the home while providing a "spiritual focus" for the family. At each meal, offerings of salted flour or libations of wine or olive oil were sprinkled into her flame. This ritual did more than symbolically "feed" her spirit. It nourished and strengthened the family bond while bringing tranquility to the household.

Modern followers of Vesta typically have a Vestal candle on the table and make similar offerings. It is a simple family ritual that makes the home a sacred space, and that reinforces a sense of family solidarity. As well as meal-time offerings, New Vesta adherents usually have a lararium or family altar located near the entrance to the home. Mementoes of family members—living and dead—are kept here, as is a Vestal candle. The position of the lararium—near the home's entrance—serves to "bless" the comings and goings of family members, and to serve as a visual reminder than home really is where the heart is.

Despite having been brainwashed to fear and loathe pagans, my husband did a bang-up job of accepting this tradition into our home. Why? Because it didn't raise any of his "religious red flags." It didn't ask for money or reject science. It didn't require us to outsource the morality we imparted to our son, and it didn't involve him being indoctrinated into supernatural belief. It wasn't angry or judgmental and it didn't put anything—man or god—above our own marriage and family.

Obviously, this is only a superficial look at New Vesta [See Part 6], which itself is only one expression of Paganism. "Contemporary Paganism" is an umbrella term for many beliefs, which are as diverse as they are rich. There is insufficient space here to do justice to the practices that many people hold dear. This is a snapshot of what modern Paganism looks like in our home. There are no human or animal sacrifices in our basement. There are no mystery chants, secret rites or orgies. There is just a family who really loves watching *Battlestar Galactica* re-runs and who is doing its best to tread lightly upon the Earth while being decent to our fellow travelers.

I think it is time to challenge the stereotypes surrounding modern Paganism and its various beliefs. It has so much to offer, from its fascinating history and cultural influence to its contemporary efforts to create a better world.

Pedestal of Tukulti-Ninurta I, Ashur, c.1243-1207 B.C.
(Staatliche Museen zu Berlin)

## Part 9: Looking Back: Non-Theistic Pagans in History

A frequent complaint brought by some polytheistic Pagans against non-theistic Pagans is that they have misappropriated the name "Pagan." Ancient paganism, they argue, was synonymous with polytheism, and thus contemporary Paganism should be polytheistic as well. Humanistic and Naturalistic Pagans tend to be more forward-looking than backward-looking. Unlike forms of Paganism which seek to reconstruct the religions of ancient pagans from surviving sources, Humanistic and Naturalistic Pagans have largely abandoned attempts to legitimize their beliefs by appeals to the past. For them, the value of a religious practice lies in its usefulness to people in the present.

Having said that, Polytheists and Pagan Reconstructionist do not have an exclusive claim to the pagan past. While belief may have been the norm (as it is today) among ancient pagans, there were atheist pagans in antiquity. Most of the examples we have come from ancient Greece and Rome, due to the abundance of records we have from that time and place. (More material survives in Greek than in all other ancient languages put together.) Nevertheless, there were atheists among the heathen peoples of northern Europe, as well as among ancient Indian philosophers and Buddhist thinkers. It is likely that, wherever and whenever there have existed people who believed in gods, there have also existed people who did not. Some contemporary non-theistic Pagans look back to and find inspiration from these ancient predecessors.

## The Forgotten History of Atheist Paganism
### by John Halstead

The argument that modern Paganism should be polytheistic because ancient pagans were polytheistic mischaracterizes how the word "pagan" has been used in history. The term "pagan" was invented by Christians to stigmatize non-Christians. It was applied first to polytheistic people in the Roman Empire, but it has also been and continues to be applied to animistic indigenous peoples, to polytheistic Hindus, monotheistic Muslims...and to atheists. Like other words which have been reclaimed by an oppressed group, like "queer" or even "geek," the word "pagan" might also be reclaimed by any group it has been used against.

Some Pagans today feel that "atheist Pagan" is a contradiction in terms. But as it has been applied by Christians historically, "atheist pagan" was not an oxymoron, but a redundancy—to be "pagan" and to be "atheist" both meant being someone who disbelieved in *the Christian god*. Early Christians were as likely to call their polytheist neighbors "atheist" as they were to call them "pagan."

The argument that atheist Pagans are misappropriating the name "pagan" also overlooks the fact that there were atheists and other non-theists in antiquity. In *Battling the Gods: Atheism in the Ancient World* (2015), Tim Whitmarsh traces the history of atheism from Classical Greece to the early Roman Empire, beginning with the pre-Socratics, who looked for the origins of the universe, not in supernatural theogonies about the birth of gods, but in physical matter.

In the 5th century BCE, Xenophanes of Colophon argued that the gods were projections of human qualities, anticipating 20th century cognitive theorists who would explain the origins of religion in terms of the human desire to render a mysterious nature familiar. While Xenophanes and other Pre-Socratics spoke of "God" (in the singular), their one "God" was more or less synonymous with nature or the rational order of the universe.

Other naturalistic philosophers followed. Anaxagoras may have been the first to be put on trial for impiety because of his atheism. Hippo of Samos argued that the soul was nothing more than the corporeal brain. Similarly, Democritus believed that the mind was made of atoms and disbursed after death. And Thucydides was the first to write a history without reference to supernatural agents, which Whitmarsh describes as "the earliest surviving atheist narrative of human history."

Any or all of these individuals may have been referred to as *atheoi*, yet they probably did not refer to themselves in this way. The first references we have to *atheoi* are actually not to those who disbelieved in the gods, but to those who had been abandoned by the gods, i.e., the "godforsaken," and to those who lived without the civilizing order of the gods. As Whitmarsh explains, only later did the term become "a social category constructed by self-styled protectors of religious orthodoxy as a receptacle for those whose beliefs they do not share." It included those who disbelieved in the gods, as well as those whose conception of deity was radically different from the orthodox view.

Take, for example, the Epicureans, who were commonly called *atheoi*. While they claimed a belief in the gods, and rejected the atheist label, they nevertheless denied that the gods created the universe or that they intervened in the world. They also believed that worshipping the gods did not influence them. The gods of the Epicureans were practically irrelevant to humanity, except for their occasional appearance in dreams.

Other pagan philosophers, while not self-styled atheists, adopted allegorical interpretations of myths, seeing the gods as metaphors for natural phenomena or human attributes. Theagenes of Rhegium, for example, associated Apollo and Hephaestus with fire, Poseidon with water, Hera with air, Athena with the intellect, Ares with folly, Aphrodite with desire, and so on. Prodicus of Ceos said that ancient people had deified all things beneficial to humankind, so that bread became Demeter, wine Dionysus, water Poseidon, fire Hephaestos, and so on. Later, the Stoics, like Zeno, Cleanthes, and Chrysippus, also associated different gods with different elements and qualities.

As with many other epithets, though, what began as an insult was eventually reappropriated. Diagoras of Melos may have the honor of being the first self-professed atheist, to be followed by others like Theodorus of Cyrene. But it was Clitomachus, the 2nd century BCE skeptic, who was responsible for the idea of atheism as a coherent movement with its own philosophical history. Clitomachus likely wrote a book called, *On Atheism*, which is now lost to us, but he was a prolific writer, so other of his writings survive. He collected atheistic arguments, identified atheism as a distinct philosophical school, and categorized its varieties. He also compiled a compendium of philosophical atheists, which included Protagoras, Prodicus, Diagoras, Critias, Theodorus, Euhemerus, Epicurus, and others—thus giving atheism its own intellectual history. According to Whitmarsh, his "inventive doxography of atheistic argumentation created, for possibly the first time in human history, an intellectually coherent and substantial set of arguments against the existence of the divine."

But were these individuals "pagan"? As has already been discussed above, the question is anachronistic, since the term "pagan" was invented by Christians centuries after atheism emerged in Greece. Perhaps, then, we might ask whether these individuals were religious. Certainly some of them were. Some of them spoke of "God" or "gods," albeit in radically different ways from the traditional understanding of anthropomorphic divine beings.

In addition, many of the individuals identified as atheists continued to engage in public worship of the gods. The early Stoic, Persaeus of Citium, for example, insisted that the gods of the city should be worshipped in the traditional ways, even while denying their literal existence. Similarly, the second century AD Roman skeptic, Sextus Empiricus, stated that honoring gods by performing ritual sacrifices did not require believing that they exist, and he argued that skeptics could and should take part in public religious activities. The Epicureans also continued the practice of prayer, but with the understanding that it benefited, not the gods, but the humans performing the prayers.

While this position appears contradictory from the perspective of 2000 years of subsequent Christianity, we must remember that religion had a very different meaning in antiquity. The religion of the ancients was not so much a matter of personal belief as public performance. Due largely to the influence of Protestant Christianity, the notion of personal communion with the gods is central to the modern conception of religion. But this was not the case for people in the ancient world, for whom religion was primarily a communal activity, one concerned with maintaining a beneficial relationship between the community and its gods. Viewed from this perspective then, it is the cultivation of personal relationships with gods by contemporary polytheistic Pagans which is anachronistic.

In addition, ancient religion was less concerned with belief, than with practice. In the parlance of students of religious studies, it was "orthopraxic," rather than "orthodoxic." For this reason, atheism *per se* was never criminalized in ancient Greece, in contrast to "impiety." To be sure, charges of impiety were brought against atheists, but impiety referred not to the absence of belief in the gods, but to the failure to perform sacrifices—because it was the failure of outward performance, not the absence of belief, that was thought to have a deleterious effect on the wellbeing of the community.

The concern with orthodoxy may have first arisen with the Orphic mystery cults, which were uniquely concerned with the salvation of individuals. Later, Christianity was to follow this pattern, eventually transforming our understanding of the meaning of religion.

When Paganism was revived in the 20th century, contemporary Neo-Pagans followed the pattern of their ancient pagan predecessors in emphasizing practice over belief. While polytheism was a significant element in many of the spiritualities that were emerging under the tent of

Paganism at that time, in many cases these polytheisms were of a new kind—the many gods of the polytheist pantheons were understood as aspects of a single Great Goddess, or of a Goddess and her male counterpart, or else as archetypes of the collective unconscious. In fact, literal belief in gods may have been more the exception than the rule among 20th century Pagans for several decades.

Thus we see that atheistic and non-theistic Paganism has a long history dating back to Classical Greece and Rome. If we had better sources for other pagan peoples, we would likely find atheists among them as well. Literal belief in the gods was never a prerequisite for participation in ancient pagan religions, nor is it necessary for Neo-Pagans today.

## Bibliography

Bremmer, J. "Atheism in Antiquity," in Martin, M., ed. *The Cambridge Companion to Atheism.* Cambridge University Press (2006)

Brisson, Luc. *How Philosophers Saved Myths: Allegorical Interpretation and Classical Mythology* (2004)

Drachmann, A. B. *Atheism in Pagan Antiquity* (1922)

Anne Bates Hersman, *Studies in Greek Allegorical Interpretation* (1906)

Whitmarsh, Tim. *Battling the Gods: Atheism in the Ancient World* (2015)

## Exploring the Historical Roots of Naturalistic Paganism
### by B. T. Newberg

Many may assume that Naturalistic Pagans, who tend to be agnostics or atheists, are an exclusively modern phenomenon. I have made a project of questioning that assumption, probing various historical Pagan traditions for something resembling naturalism. The significance of this project goes beyond naturalism. Indeed, it calls into question the historical consciousness of Pagans in general. If there were naturalists among ancient Pagans, how might that change the way we see the myths and traditions on which Pagans of all styles of belief base their practices?

First, a note about biases: all historians are prone to them; the best one can do is acknowledge one's own. I, for my part, am not without an "agenda." As a Naturalistic Pagan myself, the fostering of a historical consciousness for those like me is a vested interest. Yet, I also have a more disinterested concern with accurate history, and wish to add to the many laudable efforts of others by filling out a little bit more of the picture.

### Terms, briefly

A *Naturalistic Pagan* is someone whose spiritual path belongs to or is inspired by ancient Pagan cultures, and who holds naturalism as a worldview.

*Pagan*, for present purposes, can be defined in the broadest sense as describing any non-Abrahamic cultural-religious tradition. This looseness is no comment on recent debates on Pagan identity; rather, it is justified by the simple futility of drawing stark dividing lines between historical traditions. All ancient cultures are caught up in a web of mutual influence, such that disentangling the Pagan from the non-Pagan bears relatively little value.

*Naturalism* is a worldview with numerous technical definitions, each with their own problems. For the purposes of this essay, we can quote Littré's 1875 *Dictionnaire de la langue française*, which defined naturalism as: "the system of those who find all primary causes in nature" (Furst and Skrine, 1971).

Variations on this definition continue to enjoy popularity today. Concentrating on *causes* it allows analysis to focus on how different people explained events, which makes it more or less portable across historical eras. We will not be able to escape the question of differing concepts of *nature* in different eras, much less the question of the so-called *supernatural*, which remains problematic in Pagan contexts today. [See Part 2.]

## Naturalistic Traditions

Here is a glimpse of what I have explored elsewhere at length. (See my "Naturalistic Traditions" series at Patheos.com, republished in modified form at SpiritualNatualistSociety.org.)

Traditions resembling Naturalistic Paganism appear to date at least as far back as the Axial Age (roughly 800-200 BCE). Around this time, a number of peoples simultaneously developed an increased interest in second-order thinking or "thinking about thinking" (Bellah, 2011). Most developed metaphysical theologies, increasingly transcendent, but some went the opposite route, focusing sharply on the here and now. Among the latter were the first naturalistic ideas.

Axial developments were noteworthy across Greece, India, China, Persia, and Israel, with naturalism emerging in the first three. Greece can serve as an example.

In Greece, a variety of poets, historians, healers, philosophers, and others began to focus on human affairs and the natural world. For example, Sophocles wrote plays in which the consequences of human action were sufficient to account for events, with divine influences mostly off-stage and secondary. Thucydides told history largely without divine explanations. The Hippocratic tradition of healers explained diseases such as epilepsy without invoking divine influence. Anaximander and the Ionian philosophers crafted views of the natural world without reference to the divine or magical. The Epicureans' atomistic philosophy was particularly naturalistic; likewise were certain elements of the Stoics and Academic Skeptics.

At the same time, apparently few of these people abandoned what we would label "religion" (Greeks had no such term at the time). For example, we have records of Epicureans, perhaps the most naturalistic of all, holding priesthoods. Most of them didn't even deny the existence of the divine *per se*. Rather than reject religion, most seemed to recognize its continuing value, albeit with new interpretations. Allegorical, cultural, or material understandings integrated religious practices with the naturalistic science of the day. (While historians disagree as to whether these ideas should yet be labeled "scientific," we can follow David L. Lindberg in defining by context: they were non-supernatural contemporary equivalents to and historical ancestors of what would become Western "science.") This integration can appropriately be called *Naturalistic Paganism*.

Naturalism never comprised more than a minority in any culture, including the Greeks, but its influence struck the ancient world. It spread through the Roman Empire, and changed the development of the West. It is possible, though difficult to establish, that it may have influenced some among the Celtic, Germanic, and Slavic peoples as well. No part of the West remained untouched.

Naturalistic Paganism survived from the ancient world to the modern day, though not in any unbroken lineage. Naturalism continued to develop, aided paradoxically by the explicitly supernaturalistic theology of Thomas Aquinas. Meanwhile, Pagan allegory developed under subordination to the Christian God, and later contributed to the Neo-Pagan revival.

In the 20th century, Occultists such as Dion Fortune and Israel Regardie attempted to integrate the science of their day, especially the psychology of Jung. This archetypal influence remained strong for much of the century. Now, fields like cognitive science, neuroscience, evolutionary approaches, and physical cosmology are coming to the fore. As in the ancient world, today's Naturalistic Pagans integrate the current most compelling scientific developments.

For almost all of its history, this disparate movement has had no common name. That changed in 2005 when Jon Cleland Host coined the term "Naturalistic Paganism" and founded a Yahoo group of the same name. There is no central organization or structure, but many independent authors and leaders push forward the community in different ways.

## Bibliography

Bella, R. N. (2011). *Religion in Human Evolution: From the Paleolithic to the Axial Age*. Cambridge: Belknap Press.

Brisson, L. (2004). *How Philosophers Saved Myths: Allegorical Interpretation and Classical Mythology*. Chicago: University of Chicago Press.

Furst, L. and Skrine, P. (1971). *Naturalism*. London: Methuen.

Hankinson, R. J. (1998). *Cause and Explanation in Ancient Greek Thought*. Oxford: Oxford University Press.

Hippocrates. (2009). *On the Sacred Disease*. Trans. Adams, F. *Internet Classics Archives*. Retrieved January 1st, 2013, from: <http://classics.mit.edu/Hippocrates/sacred.html>

Jones, P. and Pennick, N. (1995). *A History of Pagan Europe*. London: Routledge.

Lindberg, D. C. (2007). *The Beginnings of Western Science*. Chicago: University of Chicago Press.

Parker, R. (2011). *On Greek Religion*. Ithaca, New York: Cornell University Press.

Prado, I. (2006). "Ionian Enchantment: A Brief History of Scientific Naturalism." Naturalism.org. Retrieved December 31st, 2012, from: <http://www.naturalism.org/history.htm>

Saler, B. (1977). "The Supernatural as a Western Category." *Ethos,* 5(1), pp. 31-53.

Thucydides. (2009). *The Peloponnesian War.* Trans. Hammond, M. Oxford: Oxford University Press.

Wians, R. W. (2009). *Logos and Muthos: Philosophical Essays in Greek Literature.* New York: State University of New York Press.

Woodruff, P. (2009). "Sophocles' Humanism." In Wians, R. W., (2009), *Logos and Muthos,* New York: State University of New York Press.

## Was the Buddha a Humanistic Pagan?
### by Tom Swiss

#### "So Siddhartha sat down under a tree"

Let's start with a quick overview of the Buddha's story. About 2,400 or 2,500 years ago a young prince in what is now Nepal, Siddhartha Gautama of the Shakya clan, became more interested in spiritual matters than in politics and government. (Or perhaps his father was an elected chieftain in a sort of republic rather than a king—the history is at best shaky.)

The legendary version involves a prophecy made at his birth, an incredibly sheltered childhood, and his sudden discovery as a young man of the existence of old age, sickness, and death. Almost overcome by the shock, Siddhartha discovered the existence of spiritual traditions. Thinking these must hold an answer as to how to deal with the suffering he had just learned about, he left home—abandoning his wife and son—to go study various meditation systems.

He sought out the best teachers and quickly mastered their techniques for altering consciousness, but wasn't satisfied. Looking for another option, he gave extreme asceticism a try. He completely overcame all his fleshly desires and, becoming immune to the desire to eat, came within a hair's breadth of dying from starvation. That wasn't the answer either.

So Siddhartha sat down under a tree (later known as the Bo Tree or the Bodhi Tree) to figure things out.

He eventually had a mystical enlightenment experience and a conceptual breakthrough which he expressed as the Four Noble Truths:

1. Life is marked by "dukkha"—suffering, stress, out-of-jointness, dissatisfaction.
2. The origin of this suffering is our desire that things be other than they are, our clinging to some of the temporary phenomena we encounter and our fear and aversion to others.
3. A solution to this is possible.
4. The way to this solution is a program of intellectual understanding, ethical living, and mental training—the Eightfold Path.

He started giving lectures on these ideas, and attracted a large group of followers who started calling him the "Awakened One"—the Buddha. He spent the rest of his life teaching these concepts and developing a religious community (which eventually included his abandoned wife and son) to propagate it.

### The Buddha's "Apatheism"

Now, the story as I've given it here makes the Buddha sound like a philosophical naturalist, and that's probably not the case. The stories of his birth and enlightenment feature various deities and demons, and there are also tales about his supposed "past lives" that would, if taken literally, require some sort of supernatural soul. Mahayana Buddhism in particular was happy to absorb deities and spirits and tales of the supernatural as it spread to other cultures, and its sutras are as full of miracle stories as the scriptures of any world religion.

The earliest written records of Buddhism weren't created until centuries after the Buddha's death, so it's hard to know how much of this supernaturalism originated with the Buddha himself and how much was retconned in later. But it's likely that the Buddha believed in at least some sort of supernatural phenomena.

But it also seems from the scriptures that, when the Buddha was directly asked about such matters, he would reply that they were irrelevant to the point he was trying to make. We might call him "apa-theist"—he was apathetic regarding the existence of deities and other supernatural phenomena.

More importantly, it's clear the Buddha never claimed to be carrying out any sort of divine will. The core of his teaching is entirely about the human experience of suffering. And his suggested solution is not to give yourself over to a god or to pray for salvation—indeed, some of the myths have it the other way around, with gods learning from the Buddha. The Buddha's recommendation is for each of us to change our lives and our way of thinking and experiencing through our own efforts.

If we define "religious humanism" as taking a human-centered rather than a deity-centered perspective on the big questions, the Buddha's teachings definitely qualify.

## The Buddha and the Earth Goddess

There are also some striking elements of nature spirituality in the mythology of the Buddha.

The legend of his enlightenment as told in the Lalitavistara Sutra has him tempted by the demon Mara, who claims that Siddhartha has no right to seek enlightenment. Mara claims that the accolades of his army of demons show that it is he, not Siddhartha, who has the right to the prize, and challenges Siddhartha to produce a witness on his behalf. Siddhartha reaches down and touches the ground, and the Goddess of the Earth responds. He then spoke this verse:

> "This earth supports all beings;
> She is impartial and unbiased toward all,
> whether moving or still.
> She is my witness that I speak no lies;
> So may she bear my witness."

As soon as the Bodhisattva touched this great earth, it shook in six different ways. It quivered, trembled, and quaked, and it boomed, thundered, and roared. Just as a Magadhan brass cauldron, when struck with a wooden log, chimes and reverberates, so did this great earth sound and reverberate when struck by the Bodhisattva with his hand.

Then the earth goddess, who is called Sthāvarā, in this great trichiliocosm, along with her retinue of one billion earth goddesses, began to shake the entire great earth. Not far from where the Bodhisattva was sitting, she broke through the earth's surface and revealed her upper body, adorned with all sorts of jewels. She bowed toward the Bodhisattva, joined her palms, and spoke to him:

> "You are right. Great Being, you are right. It is just as you say. We bear witness to this. But still, my Lord, you alone are the supreme witness in the worlds of gods and humans and the supreme authority."
>
> —Dharmachakra Translation Committee, *The Play in Full*, version 2.22

This strikes me as highly significant. According to the mythology of Mahayana Buddhism, the Buddha's spiritual authority comes not from a sky deity like Jehovah/Allah, Zeus/Jupiter, Amaterasu Okami, Thor, Horus, or Indra, but from an earth deity, an embodiment of the living and supportive world.

## Buddhism as a "Forest Religion"

Of course this is a legend created well after the Buddha's death, and so doesn't tell us much about his own attitude. But if we take the legend of the Bo Tree as being at least partially true, the fact that he went there rather than to a mountaintop or a cave or a desert is important.

Consider what his state of mind might have been like at this time. He had tried the spiritual paths available in his culture and found them all wanting. He had pushed himself almost to death and not found what he was looking for. This would create an intense spiritual crisis. Where could he turn for support?

He went to the trees. The Buddha achieved his enlightenment while sitting alone under a tree. Buddhism is at root (so to speak) a forest religion, and the legend of the Buddha touching the Earth may be a mythological expression of this.

Of course neither humanism nor Neo-Paganism were established ideas in the Buddha's time. But there are enough resonances that Humanistic Pagans might legitimately claim him as a forebear, bringing a human-centered and nature-appreciative perspective to the spiritual quest millennia before science and the unpleasant side-effects of industrialization started pushing Western thinkers in that direction.

## "A Goðlauss Kind of Guy":
## An Interview with T. J. Fox

This interview with T. J. Fox took place in 2015.

**How did you come to Paganism?**

I was raised in a skeptical, atheistic family; we gave each other presents at Christmas and hunted for Easter eggs, but I never attended any church nor had any form of religious education. Also, my Dad was an actor, a director and a stage magician, so I grew up with a "behind the scenes" understanding of how to conjure suspension of disbelief.

I first learned about Paganism from Tom Robbins' counter-culture novels, *Another Roadside Attraction* (1971) and *Even Cowgirls Get the Blues* (1976)—I would have been in my very early '20s at the time—and I was powerfully intrigued by his description of a secret tradition, a native European spirituality that was deeply connected to nature. Or perhaps not so much a secret tradition, as just a new perspective from which to view things like wishing wells and Christmas trees. The most "transcendent" experiences I'd ever had up to that point had been during intensive martial arts training in natural environments, so Robbins' writing on that subject made intuitive sense.

From my martial arts studies I knew a bit about Shugendo, which is an ascetic Japanese nature religion combining elements of Taoism, Shinto and esoteric Buddhism. I also knew a little bit about Native American religion and so-on, but my immediate frame of reference was actually the *Robin of Sherwood* TV series, which had featured the character of Herne the Hunter as a deer-antlered shaman in Sherwood Forest. What Tom

Robbins wrote seemed to offer me a way to temporarily live inside that fiction, which was very appealing at the time.

I found a copy of Margot Adler's book, *Drawing Down the Moon* (1979, 1986), in the local library and devoured it. It made me hungry for a community, but this was long before the Internet, so I wasn't sure how to find others who might be interested. I ended up slipping a general inquiry note with my phone number inside the Adler book, on the assumption that other "seekers" might find it and get in touch, which is what happened.

I joined their vaguely Wiccan circle but found that their ritual was in the vein of dancing around a cloth altar in the living room while Clannad played on the stereo. I eventually persuaded them to actually get out into nature and we traveled to a really wild beach. It was night, I gathered wood and lit a bonfire, the wind was high and the waves were crashing in, and then I turned around to find the others starting to lay down their ritual cloth and their feathers and jars of salt…I felt that they were really missing the point. "We're here! Here's the ocean, here's the earth, here's the fire! We don't need the symbols anymore!"

We ended up performing what was, to me at least, a really good, effective Pagan ritual. It was mostly improvised. There wasn't much said, but there was ecstatic dancing around the fire, lots of chanting, lots of drumming. I ended up spinning around in circles and got so dizzy that I accidentally fire-walked straight through the flames—fortunately, my feet were so cold and wet that I didn't get burned—and then I charged into the sea and let the ninth wave carry me back to shore. It was very cathartic.

**How did your Paganism evolve from there?**

From then on, I craved more of those experiences, which led me away from bureaucratic "ceremonial magic" and the Wiccan circle and more towards a sort of self-devised, quasi-Shugendo-style initiation, somewhat inspired by Norse and Celtic myth and folk practices. It always required extreme physicality and took place solo in wild space—free-climbing cliffs to construct hidden altars, standing in rune-stances underneath waterfalls, midnight drumming and swinging sacred sledgehammers on mountaintops. Berzerker wilderness parkour, though this was long before parkour came along.

It was all about *rammaukin*, which is Old Norse for "augmented strength"—somewhat shamanic and frequently dangerous, but that was part of the point. I strongly felt that this sort of thing *had* to be dangerous in order to be real.

Basically, I was a young man and a new father and I needed to test myself, and in the absence of any meaningful initiations offered by secular, modern society, I had to invent my own. I think I was lucky to have found Paganism at that time, because many young men in non-tribal societies act on the same initiatory urges without that mythopoeic context and end up really harming themselves, or hurting other people. Too many of them don't survive the ordeal.

After a few years, what I was doing coalesced into a statement of ethics—"the strong shall protect the weak," and so-on—and a reliable set of wilderness practices. I initiated one other person and also used an element of my practice to help out a friend who was going through a very tough time, but I wasn't motivated to evangelize and never even wrote most of it down. For that matter, I think that my practice would only ever appeal to a very niche audience. It was much more of a thing to do—a *way* in the Taoist sense—than a belief system, and it was far outside of even the Pagan "mainstream." Eventually I just didn't feel the need to keep testing myself, so I guess the initiation worked. I haven't had much connection with Paganism since then.

During the early 2000s, though, I started traveling a lot, to the point that I was away from home at least six months out of any given year—moving through Europe, North America, Australia, Japan. That was the time when the godless philosophy, if I can call it that, really sank in and became part of me. "He hath need of his wits, who wanders wide...

**How do you view Pagan ritual?**

I enjoyed neo-Pagan rituals (the really good ones, anyway), myths and community on an "as if" basis, having realised the real-world benefits of behaving, ceremonially, as if magic and gods were real. I also loved the poetry and theatre of Paganism and the challenges and rewards of "creative spirituality," but I was ultimately put off by the irrationality (mystic literalism) of some of my fellows. They were mostly nice people but I couldn't take the woo.

**What do you see as the "real world benefits" of behaving "as if" in ceremony? And how would you respond to those who say it's disingenuous?**

I see it as having the same benefits as suspension of disbelief in theater, or in reading a novel or watching a magic show. A given story may not be literally true, but it may still be profoundly moving, or even reveal unconsidered truths. I see ritual and mythology as participatory fiction; one gets the most out of them by deciding to behave "as if," at least for the duration. One isn't required to believe in the literal reality of ghosts and monsters in order to enjoy reading (or writing) a good horror story.

Actually, I'd go further than that; as much as I enjoy horror stories, I get at least as much out of learning about the skeptical, scientific responses to ghosts and monsters. It may be relevant that my dad was an actor and a stage magician, so I grew up with a strong awareness of the "backstage" side of things—the mechanics of how illusions were created and how to conjure suspension of disbelief in an audience. I'm inspired by people like Harry Houdini and James Randi, who devoted so much time and effort to countering superstition, and especially to combating people who would cynically exploit the superstitions of others.

During the early 1920s, in the wake of the horrors of the First World War and then the lethal Spanish Flu pandemic, a lot of people felt they had cause to believe that the world was coming to an end. That period saw a strong revival of Spiritualism. Houdini, who had recently lost his beloved mother, became obsessively interested in trying to contact her spirit, but because of his training in stage magic and the psychology of deception, he instantly saw through the tricks of fraudulent mediums. He felt that the trickery was a perversion of his art; it infuriated him and he dedicated himself to exposing the fraudsters. His life was threatened several times as a result.

Houdini, interestingly enough, had no issue with genuine Spiritualists—that is, people who were sincere in their beliefs—as long as they did no actual harm. He may have felt that they were deluded, but his real ire was reserved for "ghost racket" con-artists, who were willfully "playing" the bereaved for their own benefit. I feel much the same way about New Age hucksters.

**Can you explain more what you mean by "creative spirituality"?**

Given that I don't believe in literal metaphysics, it follows that people create their own sense of spirituality and spiritual practices.

I do believe that Coleridge's famous insight—"that willing suspension of disbelief for the moment, which constitutes poetic faith"—has profound implications. Surely naturalistic Paganism is a form of Ecopoetic Faith; it allows us, temporarily but passionately, to imagine, create and behave "as if," in the spirit of Peter Pan's urgent plea to clap if we believe in fairies.

For all that Sir Arthur Conan Doyle created a master rationalist in Sherlock Holmes, he also believed implicitly in the literal reality of fairies, which led to his being thoroughly and publicly hoodwinked by a schoolgirl prank. On the other hand, perhaps it's also important to remember that Conan Doyle and Peter Pan creator J.M. Barrie were friends, who played on the same cricket team!

**You wrote an article about the goðlauss of antiquity for a progressively-oriented Ásatrú magazine in 1992 which caused a bit of a stir. Tell us about that.**

It was inspired by the curious tradition of spiritual atheism particular to nomadic warriors in Medieval Iceland. Various scholars, including Jacob Grimm, J.R.R. Tolkien and especially E.O.G. Turville-Petre, had written (and speculated) about the "godless," who either did not believe in or simply did not trust the gods, relying instead on a combination of luck, pragmatic skill and gnomic wisdom. I wondered if my article was the first to try to recontextualise that concept in the (then-)contemporary Pagan milieu. As I recall, it wasn't a very popular article and led to my being obliquely described as a "worker of evil magic." *C'est la vie*, but two decades later, I'm still a goðlauss kind of guy.

**Why do you think it was controversial?**

It was controversial because it was a statement of atheistic, anti-supernatural intent framed in terms of genuinely ancient knowledge. It's understandable that, to "true believers" in supernaturalism for whom, say, the Icelandic sagas were a major frame of reference, that idea kind of came out of left field and may have felt threatening. I'd only vaguely sensed that might be a problem when I wrote the article.

**What can you tell me about the goðlauss of antiquity?**

Not very much, really. We know that there were some people referred to as having been godless in various Norse texts. It may well be that the Christian writers who recorded their stories made more of their atheism or misotheism than may have been warranted. The Christian sentiment may have been that having no gods at all, or just disliking them and refusing to sacrifice to them, was better than worshiping Odin, Thor and Freya.

That said, the godless people do seem to have shared a common set of circumstances and even a common set of beliefs and values that went beyond plain-and-simple atheism. Most of them seem to have been exiles in one way or another—cut off from their ancestral lands and therefore from their ancestral religions, which were closely tied to those lands. A lot of them were wanderers and there was a fair proportion of mercenaries.

In the absence of belief in the gods, or at least of *faith* in the gods, they seem to have valued other things—worldly wisdom, skill, codes of honor, and especially the lasting value of a "good name"—the idea that, since we can't expect an afterlife, what we do in this life really counts. It's a bit like the classic Talmudic prescription for immortality—"Write a book, plant a tree, have a child."

The godless responses to the question "what do you believe in?" were "I believe in my own might and main," or just "I believe in myself." There was also a pervasive sense of fortune (or "wyrd," fate) favoring the bold.

**Can you recommend some books for learning more about the goðlauss in antiquity?**

There are some scattered references in Grimm's *Teutonic Mythology* and in at least one of Tolkien's academic works, but otherwise the only source I can recommend is the "Godless Men" chapter in Turville-Petre's *Myth and Religion of the North.* For practical purposes, if you read that one chapter, you'll know as much about the godless Old Norse as anyone does.

That said, I think it's very likely that most of the *Hávamál*—the collection of gnomic poems traditionally attributed to Odin himself—was written from the godless point of view. Apart from the highly mystical *Rúnatal* and *Ljóðatal* sections, which describe Odin's self-sacrifice to gain magical powers, the *Hávamál* offers entirely pragmatic, worldly wisdom. Things like not getting too drunk, not trusting people until they're twice-proven, the tactical value of being generous to friends, etc. A lot of it is still very sound advice, but obviously, it was written about a thousand years ago, so you have to be judicious in how you interpret and apply it.

There's also a rather mournful Anglo-Saxon poem, *The Wanderer*, which seems to come from the same perspective.

**What would you hope for the future goðlauss of contemporary Paganism?**

Perhaps it's inevitable that, given the influence of people like Ronald Hutton, let alone Neal deGrasse Tyson, some contemporary Pagans should want to move beyond mystical literalism. Perhaps a good number of Pagans have always felt that gods and magic are actually metaphors or psychological constructs, but recently they've felt more free to identify themselves as humanists or atheists—I don't know.

That said, I hope that the realization leads to more actively creative approaches to spirituality, perhaps a more realistic or sophisticated sense of Pagan history and a syncretic approach towards science, nature and mythology. Especially the sense of history, actually—I agree with Hutton that modern Paganism is largely a literary and counter-cultural phenomenon, reaching back to Romantic poetry and to all manner of Utopian experiments. That's a proud heritage and it should be more widely understood and embraced.

Pinwheel Galaxy
(European Space Agency & NASA)

# Part 10: Looking Forward: Non-Theistic Pagan Community

> "In some respects, science has far surpassed religion in delivering awe. How is it that hardly any major religion has looked at science and concluded, 'This is better than we thought! The Universe is much bigger than our prophets said, grander, more subtle, more elegant?' Instead they say, 'No, no, no! My god is a little god, and I want him to stay that way.' A religion, old or new, that stressed the magnificence of the Universe as revealed by modern science might be able to draw forth reserves of reverence and awe hardly tapped by the conventional faiths. Sooner or later, such a religion will emerge."
>
> — Carl Sagan, *A Pale Blue Dot: A Vision of the Human Future in Space*

Recently, in an article on the growth of Paganism on college campuses in the online magazine, Inverse, reporter Sarah Sloat described Humanistic Paganism as possibly "the least organized faith of them all." That was a gross overstatement, but Sloat was correct to say that, by conventional standards, Humanistic Paganism is not an "organized" religion. While there have been some efforts to gather Humanistic and Naturalistic Pagans in recent years, we have very little in the way of institutions.

There are several reasons for this. Since we are a minority within a minority religion, our geographical dispersion renders the internet the only form of community for many. Of course, this is not all that unusual for Pagans generally. It is also possible that Humanistic and Naturalistic Paganism attracts more introverted personality types. In addition, many Humanistic and Naturalistic Pagans tend toward the "minimalist" end of the spectrum of Pagan practice, so they may feel less of a need to find others with whom to practice IRL ("in real life").

Finally, it is possible that a significant number of Humanistic and Naturalistic Pagans simply find their community among other Pagans of different theological orientations. As has been explained elsewhere in this book, many Humanistic and Naturalistic Pagans are comfortable practicing alongside theistic Pagans, even in rituals which are outwardly theistic. They approach participation in these rituals with the same sincere and reverent attitude as their theistic co-religionists.

Despite these challenges, a sense of community has begun to develop among Humanistic and Naturalistic Pagans. We share our experiences and ideas on the Naturalistic Pagan Yahoo group. Many have written essays and poetry for the HumanisticPaganism.com community blog. And we have gathered for ritual and community at PantheaCon.

So what does the future hold for the Humanistic and Naturalistic Pagan community? The founder of HumanisticPaganism.com, B. T. Newberg, recently shared his vision of what the future holds for our community in following years and decades, which included:

- **The discussion moves beyond the "Paganism 101" phase of who we are as Naturalistic Pagans** and shifts toward how we deal with real-life issues and struggles, such as parenting, grief, gender issues, environmental challenges, and activism. The tone of our discourse becomes less abstract and more personal, exploratory, and vulnerable.

- **Sustainable living is taken for granted as part of the Naturalistic Pagan way of life**, and individuals publicly share how they "walk the walk" in terms of environmental consciousness. The various Naturalistic Pagan groups and individuals collaborate to address urgent environmental issues, focusing on applying naturalistic, evidence-based views to policy change, activism, and the relationship of self to nature.

- **Face-to-face groups of Naturalistic Pagans exist in many major cities and regions**, thanks to the initiative of local volunteers, especially parents wishing to share a naturalistic perspective with their children. These groups and other local groups of naturalistic spiritualities communicate with each other, share overlapping membership, and collaborate on public projects. The first annual conference is held for Naturalistic Pagans.

- **A new generation growing up naturalistic begins to assert itself,** no longer stuck in reactionary mentalities but rather evolving more nuanced, relevant, expressive, and self-critical forms of Naturalistic Paganism.

## The Care and Feeding of Your Atheist Pagan
### by Jeffrey Flagg

I've been meaning to write an article like this for a while now, and in my mind, I've done it under a number of different titles. It started life as "What is an Atheist Pagan, Anyway?" Over time, though, I've realized that's really not the most satisfying tack for such an article. Nobody elected me Emperor of Atheist Pagans, so I can't make statements about what we all are. Finally, a series of email exchanges with one of my fellow mystic friends brought the structure of this article to its forefront, because I've noticed that there is a predictable mutual confusion in our interactions. The reason why I feel something of a "care and feeding" style article is better is that the theme is a bit more fun, casual, and personal. I can't speak for others, but I don't require actual care and feeding, though I do sometimes enjoy being a pet.

So, let's start back at the beginning. If you're reading this, and if you're Pagan, and if you're associated with a somewhat diverse Pagan community, there is a distinct possibility that someone you know through that community is an atheist Pagan. This may or may not come as a surprise to you. Amidst the vast diversity of people working with different pantheons, with the God and Goddess, with the divine intelligences of Qabalah, the hordes of spirits in Goetia…there are a few of us who went up to the smorgasbord of divinity and actually concluded our plates were beautiful when empty. We are among you, we know your gods and your spirits and all the rest, and we might even engage with them, but we don't identify with them as being our gods. We might not even consider divinity to exist "out there." But we still find a deep, powerful connection to the practices, to the blending of ideas and thoughts, to the experiences we gain, and from the community we keep. We might even engage with some of those gods you do, but just think about them differently. I'm one of them, and I use the term "atheist Pagan" to describe myself and the others like me I've met on the way.

And I think there's one thing I think we could agree on (other than agreeing that we're atheists), and that's this—other Pagans don't always know what to do with us. There are a number of very good reasons why this happens, and I'm not going to hash them out too much here. Instead, I'd like to just focus on some things that you, my dear reader, can do that could mean a lot to any of the atheist Pagans in your community. Please keep in mind that you might have some atheist Pagans in your community right now and not know it. I've met more than a few who don't speak very loudly about their atheism.

So, without further ado, care and feeding of the atheist Pagan in your life.

**<u>Don't</u> challenge your atheist Pagan about why he or she doesn't believe in your gods/deities/spirits/etc.**

I know it may seem really strange to have a conversation with someone who's a Pagan and an atheist. You might also genuinely want to know how this person came to reach his or her particular perspective. It's totally fair to ask in a warm and friendly way, the way you might ask your Ásatrú friend what attracts him or her to the Norse pantheon. It's very important, though, that you not ask your atheist Pagan as if you're demanding he or she defend his or her choices. Don't ask like you've encountered something weird.

Go back in time a bit to when you began to identify yourself as Pagan to others. No doubt you remember some people in your life treating you like you were full of strange ideas because you wanted to believe in many gods (or in some all-encompassing deity of nature, or some other non-mainstream theology). It sure must have felt exhausting to have to explain and defend yourself over what was, quite honestly, your truth. Atheist Pagans go through this, too. We often get it from Pagans over our atheism, from other atheists for our Paganism, and from mainstream people over both. Beyond that, consider this—Pagans want the tolerance of diversity. This means monotheists, polytheists, pantheists, and atheists, too.

**Don't tell your atheist Pagan that he or she isn't "really" an atheist or "really" a Pagan.**

This actually comes up more than you might think, usually in the nicer version of "you're not really an atheist." It's almost meant as a compliment, often from someone who's taken crap from particularly adversarial atheists in the past. There's a stereotype about atheists that we're all loudmouths who won't rest until we've destroyed everyone's favorite spiritual beliefs and paved the entire noosphere over with a fresh coating of empirical materialism.

Atheism is actually a very, very simple standpoint—you become an atheist when you have no deity, and that's it. The definition itself is very, very general, and throughout history, there have been many, many different ways to arrive at that state. An atheist might believe that deity does not exist, that the metaphysics of the universe simply does not define a place for deity, that deities exist but should not be treated in the customs one gives deities, or any of a number of other positions. Most of the atheist Pagans I've had the pleasure to meet do tend to have a pretty strong materialistic streak to their worldview (and, honestly, most Pagans do too, in general), but not many of them are out to constantly criticize every religious belief or superstition they come across.

On the other hand is the assertion that atheist Pagans aren't "really Pagan." While atheism and Paganism may seem, to some, irreconcilable, there isn't a theological test associated with being Pagan. Generally, Pagans are respectful of one another's pantheons while focusing on their own. This doesn't actually preclude having a personal pantheon with zero gods in it. Atheist Pagans are like any others who don't necessarily share your personal pantheon.

**Don't presume your atheist Pagan is less spiritually capable or fulfilled.**

How I got to be an atheist is a fairly long and winding story, so I'll give you the "tl;dr" version—I was finally honest about myself that "the gods" just "weren't there." I spent several years trying very hard with a number of practices, and had a lot of very interesting experiences along the way, but I just never really felt anything that really left me feeling strongly driven to the reality of deity. This is the opposite experience of most Pagans, but it's just as real and credible.

It actually takes a lot, in a community that takes its spirituality so personally, to admit that. I just don't feel the same connections others do, and it's inauthentic and painful for me to make myself try to be any other way about it. The first thing Pagan theists tend to inject into this is that I'm "just blind." This is basically an assault on my own sense of authenticity, and the only authority to that position is that the theism is seen as the default. If atheism were the default position, theists would be accused of hallucinating their deities. So, no, I'm not "just blind," and neither is any other atheist. Because the theistic position is the default one, pretty much all atheists have explored it and explored what it might mean to them, and they ultimately reject it.

**Don't assume that our lack of gods means we're ignorant, stubborn, or magickally handicapped.**

It's easy to think that, because you see or hear spirits or deities or whatever, that we must be "blind" or "deaf" to them. The metaphor is a problematic one, especially since it actually claims that anyone with a different experience (a Buddhist, perhaps) is just as "blind" to your reality. An atheist Pagan may not experience the same things you do, but in the incredible mess of subjectivity that makes up human perception, remember that it's really hard to hold claim to having an objective opinion. Also, remember that Christians used to claim the default position and ascribe madness to those who talked to ghosts or received messages from old gods.

**Don't presume that being an atheist means rejecting all magick, all religion, or all new age thought.**

This is yet another stereotype. Certainly, some atheists are just like that. That sort of atheist, though, is also probably not going to get a lot of joy out of also wanting to be part of the Pagan community. Again, atheism is mostly a position about the existence of deity, and that particular question can be addressed in many ways. The question of deity has little to do with the question of the soul, of an afterlife, of the existence of magickal "energy," of the mechanism and efficacy of astrology or other means of divination, or really any other subject that's applicable to most magick, mysticism, or other Pagan practices. On these subjects, atheist Pagans have just as much philosophical, cosmological, and practical diversity as anyone. Your atheist Pagan may enjoy taking part in many of the "conventionally Pagan" practices out there, and may do so for reasons very much like your own or ones very different from yours. You can't infer a person's complete magickal identity based solely on their perspectives about divinity.

**Do understand that your atheist Pagan is attracted to Paganism.**

That may seem really strange to you, but there is probably a lot more going on in your own flavor of Paganism than you realize. There can be all sorts of wonderful reasons an atheist may continue to choose a path mostly regarded as Pagan. Your atheist Pagan may feel very strongly acculturated to Pagans and their ways. He or she might follow a path that doesn't include the worship of deities, but which is heavily built from the fabric of contemporary Paganism. He or she may work with a "sacred non-entity" much like Tillich's "Ground of Being." He or she may actually still work with deities, but see them as emotionally moving fictional characters or symbols. The reasons are myriad, but there is one thing for certain—your atheist Pagan hangs around you because he or she wants to. There is something in the connection you share that's important. That goes for your common community, too. It may seem strange because an atheist Pagan seems at odds with stereotypes about atheists, but there are already many fine atheist communities out there, and yet there are many atheists who'd rather be with the Pagans.

**Do invite your atheist Pagan to your rituals, ceremonies, and festivals.**

Have you ever gone with one of your Christian friends to a church, or perhaps to a temple with a Jewish friend or to a mosque with a Muslim friend? Maybe you went along to a Buddhist temple once or twice. Maybe you even hung out in a Scientology center or drummed with some Hare Krishnas because someone you knew and liked asked you along. No doubt, you were respectful of your hosts and possibly participated a little. Maybe you even learned something.

Many, if not most, atheists are just as capable of joining in a religious service at a level somewhere between respectful detachment and enthusiasm. One of the most wonderful things about the Pagan community is its diversity of ideas and experiences available for those of cosmopolitan mindset to enjoy. Just because someone doesn't experience your closest deity doesn't mean he or she won't enjoy experiencing your expression of that divine connection. Rituals are stimulating and fascinating things to be a part of. Anyone who's going to proselytize about gods not existing at a ritual is a real jerk, and since you probably don't have jerks for friends, your atheist Pagan friend is probably not a jerk, either.

Let's say that your atheist Pagan passed up on coming to your big Freya working. That doesn't mean the invitation wasn't welcome! It's nice to be invited to things. It's a sign of friendship. It shows you're thinking about that person and wanting to see them happy. That alone is worth it.

**Do ask your atheist Pagan about his or her story, and be open to sharing yours.**

It's not a fast or straight path to an atheistic position, let alone one that still carries the Pagan flavor. Like many Pagans, your atheist Pagan is probably very happy to talk about his or her path. It's probably one that's very personal, idiosyncratic, and heterodox, and since atheist Paganism, unlike Wicca or Golden Dawn or other paths, doesn't really have any manuals, your atheist Pagan has been finding his or her way alone for quite some time. We like sharing our truth, just like other people do.

At the same time, there's a good chance an atheist Pagan you know wants to know about your own path, your own history, and your own truth. Most Pagans I have known geek out on spirituality, even if it's from an informally anthropological point of view. Empathy and friendship carry an aspect of seeing the world through someone else's eyes. Don't be afraid to lend yours. Do feel free to compliment your atheist Pagan from your own worldview.

I don't mean to sound like a braggart, but I do get compliments on the way I comport myself in ritual. When I feel a connection to a working, I am absolutely voracious for it. I just want to take it and make every last little bit of it become part of me until performing that working is as natural to me as making a cup of tea. I want to live in the working. I want to blur the lines of where I end and where my performance begins.

In my own little cosmology, I don't really consider (or, despite years of working on it, even experience) common magickal concepts like "energy." In fact, my adopting a paradigm that doesn't really focus much on energy is due to my own lack of experience with it…or at least in my not experiencing it in the way so many others around me have. But, when someone comes up to me after ritual and says I was working the energy well, does it bother me? Of course not. I know those people are speaking their truth, and that they ultimately are trying to tell me how my own work made them feel moved. That's a wonderful, wonderful thing. Of course, not all people are the same, and I'm sure you'll find some atheist Pagan out there who will get uncomfortable or try to correct you, but it's still a far better thing to try to share yourself with others than to not; the latter means not making an important personal connection with someone in your community.

Conversely, a compliment from an atheist might not share your own spiritual vocabulary. Remember, though, that the compliment is still genuine and meant with love, and it is not a dismissal of your own experiences simply because it doesn't reflect your experiences. You may genuinely feel you're "running the energy," while another person might think you're "a talented performer." Recognize atheism as a philosophy that shapes, rather than contradicts, spirituality.

Ultimately, this is what all the other things come down to. There have been atheists who've strongly contributed to every major religion of the world. (Yes, even Christianity. If you haven't read of the existentialist Christianity of Paul Tillich, you should check it out.) Atheism has, over the past century or so, seen a very serious restriction in its definition. There are many reasons for it, not the least of which are religious interests in America using politics to attempt to restrict science and science education. In a broad historical perspective, though, there have been atheist philosophies within every religious tradition and several religious traditions that classify the cosmos in such a way that there's simply no room for deities to exist.

Your atheist Pagan might take a highly psychological viewpoint on divinity, or may believe that divinity isn't an entity and thus not subject to existence, or may think divinity is simply "the absolute," or may simply not really feel concerned with questions about divinity. As much as atheist philosophers have shaped the history of Hinduism, Buddhism, Judaism, and various aspects of Christianity, atheists in the Pagan community are there, keeping things from becoming ossified into some canonical form of religiosity. Our lack of commitment to existential divinity is a feature, not a bug, and there's a good chance that we were quite welcome to the discussion before we brought up that whole atheism thing. Let us hang out. Tell us if we're telling you what your spiritual reality should be; let us have our spiritual reality and speak from it. We'll get along fabulously. I promise.

## Atheopaganism and the Broader Pagan Community
### by Mark Green

It's never going to be a completely comfortable fit.

Just as the suggestion of religious ritual and other symbolic, poetic, metaphorical practices will always be dismissed by some in the atheist community, Atheopaganism is always going to be viewed by some in the Pagan community as not rightfully belonging.

Let me stop there and say that, in my experience, that is a distinctly minority position. Most of the Pagans I have come out to as Atheopagan have been curious and interested in talking about the details of what I believe and do, and they have shown no interest in showing me the door. So let's start there: this appears only to be an issue for those who are either preternaturally cranky or who take offense (or feel defensive) at the idea that we don't believe in their gods.

Still, nobody likes being confronted with that sort of thing, and it's a little uncomfortable when it occurs. So why should Atheopagans want to continue to participate as a part of the broader Pagan community?

Well, I start with the principle of the thing. A community which tells itself that it is radically inclusive and devoted to the Earth really has no business deciding to kick out an Earth-honoring path that shares its values and practices in more ways than it does not.

Then, there are the people. Community and fellowship with interesting, smart, creative, playful people who share most, at least, of your values is just a great thing to have in your life. And what I find is that the longer I hang out with them as an "out" Atheopagan, the more Pagans come to me to "confess" that they, too, are unbelievers.

There are resources, too. Paganism has been around for a long enough time that there are groups, classes, venues that are open to being used for rituals, and lots of books and online information. There are chants and songs and poetry, some of which are not focused on gods.

By and large, we share a lexicon with the Pagan community. They know what a ritual is, what a circle is, what an invocation is. Most celebrate some variation of the Wheel of the Year.

We also have a (mostly) shared set of values. Though it is a subculture, the Pagan community's values are notably different from those of the mainstream American society in several ways. On issues relating to diversity, sexuality, and caring for the Earth, most Pagans are simply more open-minded and progressive as a group than are mainstream Americans. The Atheopagan Principles [see Part 1] as I articulate them (your mileage may vary) reflect the Pagan community's values far more than they diverge from them.

But here is the kicker for me: Skill, lore, knowledge and artistry in creating rituals.

Pagans have been working on the art of ritual for decades. Many of us are really good at it, skilled at the moving of group energy into a pattern of reverence and flow, exaltation and release.

Regrettably, the atheist community has little of the sort to offer us, except that in being godless/supernatural-free as we are, their example extends to us the *freedom* to innovate, to bend whatever might be traditional to fit our own purposes, and there are some in the atheist community who are doing exactly that. Atheists have no loyalty to traditions beyond those of logical discourse and the scientific method; in that lack of allegiance, there is liberty.

The Pagan community is a socially and culturally rich milieu. Being in it opens the possibility of many interesting areas of study, art, craft and lore. But if I had to pick one quality that really makes it worthwhile to remain, it is that the accumulated experience of thousands upon thousands of rituals in the Pagan community has distilled into peerless technical expertise in how to work with human consciousness in a group setting. And that skill, combined with commitment to practice, has led many in the community to develop over time genuine human wisdom.

The Pagan community has much it can teach us. We have a thing or two to offer in exchange, and it seems that many in the community are finding it so. But as grateful as I am for the love, community, creativity, solidarity, diversity and kindness I find in the community, I hold out its ability to work with human consciousness and its frequent human wisdom as its brightest gems.

# Ehoah
## by Rua Lupa

As an atheist who was seeking to live harmoniously within Nature, the practices closest to my beliefs were Indigenous and Neo-Pagan. Because I live near Indigenous communities, I was able to learn those practices through participation, often volunteering as a helper at events. Because I am Metis (Canadian of mixed European and Indigenous heritage), I was accepted to attend and participate at such events, but it ultimately depended on who is leading it and how open they are to outsiders.

One of my most prominent inheritances on my European side is Celtic, which influenced my interest toward Druidism when it comes to Neo-Paganism. There being no Pagan community where I live, most of my learning about Pagan practices came from books and the internet.

Through these studies, I found that Druidism, specifically the Reformed Druids of North America (RDNA), best suited my quest for *complete harmony within Nature*. The RDNA strongly informed my approach, which led to creating an off-shoot of the RDNA that was influenced through my interactions with the Anishinaabek, the local Indigenous culture.

This offshoot was called "Ehoah," the name being based on the sounds of breathing, the sounds of life (pronounced "Eh", as in able, "O", as in oak, "Ah", as in dawn), and given the meaning *"complete harmony within Nature."* The practice is based on the following the philosophy (being an adaptation of the RDNA philosophy, hence its off-shoot) called the "Saegoah's Three Basic Tenets":

1. Through Nature fulfillment can be found.
2. Nature, being inseparable from humanity's existence, is important in human pursuits.
3. As humans are part of Nature it is important to ensure our connections within it are harmonious.

The last tenet is what determines our actions, which is to work towards ensuring that all our connections within Nature are harmonious, in everything we do and use, maintaining an awareness of and respect for our interconnections, and creating a lifestyle that reflects this. It is a process that is continually improved upon with no end point.

Those who follow this path are Seekers of Ehoah, or Saegoahs (pronounced 'say-go-ah', "saeg" being the root word for "seek"). The path has no other requirements than to agree with its philosophy and strive to practice it consistent with the scientific method. From there, there is no strict requirement of how a Saegoah should go about practicing their beliefs, being open-ended to allow for creative exploration, diverse solutions to problems, and reflection of one's own environment, wherever they are on Earth. The foundation is the scientific method. Each individual or group can then build on it in their own way, working toward Ehoah. That way diversity is preserved—something that has consistently been shown to ensure resilience and prevent stagnation in ecological communities. Maintaining such diversity encourages positive creativity between Saegoahs and allows for better reflection of our regional ecosystems, aiding in our goal in achieving Ehoah.

For the general outline of the Ehoah ceremony, I drew inspiration from Anishinaabe ceremony, but the words and meanings are changed to reflect what science has revealed about our place in the cosmos and how we relate to it. I made the ceremony outline like this so that anybody can participate, no matter one's background or way of practice as a Saegoah.

## Ehoah Breathing Exercise and Mantra

This is an optional chant to begin and end the ceremony. As an exercise it is very simple and can go on for however long you desire. Fifteen minutes is recommended to get the minimum full effect, yet can be used in shorter time frames to treat stress.

In a comfortable, relaxed position, take a deep breath through your nose and breathe out of your mouth. Take another deep breath through your nose and say "Eh" (as in able), "O" (as in oak), and "Ah" (as in dawn) for about 8 seconds each, all in one exhale. Take a deep breath through your nose and begin again. With practice, you can extend the length of time for each syllable.

## Ehoah Awareness Meditation

In a comfortable upright position, relax and leave your eyes open. Start with your core and work your way out:

**Heartbeat:** Focus on your heartbeat. Feel it. Then let your mind empty while remaining conscious of your heartbeat.

**Breath:** Feel your breath coming in and out. Then let your mind empty while remaining conscious of your breath.

**Touch:** Sense all that touches your skin: the wind, the sun, the grass. Feel the stillness. Then let your mind empty while remaining conscious of your sense of your sense of touch.

**Ground:** Whatever part of you is touching the ground (your feet if you're standing, your bottom if sitting, etc.), feel the sturdy ground beneath you. Embrace it. Then let your mind empty while remaining conscious of the ground.

**Sound:** Listen to whatever sound you hear: leaves and grasses in wind, birdsong, etc. Don't focus on any particular sound. Let the sounds come to you. Then let your mind empty while remaining conscious of your sense of sound.

**Sight:** Widen your vision to include everything up to your peripheral vision. Take in what you see. Maintaining a wide view, notice any stillness or movement, without turning your vision directly on it. Then let your mind empty while remaining conscious of your sense of sight.

Try to maintain this state for as long as possible, over time and with much practice, you will be able to reach Awareness faster and easier.

## Ehoah Ceremony Outline

["Spoken words are in quotes."]

Beginning an Ehoah Ceremony:

Walk onto the grounds from the West. Walk in one full circle around the perimeter going the direction of the earth's spin. (The direction of circling the grounds depends on which hemisphere you are on: counter-clockwise on the Northern Hemisphere, clockwise on the Southern Hemisphere.) On the second go around, gather in loose circular clump around the center, which could potentially have a fire or altar. Children, and pets that have been socialized with the group, can move freely about. Once everyone is gathered, collectively do a verbalized deep inhale.

Chant Eh-O-Ah thrice or hum, led and stopped by a designated organizer, stopping when the feeling is right.

Acknowledge the directions in open stances:

> "I/We acknowledge the East, the direction we turn to, toward our host star at dawn and deep space at dusk."
>
> "I/We acknowledge the Sky (face the nearest pole); from plants we have the ocean of air that envelops us, our shield, our breath."

"I/We acknowledge the West, the direction we turn from, where we last see our host star before night, and deep space before day."

"I/We acknowledge the Earth (face the equator)."

Place your left hand on your heart, and right hand on other kin (whether it be human, pet, plant, or soil organisms—by touching the ground).

The resulting group position is called the Web of Life.

*While in Web of Life:* "From star dust, a new star, planets—this planet, developing from its oceans, along a long lineage of life, now exists all current life on this planet. We are all made of this place we call home."

Turn to face the nearest pole or the Center and begin the ceremony focus, which may be rites of passage like birth, bonding, and diffusion, or Solterra Festivitas (seasonal celebrations).

Closing an Ehoah Ceremony:

> Position into the Web of Life
> Chant Thrice or Hum
> Verbalize Deep Exhale
> "As we go our separate ways, know that we are not truly divided."
> Leave toward the East, the direction the earth turns toward.

# Earthseed
## by John Halstead

*We are Earthseed*
*The life that perceives itself*
*Changing.*

Earthseed is an emerging Humanistic Pagan tradition which is just beginning to be Shaped. Like the Pagan Church of All Worlds, which began as a fictional religion in Robert Heinlein's *Stranger in a Strange Land* (1961), Earthseed also originated with a work of science fiction. Earthseed is the brainchild of author, Octavia Butler, which she describes in her books, *Parable of the Sower* (1993) and *Parable of the Talents* (1998). Butler (1947-2006) was one of the first Black science fiction writers and one of the first women to break the science fiction gender barrier. The protagonists of many of her books are strong Black women.

Butler's Parable series is set in the near future when the rule of law in the United States has all but collapsed due to economic pressures, to be replaced by social chaos, corporate slavery, and violent religious fundamentalism. The heroine, Lauren Oya Olamina creates a new religion, which she calls "Earthseed," and which attracts a small community of refugees, who come to call themselves "Acorn." The Parable books include many verses from a fictional book of scripture authored by Olamina, called "The Book of the Living," which describes the theology, ethics, and vision of Earthseed. Although Olamina uses theistic language to describe the beliefs of Earthseed, it is a naturalistic and humanistic religion.

Earthseed's three main tenets are—

1. God is Change.
2. Shape God.
3. The Destiny of Earthseed is to take root among the stars.

## God is Change

The first tenet of Earthseed, "God is Change," is literal truth. The one inescapable fact of existence is Change. Everything in the universe changes. One of the verses of the Book of the Living which explains this principle closely resembles a familiar Pagan chant by Starhawk:

*All that you touch*
*You Change.*
*All that you Change*
*Changes you.*
*The only lasting truth*
*Is Change.*
*God*
*Is Change.*

The statement, "God is Change," is radical from the perspective of monotheistic religion. When most people think of God, they think of something immutable in which they can place their unqualified trust in the face of a changing world. But the first tenet of Earthseed denies God the quality of unchangeableness and raises Change itself to the status of God.

The God of Earthseed is not a person. The God of Earthseed does not love us or watch over us and is not even aware of us. The God of Earthseed just *is*. Change *is*.

Earthseed is not a very comforting religion. Change is often frightening. We humans crave predictability and stability. The God of Earthseed is wildly dynamic. "Trickster" and "Chaos" are some of the names used for God in the Book of the Living. Change is faceless, implacable, and sometimes terrifying. Earthseed's God is not a God to be loved or worshiped. It is a God that is perceived, attended to, learned from, shaped, and ultimately—at death—yielded to:

> *We do not worship God.*
> *We perceive and attend God.*
> *We learn from God.*
> *With forethought and work,*
> *We shape God.*
> *In the end, we yield to God.*

But why say "God" then? Why not say, "The world is Change" or "Nature is Change"? That is what religious naturalists mean, after all, when we say "God." In her Parable series, Butler explains that one reason to retain theistic language is so that we won't be tempted to (consciously or unconsciously) imagine another, supernatural agency and call that "God." "God" is a powerful idea, and if we don't give a place for that in our life, if we do not find "God" in this world, then there is a human tendency to project it onto the supernatural.

## Shape God

What's interesting about Earthseed's conception of God is not that God changes us, *but that we also can change God*. In this view, life is a reciprocal interaction between the universe and ourselves, a notion which Butler may have borrowed from process theology.

According to the second tenet of Earthseed, God is malleable. "Clay" is one of the names given to God in the Book of the Living. Earthseed empowers us to "Shape God." This is why members of Earthseed are called "Shapers."

> *God is Change.*
> *Beware:*
> *God exists to shape*
> *And to be shaped.*

Change is unavoidable, but we can sometimes shape the direction or speed of Change:

*Chaos*
*Is God's most dangerous face—*
*Amorphous, roiling, hungry.*
*Shape Chaos—*
*Shape God.*
*Act.*
*Alter the speed*
*Or the direction of Change.*
*Vary the scope of Change.*
*Recombine the seeds of Change.*
*Transmute the impact of Change.*
*Seize Change.*
*Use it.*
*Adapt and grow.*

Starhawk has described the Neo-Pagan Goddess in similar terms. She is

> "the ever-diversifying creating/destroying/renewing force whose only constant is, as we say, that She Changes Everything She Touches, and Everything She Touches Changes…The Goddess is not some abstract thought whose qualities we can decide. She is real—meaning that when we call Her in Her various aspects, 'shit happens,' as the T-shirt says; the rivers of life-force burst the dams and it's paddle-or-die…Ultimately we don't decide who or what the Goddess is; we only chose to what depth we will experience our lives."

In Starhawk's post-apocalyptic science fiction novel, *The Fifth Sacred Thing*, the protagonist, Madrone, wrestles with this conception of deity:

> "One of the names of the Goddess was All Possibility, and Madrone wished, for one moment for a more comforting deity, one who would at least claim that only the good possibilities would come to pass.

" 'All means all,' she heard a voice in her mind whisper. 'I proliferate, I don't discriminate. But you have the knife. I spin a billion billion threads, now, cut some and weave with the rest.' "

In other words, God/dess is the force of both preservation and destruction at the heart of nature. If we want to survive, we have to fight for it like the rest of creation. "It's paddle-or-die," as Starhawk says. The Goddess does not discriminate, but that does not mean that we should not. As Starhawk writes, we have the knife—the power to discriminate. And this power to discriminate gives us the power to shape God:

*A victim of God may,*
*Through learning and adaption,*
*Become a partner of God,*
*A victim of God may,*
*Through forethought and planning,*
*Become a shaper of God.*
*Or a victim of God may,*
*Through shortsightedness and fear,*
*Remain God's victim,*
*God's plaything,*
*God's prey.*

When we say that God can be shaped by us, we are denying that our lives are entirely determined, either by an all-powerful deity or by our material circumstances, and at the same time affirming that we have only ourselves and each other to look to in order to shape a better future. This is what makes Earthseed humanistic. "God is change—Shape God" is a challenge, to work to shape our reality, just as we are shaped by it:

*All successful life is*
*Adaptable,*
*Opportunistic,*
*Tenacious,*
*Interconnected, and*
*Fecund.*

*Understand this.*
*Use it.*
*Shape God.*

While Earthseed's Shapers don't "worship" God, per se, we do use prayer and ritual to help us accept what we cannot change and to focus our work to change what we can. But prayer and ritual are useless without corresponding action. "Pray working," says the Book of the Living.

### The Destiny of Earthseed

But in what direction should we shape God? This brings us to the third tenet of Earthseed: "The destiny of Earthseed is to take root among the stars" or "the Destiny" for short.

*The Destiny of Earthseed*
*Is to take root among the stars.*
*It is to live and to thrive*
*On new earths.*
*It is to become new beings*
*And to consider new questions.*
*It is to leap into the heavens*
*Again and again.*
*It is to explore the vastness*
*Of heaven.*
*It is to explore the vastness*
*Of ourselves.*

According to the Destiny, our ultimate aim should be to discover, travel to, live, and thrive on new planets.

The Destiny is an alternative vision to the post-peak world which Butler imagines, where the United States has exhausted its physical and moral resources; where education has become a privilege of the rich rather than a basic necessity; where convenience, profit, and inertia excuse greater and more dangerous environmental degradation; where poverty, hunger, disease have become inevitable for more and more people; and where people have become commodities—a world that looks increasingly like our own present.

The Destiny has the potential to create a kind of species-consciousness for humankind, to bring us together to work toward a common goal, and to do so in a sustainable way with the Earth. It is a goal which is both lofty enough and challenging enough to drive us to transcend our current self-destructive ways.

The Destiny might be thought of as the next chapter in what some have called the "Great Story" or the "Epic of Evolution," the 14 billion year narrative of the evolution of the cosmos, the planet Earth, biological life, and human culture. Like other religious myths, the Epic of Evolution tells us where we came from. It teaches us that there is something greater than ourselves: the evolutionary process of life itself—but it is a greatness that we are a part of and share in the dignity of. And it teaches us that we are all connected: to other humans culturally, to all other life on the planet biologically, to the earth itself chemically, and to the rest of the cosmos atomically. But while the Epic of Evolution explains our past and how we got to the present, the Destiny offers a vision for the future.

The Destiny is Earthseed's vision of heaven or immortality. Because Earthseed is a naturalistic religion, Earthseed's heaven is literally in the "heavens"—i.e., in space. Unlike the Christian heaven, we don't get there by dying, though. And none of us alive today will likely reach it in our lifetimes. In fact, it may not even be the human species that reaches it, but our evolutionary successors or another form of Earthlife. While there is no personal immortality in Earthseed, the Destiny creates the possibility of immortality for Earth-life as a whole:

*Alone,*
*Each of us is mortal.*
*Yet through Earthseed,*
*Through the Destiny,*
*We join.*
*We are purposeful*

*Immortal*
*Life!*

The Destiny offers the only true immortality: the seeds of the Earth becoming new life, new communities on new earths.

The Destiny is not about irresponsibly seeking to escape the environmental problems we have created on this planet. Fulfilling the Destiny requires learning to live in partnership with one another in small communities, and at the same time, working out a sustainable partnership with our environment and the other-than-human species we share it with.

> *Partnership is giving, taking, learning, teaching, offering the greatest possible benefit while doing the least possible harm. Partnership is mutualistic symbiosis.*
> *Partnership is life.*
> *Any entity, any process that cannot or should not be resisted or avoided must somehow be partnered.*
> *Partner one another.*
> *Partner diverse communities.*
> *Partner life.*
> *Partner any world that is your home.*
> *Partner God.*
> *Only in partnership can we thrive, grow, Change.*
> *Only in partnership can we live.*

The Earth-*seed* metaphor is key here. If we want to spread the seeds of a tree, we don't chop down the mother tree. Instead, we must care for it and nurture it so that it can continue to produce seeds. The Earth is the mother tree which gives life to Earthseed.

The Destiny might seem like science fiction. But there is nothing logically impossible or unscientific about it. Of course, it will be unimaginably difficult to achieve—but that's the point. We need something big, something *mythic* in scale, *but yet still possible*, to bring us together in a way that not even the immanent destruction of Earth's biosphere has been able to. The Destiny may just be what we need to force a paradigm shift. It might enable us to move beyond the idea of international cooperation to a truly global community. And because every human being might potentially provide a breakthrough necessary to achieve the Destiny, health care and education might come to be seen as a necessity for all, not the privilege of a few.

## The Earthseed Community

In addition to inspiring Earthseed, Octavia Butler's Parable series, especially the Destiny, has inspired other religious movements, including the naturalistic Solseed Movement and the transhumanist Terasem Faith. These movements are similar to Earthseed, but Earthseed is unique in emphasizing all three Earthseed tenets.

Earthseed begins with creating small, but diverse communities of people that urge one another toward the Destiny and to live sustainably with the environment. The essentials of being a good member of the Earthseed Community are to:

1. Learn to shape God with forethought, care, and work.
2. Educate and benefit your community, your family, and yourself.
3. Contribute to the fulfillment of the Destiny.

If you would like to become a Shaper of Earthseed, you must simply agree to follow the three essentials above and recite the "Words of Welcoming" to another Shaper:

*I am Earthseed—*
*One of many*
*One unique,*
*One small seed,*
*One great promise.*
*Tenacious of life,*
*Shaper of God,*
*Water,*

*Fire,*
*Sculptor,*
*Clay,*
*We are Earthseed!*
*And our Destiny,*
*The Destiny of Earthseed,*
*Is to take root*
*Among the stars.*

To find out more about Earthseed, visit godischange.org.

$$\infty = \Delta$$

## A Poetry of Place:
## An Interview with Glenys Livingstone
## of PaGaian Cosmology

Dr. Glenys Livingstone is leader of the thriving PaGaian community of naturalistic spirituality, and author of *PaGaian Cosmology* (2005). This interview took place in 2011.

**B. T. Newberg:** What makes PaGaian different from other Neo-Pagan paths?

**Glenys Livingstone:** PaGaian is understood as an "evolutionary" spirituality because it is grounded in the evolutionary story, and the practice of ritual at seasonal points celebrates that Cosmic unfolding, as well as the regional phase of the year—there is not understood to be any separation of Creativity.

**BTN:** What do you mean by "no separation of Creativity?"

**GL:** The same Creativity that unfolds the Cosmos manifests in the extant Creativity of the Seasonal cycle, and in any cycle of being—including personal. All layers of Creativity may be celebrated at once—may be understood to be woven into each other.

Thomas Berry and Brian Swimme define three qualities of Cosmogenesis in their book *The Universe Story* (1992), which I have linked with an ancient Triplicity—as Marija Gimbutas notes in *The Language of the Goddess* (1989), expressed in later times (evidenced in the last several thousand millennia) as three qualities of the Triple Goddess and also in the Triple Spiral of Irish indigenous tradition.

In *PaGaian Cosmology*, I have re-visioned the three faces of Goddess (based in female biology and lunar phases) as Cosmic Dynamics innate to being, no matter your gender or species, and suggest that the Triple Spiral and the ancient notion of a Cosmic Triplicity may have embraced such a notion of Cosmic Creativity.

Such Cosmic Creativity was also understood to be symbolised and microcosm-ed in the female body which may conceive, give birth, and lactate—bring forth new life: surely a central impetus to being and becoming. Indigenous cultures have no problem with this—She includes all (we all have navels that may remind us of connection to a birthing Cosmos).

PaGaian Cosmology is a synthesis of all that: the science, the Pagan and female metaphor.

And it is a practice—of Seasonal rituals that align one's small self with regional and Cosmic creativity: that is how it happens in our small particular lives—in Conversation (ceremony) with our Place which is understood to be alive and sentient. So PaGaian Cosmology is not just an idea or thought. It has to be practiced in ritual in some way—that is the nature of the Cosmos we are in…it is an Event.

For change to really happen one's cosmology must be embodied—it can be really simple or with high drama, but it expresses relationship with Place, helps us come Home—not just talk about it.

**BTN:** And that capital "P" in "Place" is there for a reason, isn't it? You've said that PaGaian is not even about gods, it's about Place. The Goddess is a metaphor: "a place, not a deity." What does that mean?

**GL:** The term "Cosmology" is used decidedly because what is being discussed here and what *PaGaian Cosmology* is about, is a *Place*—the Cosmos—as sacred (as many of our ancient forebears apparently knew their Place to be). It is not a theism of any kind—be that atheism, pantheism, panentheism or whatever, nor even a "thealogy." Any references to deities is understood to be metaphor: Poetry is all we have to attempt to express the multivalent awesome Universe.

As I say in my book: "Cosmos is a Place, dynamic and moving, alive and changing, which is indistinguishable from participatory selves, which remains ultimately mysterious and indefinable; thus ultimately only able to be spoken of metaphorically. This then is Poetry."

**BTN:** So, if we're talking about Place, then why continue to use the word "Goddess?"

**GL:** Most people who use the word "God" forget that "God" is a metaphor—and it is perhaps past its "use-by" date. Some may not find "Goddess" helpful either, but I am of the opinion that the word needs trotting about—to put a sense of "Her" back on our lips and in our minds: the lack of language that may express or do that is symptomatic of the problem of "Her" invisibility—that we don't have words to conjure a sense of femaleness to the sacred, and most people on the Planet have forgotten that that is possible.

I also want to say that some may be put off by the sub-title of my book ("Re-inventing Earth-based Goddess Religion"). I chose to use the word "religion," because the root of the word means to connect and "cosmological celebration" is a "connecting" practice—and what I feel is required is a consistent practice of intention, attention, meditation and ritual, that enhances a personal and communal sense of belonging. I would like to write a new version however and change the sub-title to something like "Re-Creating a Gaian Poiesis" or "a Poetry of the Cosmic Mother."

**BTN:** So what does all this look like "on the ground"? How does a person practice PaGaian Cosmology? Would an outside observer notice anything different from other forms of Neo-Paganism?

**GL:** What PaGaian Cosmology looks like "on the ground" is that it involves a practice of ritual for each Seasonal Moment (as I name the "Sabbats"): that means eight a year here at my Place—that could vary according to your Place but you would have to work that out.

Essentially PaGaian Cosmology is a *practice*, not just a head-trip—it has to be *done*: it is an art form. Ritual is the art form of a living cosmology—that is where the transformation happens.

"Conversation" is necessary—and that is how I understand ritual and the creating of it—I get that term for ritual from Thomas Berry: one needs to be *speaking* with one's beloved of the soul, which may be named as the "sentient Cosmos."

The rituals here don't look/sound much like traditional Wicca or other forms of Neo-Paganism, in the sense that the central focus of the celebration is frequently quite different, and language I have used in the scripts that are offered is quite different (and I do offer scripts because language is important in my opinion—but the words are meant as guides—for a *sense*—not to be parroted, though they may also be regarded as Poetry and learned by heart with some variation of one's own).

For example, in terms of language, when the elements are "called," I speak of "remembering" that we are Water, Fire and so on; and/or that we are expressions of these Cosmic Dynamics. The elements are qualities of Earth/Cosmic manifestation, always present and *felt*.

In PaGaian Cosmology, the language of ritual needs to express that we *are* the Earth…so that we may re-learn it more deeply.

In terms of an example of the central focus of a Seasonal ritual being different from other forms of Neo-Paganism: at Beltaine the PaGaian ritual essentially celebrates Desire—not just a simple notion of "Goddess and God" or even a simplistic version of "Beloved and Lover," but yet still deeper to a Cosmic essence that is multivalent, and that is felt in the Power and Creativity of Earth-Sun-Moon interaction. Aphrodite *is* named particularly—as representing this Power (of Allurement/Desire) but need not be: it may be felt as distracting, or there may be other deities (zoomorphic or anthropomorphic) that one may find helpful for personal or collective aesthetic reasons.

PaGaian Cosmology may be summed up in the practice of what I call the "Triple Goddess Breath Meditation" which I teach here on the ground, and is also described in the Introduction to my book (*The Yoga Mudra as In-Corporation of Gaia's Breath*). I have made a DVD of it for my online students, so they can see it and associate it with imagery—which of course will take off and vary in their own minds. The words, more or less, are on the final pages of Chapter 8 in my book. It expresses the sense of each being (one's personal being) as a "Place of the Cosmological Unfolding."

**BTN:** Speaking of online students, is there a training program? Are there local or online PaGaian groups? How does one become more involved in PaGaian Cosmology?

**GL:** I teach and facilitate a year-long course called "Celebrating Cosmogenesis" which is a mentoring through the year-long cycle of eight Seasonal Moments: it is now available online for both hemispheres. There is information here. Many simply use my book as inspiration for their Cosmic/Earth rituals—and I update the online versions of the offered ritual scripts in Chapter 7 each time we change it here on the ground at my Place.

**BTN:** Where can we find your book?

**GL:** You can ask for it at any good book shop, and lots of online retailers such as Amazon. It is freely available with a Creative Commons licence at my website at http://www.pagaian.org/book and a paper copy may also be purchased there.

**BTN:** Finally, if you had just one sentence to express the heart of your path, what would it be?

**GL:** It is a practice of relationship with our Place, and the Place is at once the small self, the communal self-other, and the cosmic self-all that is.

## Non-Theism and Literal Belief in Wicca:
### An Interview by Pat Mosley

Non-theism is a hot topic in today's Pagan communities. I sat down with the high priest (HP) and high priestess (HPS) of the Wiccan coven I work with to discuss atheism and belief structure in Wicca.

**Pat Mosley:** So I've been reading a lot about atheistic or otherwise non-theist perspectives among Pagans, and I'm really curious about your understandings of how belief works in Wicca. What belief structure was maybe taught to you or intended? What role literal belief and theism or atheism play in Wicca?

**HPS:** I don't know any atheists in Wicca or Paganism, but I probably just haven't met them yet. They are all welcome. That's certainly a fascinating viewpoint to hold and still be drawn to Wicca. What is the appeal to them?

**PM:** Well, a lot of folks are drawn to a very empirical relationship with the Earth that's complemented by the poetry of Paganism.

**HP:** I think there's always been an element of that, for as long as I can remember. I love that description you just gave. I think that fits me well. Very Jungian to a degree, and I think that fits with our generation's adoption of Wicca.

**HPS:** I can appreciate that. I'd like to think we're opposed to neither strict nor atheistic encounters of the Divine. It's certainly going to be different for different folks, and over time.

I mean, lots of people are developing this atheistic relationship with the gods they were raised to believe in when they enter Wicca, and if they develop that relationship with other gods in general, I'd say that demonstrates how helpful ritual and Pagan imagery can be in encouraging psychological growth.

**PM:** My understanding of our group work has been that these sort of belief questions are left up to the individual. Our primary goals, from my perspective, have been ritually enacting community, with each other, and with nature, then growth like you're saying. Is that a correct assessment?

**HPS:** Yeah, definitely. Wicca is not dogmatic. It is a community first and foremost. We are reconstructing—taking the best from the pagan communities of the ancients. It's not church. It's not literal belief and forcing people to believe a certain way.

**HP:** And our rituals are very much based in this sort of transpersonal experimentation mindset. That's why we talk about "performing" ritual so often, and put on masks, or get naked. It's about manifesting and honoring those aspects of the mind—the great couple, the divine androgyne, the wizard, the hunter—archetypes that can be named and reclaimed from the fears of our minds…I never really thought about how much pop psychology of the `60s played into this!

**HPS:** That's a good point. And I think that's a good perspective because people who maybe need a god or goddess may have a literal belief system to support themselves, but those who don't, don't. I guess I do know atheist Pagans in that sense.

I want Wicca—it's our duty as the Wica—to welcome them both and give them community. That's how I feel.

**PM:** How was Wicca taught to you? As a religion with literal beliefs? Or from this more transpersonal or Jungian perspective?

**HPS:** Well, from the women's movement, I think most of us were coming to it very dissatisfied with gods and with this mindset that we would terrorize the dominant culture by calling ourselves Witches and basically playing to all of their fears about revolution and Witchcraft.

It wasn't as literal then as it maybe is now. I think there have always been literal believers, and many of them grew into that over the years. Especially as you were elevated to the later degrees, for me at least, it was about recognizing the power in myth and story, and learning how to manipulate that to dismantle patriculture.

We still do that. Stories are how we teach values to our children, how we can change the way this civilization views the planet and different marginalized communities.

Our teachers may have taught it very literally in the beginning, because that's how you trick the unconscious so you can start working with it at a deeper level. But I think there was a willing suspension of disbelief that our generation carried through those rituals because we were trying it to try to find Power. Does that make sense?

**PM:** Yeah, totally. Do you have anything to add to that?

**HP:** I mean, I agree. LaVey was a big inspiration to me. Crowley. It's always been more about the performance and the power we can get from that performance, that change of the way we interface with the world.

I think too there can be this disconnect between how people who have interacted with Christianity, for example, and then become atheists view "gods" versus how many Pagans view them.

Like, to me, a god is just a label assigned to these mythic characters whose stories teach us about value and culture. They aren't people, they aren't animals, they're characters, they're a role. And I think we perform that role sometimes or find meaning in the stories.

Some people definitely take it pretty far; maybe they still have a lot of baggage from Christianity or whatever. Maybe they just really need a literal being to ease their minds for whatever reason.

**HPS:** And I don't see a problem with that. I don't think we should be afraid of the meaning people find in religion, or even in their minds, if it helps them and doesn't fuck with anyone else—crazy is a stigmatized construct! Humanity was born from psychological divergence.

**PM:** Yes! That's so where I'm at right now.

**HP:** Yeah, and when atheists come from very strict religions, they sometimes seem to project that mentality on other faiths. Like in Wicca, we'd never tell you what your relationship with any given entity or god needs to be. We're not telling you that there's an all-powerful omnipresent physical force ruling over your life. I think sometimes they prescribe these very Christian beliefs about God onto all gods or religions, when they haven't even really gotten to know those other religions or gods to the same degree as the one they don't believe in…Pop culture witches aren't helping.

**HPS:** It comes down to values. I think the values are the most important part. Not beliefs. Wicca—our Wicca, our coven, is about values. We value community, we value the marginalized, we value the planet in all its glorious manifestations.

Communities will always have differing beliefs, that's what makes them communities and not cults. That's what makes them strong. My mission, I feel, as a priestess of this community, is to keep it open to a variety of beliefs and room to grow.

In the '60s, we would have said what matters is that she's a woman. She can be an atheist, an immigrant, a prostitute, a trans woman, whatever—but she's still a woman.

By the same token, you can be an atheist, a mystic, a Tarot reader, a comedian, a historian, whatever—you're part of the community, and that's who the Wica have always existed to serve and guide towards their greatest self, not a prescribed belief system.

**PM:** I love so much of what you've said there. But just to play Devil's advocate here for a minute, there are numerous references to gods and goddesses in Wiccan ritual, in Wiccan books, etc. How does that play into this openness of belief?

**HPS:** Well, it's ritual and belief for people who need it to feel whole. Like the God and Goddess—it's the ancestral memory of our great mother and father, found in basically every culture's origin myth. It's giving equality of men and women space—story—in our community.

For people who have a broken relationship with their parents or with the culture as a whole, maybe a literal reconnection with these forces is needed. And I think Paganism encourages that. For folks who have it together more, maybe these forces appear more as archetypes that influence culture, and ritual is an homage to our heritage. We welcome that too.

There's no judgment of either of those perspectives. We teach Cernunnos both as a god character performed during ritual and as a man from the community playing the role. The Goddess is both a character—a reminder that women have power, which is a subversion of patriarchal culture—performed during ritual and as an actual woman in the community.

For people who don't study Wicca long enough to reach the higher degrees and really learn how stories move with us, or for people who get very attached to the relationships they need with these roles, I can see how this could be very confusing. I hope I'm explaining it well.

**PM:** I'm following, and this is so much of what appeals to me to keep studying in this faith. There's a universalism almost in how these archetypes permeate all world cultures.

**HP:** And I think that's the beauty of Wicca. Because you can find or apply its base structure to any myth, any belief system. It transcends specificity.

**PM:** Do you think that was intentional in its design?

**HP:** Well, I think it first came into the public eye as a very British incarnation of that universalism. But if you believe it's older than Gardner's covens, then I think you can find those roots in the ease with which it slips into a priesthood's guidance through psychodrama.

**HPS:** You always cause me to question how much mess our generation has made of everything, Pat.

**PM:** Hahahaha!

**HPS:** You know, regardless of how Wicca was intended, or engineered, or even where it is today, I think the values are what give it lasting appeal, and I'm comfortable with the values we've assigned to it. I'm confident that everyone we've initiated will continue to carry those values forward.

**PM:** So, last question. Do you think the future of Wicca is more atheistic, theistic, or continuing in this sort of open-community lineage?

**HPS:** Open community. Everyone welcome. I've always thought, and I still do, that Wicca can serve as a global religion of peace and mutual respect.

**HP:** Honestly, I hope there's a stronger atheistic resurgence. This conversation is really fascinating me and making me think about what I really believe. Some of what I see today, I think we really need to keep grounded in psychological growth, empiricism, reason. That really falls on the teachers to teach, I suppose.

## Family, Extended
### by Amelia Stachowicz

The third Sunday after Beltane, I found myself shuffling forward in line to receive Communion.

...Let me back up a bit.

Of all the things in the world, my family is one of the most important to me; a rather significant part of my identity is comprised of being the daughter of so-and-so, who was given life by this person, who was the child of the person who came over on the boat, and so on and so forth. I can't recite names and titles *too* far back, but I can tell you stories: my union boss great-grandmother for whom I am named, or my great-grand-relation who missed the departure of the Titanic because he was hungover, or personal accounts of the history of Detroit. The surnames and bloodlines matter less than the history and the sense of shared traditions. When Heathens talk about kith and kin, I feel a small flare of happy recognition.

So, family is important to me, and faith is important to my family—specifically, the Catholic variety. Though they are far from fundamentalists, it nevertheless runs deep: I can point to the church off of I-75 that was built by members of my family and other members of the local Polish-American community. My great-grandmother once intended to commit suicide, but held off because she heard the Virgin Mary telling her not to. My mother taught catechism for a number of years (one of which I assisted with). Religion was never explicitly forced, but it didn't need to be: it was woven into the fabric of lineage. It wasn't theology; it was something that one simply *did*.

Only, it never quite fit me, a fact that stung. Without turning this into a screed, I was and am unsatisfied with a number of points in the worldview. As a young teenager, I was none too graceful when I resisted being confirmed, and while I cringe now at my lack of tact, I firmly hold that my misgivings were and are sound. Years later, my awe of the natural world and interest in mythology would see me investigating contemporary Paganism and hesitantly participating in rituals with other people. I am inexperienced, but eager to learn. So I read the works of Pagan authors, take long walks outdoors, and try (and often fail) to meditate regularly. There has not yet been a larger organization that I have clicked with, but Druidry as a philosophical system is a compelling one.

In some alternate scenario, I probably could have made myself fit the religion of my family, but it would have been in a put-upon sort of way, pining for something I couldn't quite name but knew had something to do with the feelings that well up in me when I look up at the night sky. These days, I'm less concerned with being a non-Catholic or a non-Christian, and more interested in being what I *am*: a spiritual naturalist and solitary Pagan; someone who practices low-key observances related to the seasons; one who looks to her ancestors for guidance as well as tales of caution. I find it to be considerably more helpful as a mindset—not to mention healthier.

This would not be a problem if I were considering only myself: being a solitary tree-hugging dirt worshiper has suited me well so far. My conundrum comes from having family ties, which explains what I was doing at a cousin's confirmation Mass when I was really craving grass beneath my feet and the heat of the sun on my face. Peeking around at my extended family arrayed around me, I felt terribly cut off from them in a way that I hadn't felt quite so keenly before. Do I take Communion? To whom exactly do I address communal prayers, if I even recite them along with everyone else? Will my grandmother, sweet woman that she is, notice if I choose to avoid doing these things? Will *anyone* notice…and would it even matter if they did?

Being a non-religious, agnostic teenager attending church with my family was one thing. Being a woman who had crowned a statue of Persephone with flowers on the first of May, after pouring a libation just a few weeks prior was quite another. The divide between myself and them felt sharper, the cut deeper. It was not the rites of passage, body of mythology, or even the exquisite art that I was sad that I had forsaken all of those years ago: rather, it was the severing of those ties relating to a core of my kin's culture. Keeping up the banner of tradition can lead to stagnation, but choosing to set that banner down can present a fearsome void.

The disconsolate feeling increased in depth through the Mass and into the coffee hour that followed. As it ended, I stepped outside and inhaled, taking a glance around to try to orient myself in the present moment. Overhead the clouds hung heavy in concordance with my mood, but as I paused to observe the way life continued around me despite my troubles, my pattering heart calmed.

All life on Earth is connected by virtue of common ancestry; the idea of everyone being family hit me hard then. It was something that I had known intellectually, but hadn't been reminded of emotionally for a while. How could I be alone when all of the world surrounded me, with all of my brothers and sisters, my grand-relations, my eternal parents? Nobody was alone, not really. Nobody could be if they tried.

I am still grappling with the implications of this: if you truly hold all living beings to be your kin in some way (however distant), then things like the razing of forests for factory farms or the blatant dumping of toxic substances into rivers are attacks against your family. One feels significantly more invested in the struggles for justice that are endlessly being fought across the globe than if the parties involved are just abstract characters. The amount of greed and lack of regard for the wellbeing of others is appalling, staggering, overwhelming. It takes resilience to keep that initial flame alive in the face of continually discouraging news.

That wasn't on my mind at the time, however, as I made my way across the parking lot. I turned my face up toward the veiled Sun.

"This is my church," I muttered to myself. "And you are all my family, too." The northbound wind blew in parallel to the road, pushing my hair back.

*Welcome home.*

# Contributors

**Áine Órga** identifies as a pantheistic Pagan. After grappling throughout her adolescence with a seeming conflict between her interest in Paganism and witchcraft and her naturalistic worldview, she realised in early adulthood that something was profoundly missing in her life—and that something turned out to be a religious practice and a deep and constantly evolving passion for all things spiritual. At her heart, she is a writer, an artist, a teacher, and a traveler of the inner world of the mind. She is currently reading towards a Master's degree in Religious Studies, and blogs and makes videos on her spiritual path on her website, heart-story.org.

**Alison Leigh Lilly** grew up a shy Irish Catholic hippie girl, exploring the woods and fields surrounding her childhood home with the same curiosity and enthusiasm she would later bring to her studies of mysticism and nature spirituality. Seeking the spiritual heritage of her Celtic ancestors, she discovered poetry and story, mud and blood mingled with the scent of peat fires and the slick feel of damp stone. Eventually, these interests landed her squarely in the round hole of Academia, where she graduated valedictorian of her class, humbly accepted her degree, and ran for it. She now resides in the lovely, rain-drizzled cityscape of Seattle, where she lives with her husband, her black cat and two pet frogs. She devotes her time to cultivating a spiritual life founded on peace, poesis, and attentive engagement with the inner and outer landscapes of wildness, wilderness and nature. She explores these themes through podcasting, essays, articles and poetry, and her work has appeared in a number of publications both in print and online, including at her blog *Holy Wild* (http://alisonleighlilly.com).

**Allison Ehrman** goes by many names: mother, wife, sister, friend, technical writer, manager, volunteer, activist, tree hugger. But when she's enveloped in the sanctuary of a forest, beach, or grassy plain, she's simply a child again. She was given many inadvertent lessons in earth-based spirituality throughout her childhood. She learned the names, colors, and songs of the birds with her grandfather. she pressed seeds into the warm soil and harvested vegetables beside her father in his garden. She frequently gazed into the starry skies with him after dark, pondering the enormity of the universe and hence the smallness of herself. She tasted wild berries and sumac and excitedly watched doodlebugs defending their formidable ant traps with her grandmothers. Eventually, she walked away from the uncomfortable pews and church buildings of her youth and found spiritual fulfillment entirely within the glory of nature. Without any knowledge that other people had done so for centuries, she cast circles aligned with the cardinal directions and celebrated her own rites of passage. She established family rituals for the solstices and equinoxes. Today, Allison finds peace and inspiration in the seasonal cultivation of her garden, and she and her husband take their sons into the forest to share everything they have learned, including a deep and lasting reverence for the earth around them. When people ask what it she believes, who she is, many names come to mind: Unitarian Universalist, Scientific Pantheist, Pagan. For her, they're all one and the same.

**Amelia Stachowicz** was raised in the Great Lakes region of the United States. She is an aspiring field biologist and amateur artist. Though she has long recognized the inherent sacredness of the world, she is relatively new to Paganism and to the notion that one can be an atheist *and* religious. In her free time, she writes poetry, takes long walks outdoors, and whittles away at her "to read" pile.

**Anna Walther** practices place-based Paganism in Austin, Texas. Her practice is inspired by the Reclaiming Tradition of Witchcraft and the teachings of Zen Master, Thich Nhat Hanh. Anna's interests include sacred spaces, ritual art, ecopsychology, biophilia, and environmental ethics. She attends First Unitarian Universalist Church of Austin with her husband and children.

**B. T. Newberg** founded HumanisticPaganism.com in 2011, and served as Managing Editor till 2013. His writings on naturalistic spirituality can be found at Patheos, Pagan Square, the Spiritual Naturalist Society, as well as at HumanisticPaganism.com. Since the year 2000, he has been practicing meditation and ritual from a naturalistic perspective. After leaving the Lutheranism of his raising, he experimented with Agnosticism, Buddhism, Contemporary Paganism, and Spiritual Humanism. Currently he combines the latter two into a dynamic path embracing both science and myth. Professionally, he teaches English as a Second Language. After living in Minnesota, England, Malaysia, Japan, and South Korea, B. T. Newberg now resides in Minneapolis, Minnesota, with his wife and cat. He currently serves as Advising Editor for HumanisticPaganism.com, and is also Education Director for the Spiritual Naturalist Society, where he created and now teaches a course for naturalists, including Naturalistic Pagans, entitled "SNS 101: Introduction to Spiritual Naturalism."

**Bart Everson** is a writer, a photographer, a baker of bread, a husband and a father. An award-winning videographer, he is co-creator of ROX, the first TV show on the internet. As a media artist and an advocate for faculty development in higher education, he is interested in current and emerging trends in social media, blogging, podcasting, *et cetera*, as well as contemplative pedagogy and integrative learning. He is a founding member of the Green Party of Louisiana, past president of Friends of Lafitte Corridor, and a participant in New Orleans Lamplight Circle. Bart is also a columnist for Mid-City Messenger and Humanistic Paganism. More at BartEverson.com.

**Blue** is, in no particular order, an atheist, Thelemite, Chaote and magic(k)ian, who has been building a relationship with Aphrodite for 25 years. Practice and labels need not be congruent. You can read more of

Blue's writing online at Garden of the Blue Apple: Musings About Aphrodite.

**Brendan Myers** loves faerie tales and space exploration. He lives in a library, next door to a forest. Brendan is a TED speaker, a successful Kickstarter (twice), and the author of fifteen books in fiction and nonfiction. After earning his Ph.D. in philosophy from the National University of Ireland, Galway, he has taught at six different institutions in Canada and in Europe, and provided policy research for government agencies, labour unions, and game design studios. Myers' ideas have been featured by the Pacific Business & Law Institute, the Scottish Environmental Protection Agency, the Order of Bards Ovates & Druids, as well as numerous environmental groups, interfaith groups, and humanist societies around the world. Originally from Elora, Ontario, Brendan now serves as professor of philosophy at CEGEP Heritage College, in Gatineau, Quebec. Follow him on Twitter @Fellwater or on Facebook.

**Cat Chapin-Bishop** has been Pagan since the late '80s, and also Quaker since 2001. Cat is the former Chair of Cherry Hill Seminary's Pastoral Counseling Department, and her essays have appeared in Laura Wildman's *Celebrating the Pagan Soul*, *The Pomegranate: The Journal of Pagan Studies*, and at The Wild Hunt blog. Cat writes about the connections between Pagan and Quaker practice at her own blog, Quaker Pagan Reflections, hosted at Patheos. She lives with her husband in Western Massachusetts, where she attempts to find peace in the midst of chaos.

**DT Strain** is Executive Director of the Spiritual Naturalist Society (www.SpiritualNaturalistSociety.org). He is a Humanist minister, speaker, and writer on the topics of ethics, spirituality, and ancient philosophy. DT also serves on the Board of Directors of New Stoa. His Humanist Contemplative group and blog inspired a similar mindfulness group at Harvard University. He is former president of the Humanists of Houston and has served in the Chapter Assembly of the American Humanist Association. DT writes for the Houston Chronicle belief page online and his work has appeared nationally in other magazines, on Houston PBS, and the journal, *Essays in the Philosophy of Humanism*. He attends Jade Buddha Temple and occasionally speaks at their English Dharma Group and other venues.

**Debra Macleod, B.A., LL.B.** is a couples and family mediator, a top-selling marriage author-expert and a popular resource for major media in North America. She is the leading proponent of the New Vesta tradition and order. Her New Vesta book series and Add a Spark women's seminars "spread the flame" into modern lives and homes. You can visit Debra's private practice at DebraMacleod.com or her Vesta website at NewVesta.com.

**Eli Effinger-Weintraub** is a Reclaiming-tradition Atheopagan rooted in the Twin Cities Watershed. She grounds her personal spiritual practice in the everyday, primarily in bike-riding, deathwork, and writing (plays, creative nonfiction, and short speculative fiction). She finds inspiration in nature, science, and the visual art of her wife, Leora Effinger-Weintraub. Eli is also a mercenary copyeditor. Try her tweets; they're delicious: @awflyweeeli

**Glen Gordon** has been in and around the modern pagan community for eighteen years. He has had formal training in both traditional British Wicca and British Neo-Druidry. However, the past few years he has no longer self-identified as "pagan." Instead, he sees himself more as a spiritual and religious naturalist with humanist leanings, and as a Unitarian Universalist. In the recent past, while residing in the Inland Northwest, he has spoken at his local UU church on topics of Bioregional Animism and Religious Naturalism. He has facilitated land-centered group ceremony which blend naturalism, humanism, neopagan, and UU influences.

**Glenys Livingstone Ph.D.** (Social Ecology) has been on a Goddess path since 1979. She is the author of *PaGaian Cosmology: Re-inventing Earth-*

based *Goddess Religion*, which fuses the indigenous traditions of Old Europe with scientific theory, feminism and a poetic relationship with Place. She lives in the Blue Mountains Australia where she has facilitated Seasonal ceremony for almost three decades, taught classes and mentored apprentices. In 2014, Glenys co-facilitated the Mago Pilgrimage to Korea with Dr. Helen Hwang. Glenys is a contributor to *Foremothers of Women's Spirituality: Elders and Visionaries* edited by Miriam Robbins Dexter and Vicki Noble (2015), and also to *Goddesses in World Cultures* edited by Patricia Monaghan (2010). She has recently produced a set of meditation CDs which are available at her website (http://pagaian.org/pagaian-prayers-invoking-her/) along with her book (http://pagaian.org/book/).

**Irene Hilldale** is a practicing atheistic Pagan living in the Midwestern United States with her husband and their endlessly amusing cat. She is an artist and writer by night, and a digital marketing specialist by day. You can find her regularly enjoying the outdoors for a hike or a run, drawing in her studio, playing classical piano, and fruitlessly attempting to keep the cat off of her altar—fortunately, nothing has been broken yet.

**John Halstead** is Editor-At-Large at HumanisticPaganism.com, a community blog for Humanistic and Naturalistic Pagans. He blogs about Paganism at AllergicPagan.com, which is hosted by Patheos, and about Jungian Neo-Paganism at "Dreaming the Myth Onward," which is hosted by WitchesandPagans.com. He is also an occasional contributor to GodsandRadicals.org and The Huffington Post. John was the principal facilitator of "A Pagan Community Statement on the Environment," which can be found at ecopagan.com. He is also a Shaper of the fledgling Earthseed community, which is described at GodisChange.org. John practices a highly eclectic and localized form of Paganism and observes the Neo-Pagan Wheel of the Year with his wonderful LDS wife and two amazing children.

**Dr. Jon Cleland Host** is a scientist who earned his PhD in materials science at Northwestern University and has conducted research at Hemlock Semiconductor and Dow Corning since 1997. He holds eight patents and has authored over three dozen internal scientific papers and eleven papers for peer-reviewed scientific journals, including the journal *Nature*. He has taught classes on biology, math, chemistry, physics and general science at Delta College and Saginaw Valley State University. Jon grew up near Pontiac, and has been building a reality-based spirituality for over 30 years, first as a Catholic and now as a Unitarian Universalist, including collaborating with Michael Dowd and Connie Barlow to spread the awe and wonder of the Great Story of our Universe (see www.thegreatstory.org and the blog at evolutionarytimes.org). Jon and his wife have four sons, whom they embrace within a Universe-centered, Pagan, family spirituality. He currently moderates the Yahoo discussion group Naturalistic Paganism. Jon is also the new Managing Editor of HumanisticPaganism.com.

**Kathleen Cole** earned a Ph.D. in political philosophy and now works as a professor at a teaching institution in the Midwest. Her research is in the areas of antiracism, feminism, and social constructivism. She was introduced to Paganism by Wiccans, but has come over time to adopt a purely naturalistic reverence for the Earth and the Universe.

**Lupa** is an author, artist, naturalist and sustainability geek in Portland, Oregon, within the watersheds of the mighty Columbia and Willamette rivers. Growing up in the rural Midwest, she was that child who was always grubbing around in the woods, turning over rocks to find garter snakes, and catching sunfish with salami in a tiny creek. As she grew older, the nonhuman natural world became integral to her sense of self and well-being, and she entered into Paganism seeking deeper connections to what she found to be sacred. After almost twenty years of exploring traditions, rituals, and structures, she has come back full circle to being most comfortable and connected through simple awe and wonder at the world around her. She is the author of several books on totemism and other nature spirituality. She has been incorporating hides, bones, and other organic materials into artwork since 1998; through this practice she is able to reclaim materials that might otherwise be discarded and give them a better "afterlife." In 2011, she earned her Master's degree in counseling psychology with an emphasis on ecopsychology and ecotherapy, and in 2013 became certified as a Wilderness First Responder (WFR). Professions aside, nothing makes her happier than being outdoors, and she is an avid hiker, camper, environmental volunteer, and explorer of her world. More information about Lupa, her writings and art, and her personal blog, may be found online at www.thegreenwolf.com`.

**M. J. Lee** was born in New Orleans, Louisiana, where she first discovered her love of Greek myth among the dusty books at local universities. It was the gods and spirits of wild places that especially captured her heart, and M. J. went on to earn a B.S. in Wildlife Science from Louisiana Tech and an M.S. in Plant Ecology from Southern Illinois University at Carbondale. It was this training in science and critical thinking along with her enduring fascination with myth and mysticism that shaped her into a Naturalistic Pagan. M. J. currently lives in west Tennessee with her husband and works as an environmental consultant. She spends her free time enjoying nature, dancing and indulging her Hellenomania.

**Mark Green** is a writer, thinker, poet, musician and costuming geek who works in the public interest sector, primarily in environmental policy and ecological conservation. He lives in Sonoma County on California's North Coast with his wife, Nemea, and Miri, the Cat of Foulness. For more information on Atheopaganism, visit atheopaganism.wordpress.com or the Atheopagan Facebook group.

**Michelle Joers** is a scientist, connoisseur of all things tea, veteran, wife and mother, beach addict, history of natural history aficionado, avid amateur botanist and herbalist, voracious reader, and canoeing fanatic. She is a co-owner of Pagan Forum, and blogs on a variety of topics at Bay Witch Musings, under the name Thalassa. She practices a bioregionally based witchcraft and considers herself to be "intellectually agnostic, emotionally pantheistic, and pragmatically polytheistic."

**NaturalPantheist** is a former Christian, who now sees himself as a Naturalistic Pantheist with an interest in Druidry and Heathenry. He blogs at NaturalPantheist.com on issues relating to scientific and naturalistic approaches to spirituality. His interests include religion and philosophy, social media and technology, current affairs, and walking. NaturalPantheist currently serves as the social media coordinator for HumanisticPaganism.com.

**Nimue Brown** has been an active Pagan and Druid for many years, having volunteered for the Pagan Federation and the Druid Network. OBOD trained, but chaotic by nature, her non-fiction work (published by Moon Books) explores spirituality as a lived experience rather than an academic subject. She has run moots, a folk club, workshops, open rituals, and meditation groups, teaches a bit, and was a founding member of Druid Gorsedd Bards of the Lost Forest, and the Contemplative Druids. Nimue blogs at www.druidlife.wordpress.com and wrote www.hopelessmaine.com—a webcomic illustrated by her husband, artist Tom Brown. As a fiction author, Nimue tends towards the gothic, steampunk and comedy, although will turn her hand to just about anything. Her Pagan music can be listened to for free at www.nimuebrown.bandcamp.com. An experienced ritual leader and celebrant, capable public speaker, and used to leading workshops, Nimue will travel to events in the UK and is also open to requests for articles, guest blogs and podcast contributions, as time permits.

**Pat Mosley** is a jack-of-all-trades, variously unknown as an author, aromatherapist, janitor, small business owner, and all-around student of the world's religions, presently living in Winston-Salem, North Carolina. He can be found on the web at patmosley.wordpress.com.

**Peg Aloi** has been researching and writing about the representation of the occult and paganism in various forms of media for years; giving talks at academic conferences, editing anthologies, and publishing essays in a number of scholarly books, including *The Handbook of Contemporary Paganism*. She was one of the original founders of The Witches' Voice, and is currently one of the editors of the organization's Facebook page. She is a practicing witch, traditional singer, adjunct professor of media studies, and guerrilla gardener.

**Rua Lupa** is a Naturalist, Saegoah, Permaculture Designer and Bioregionalist. Rua was raised on a small farm in the boreal forest of northern Ontario, Canada, and now lives on the Great Freshwater Island of the Great Lakes. Delving into learning about their ancestry led Rua to becoming involved in the Reformed Druids of North America and the Anishinaabek (Ojibway) traditions and teachings. Learning more of their cultural heritage, studying the cultures that are/were closer to the land and ways to emulate them, along with a naturalistic perspective, led Rua to following a path they called Ehoah—the word stemming from the different sounds of breathing and was given the meaning "complete harmony within Nature." With this outlook and approach Rua, obtained a Wildlife Technician Diploma, had been a board member of Bike Share Algoma; founded, ran and organized the Sault Community Drum Circle; invented the Borealis, Australis, and Globus Kalendars; became certified as a Permaculture Designer; and tinkered with many skills from glass working, welding, and drafting, to advanced wilderness first aid, life guarding, canoe tripping, winter camping, and orienteering. Better described as leaning toward a jack-of-all-trades/master-of-none, Rua is a self-described leech for learning more about these skills and new ones. Being told of having too many hobbies receives a familiar shrug, as Rua carries on with their latest fascination and experimentation toward Ehoah.

**Ryan Cronin** is an agnostic, naturalist Pagan who has studied Druidry with both OBOD and ADF. He has practiced Paganism as a solitary Druid for around five years. Ryan has an MA degree in religious studies, specialising in the psychology of religious belief and experience, and lives in the UK with his wife and two gerbils. He enjoys walking in the woods, watching *Doctor Who* and curling up with a cup of tea and a good book. Ryan blogs at www.endlesserring.wordpress.com.

**Sara Amis** has been published in *Datura*, *Moon Milk Review*, and *The Dead Mule School of Southern Literature*. Her poem series, "The Sophia Leaves Text Messages," was published as an artist's book by Papaveria Press. Her interests include sustainable living/right livelihood from a Pagan perspective, ecology, and the convergence of the pragmatic with the mystical. She has a blog on Patheos called "A Word to the Witch" and is a Faery Tradition initiate.

**Scott Oden** hails from the hills of rural North Alabama. His fascination with far-off places and times began in grade school, when he stumbled across the staggering and savage vistas of Robert E. Howard and Harold Lamb. Though Oden started writing his own tales at the age of fourteen, it would be many years before anything would come of it. In the meantime, he had a brief and tempestuous fling with academia before retiring to the private sector, where he worked the usual roster of odd jobs-from delivering pizza to stacking paper in the bindery of a printing company to clerking at a video store. Nowadays, Oden writes full-time from his family home near Huntsville. Oden is the author of the critically acclaimed historical novels *Men of Bronze* (2005), *Memnon* (2006), *The Lion of Cairo* (2010), and *A Gathering of Ravens*.

**Shauna Aura Knight** is an artist, author, ritualist, presenter, and spiritual seeker. Shauna travels nationally offering intensive education in the transformative arts of ritual, community leadership, and personal growth. She is the author of *The Leader Within*, *Ritual Facilitation*, and *Dreamwork for the Initiate's Path*. She's a columnist on ritual techniques for

CIRCLE Magazine, and her writing also appears in the anthologies: *Stepping in to Ourselves*, *A Mantle of Stars*, *Calling to our Ancestors*, and *Bringing Race to the Table*. She's also the author of urban fantasy and paranormal romance novels including: *Werewolves in the Kitchen*, *Werewolves with Chocolate*, *A Winter Knight's Vigil*, *A Fading Amaranth*, and *The Truth Upon Her Lips*. Shauna's mythic artwork and designs are used for magazine covers, book covers, and illustrations, as well as decorating many walls, shrines, and other spaces. Shauna is passionate about creating rituals, experiences, spaces, stories, and artwork to awaken mythic imagination. http://www.shaunaauraknight.com.

**Staša Morgan-Appel** is the co-founder of Roses, Too! Tradition of Feminist Witchcraft. She is active among Pagans and unprogrammed Friends (Quakers) in North America and Great Britain. She maintains an active multi-faith ministry with a focus on spiritual nurture. Staša writes about ministry/Priestessing, social justice, healing, music, life as an expat, and random other things. She blogs at *Musings of a Quaker Witch*, writes regularly for Quaker and Pagan publications, and is the co-creator *of A Winter Solstice Singing Ritual* book and CD.

**Steven Posch** is a poet, storyteller, and current keeper of the Minnesota ooser. His CD of original stories, *Radio Paganistan: Folktales of the Urban Witches*, is available from www.omnium.com. He blogs at Paganistan: Notes from the Sacred Commonwealth at WitchesandPagans.com.

**Stifyn Emrys** is an author of five books, including *Requiem for a Phantom God* (The Provocation Press, 2012), a critique of Abrahamic monotheism. His first novel, *Identity Break*, was published in 2013. He lives in California with his wife, Samaire Provost, author of the *Mad World* YA series. His books are available on Amazon and Nook. You can follow him on Facebook at www.facebook.com/semrys.

**T. J. Fox** was born in one hemisphere and now lives in another. He is technically middle-aged, but does not expect to live to be a hundred. He is a card-carrying skeptic who has written a number of books on obscure historical topics and who occasionally pines for the good old days of swinging sacred sledgehammers on mountaintops.

**Tom Swiss** describes his spiritual path as "Zen Pagan Taoist Atheist Discordian," which usually baffles questioners enough to leave him alone. He blogs as "The Zen Pagan" at Patheos, and has previously served as President of the Free Spirit Alliance. Over the past decade he has built a reputation as a lecturer on subjects spanning the gamut from acupressure to Zen and from self-defense to sexuality. He is an NCCAOM Diplomate in Asian Bodywork Therapy, a godan (fifth-degree black belt) in karate, a poet, a singer/ongwriter, an amateur philosopher, and a professional computer geek. His first book, *Why Buddha Touched the Earth*, was published by Megalithica Books in 2013. Find out more about his wacky adventures at www.infamous.net.

**Traci Laird** is an animist living in Ireland and hails from the great state of Texas (a mythic heritage she is quite proud of!). Her current academic pursuits are in Sociology and Psychology, and she engages a "sensuous scholarship" when seeking to understand Place. She can also be found online at Confessions of a Hedge Witch.

**Wayne Martin Mellinger, Ph.D.** is a Santa Barbara-based social justice activist, writer, and educator who uses spiritual practices to create a better world. Specifically, Wayne is very active in helping our neighbors of the streets transition into permanent housing and environmental issues. He has taught at the Santa Barbara, Santa Cruz, and Berkeley campus of the University of California, Ventura College, the Fielding Graduate University and Antioch University Santa Barbara.

## Environmental Impact Notice

The production, transportation, and disposal of print books consumes trees and water, produces greenhouse gases, and releases toxic chemicals into the environment. While there are no environmentally impact-free choices for book reading, some choices are better than others. In general, e-books have less of an environmental impact than print books. The manufacture of ebook readers constitutes the most significant percentage of the total environmental impact of ebook reading, but ebooks themselves have much less of an impact than print books. So every ebook you read on your device, instead of buying a print book, decreases the net environmental impact of choosing ebooks over print books. According to a 2010 article in *Slate*, reading 18 to 23 ebooks, instead of print books, will offset the environmental cost of the production of your ebook reader over its lifetime. Of course, the production of ebook readers still requires mining of nonrenewable minerals, and some readers contain toxic chemicals. So make sure to use your ebook reader lots, use it for as long as possible before replacing it, and then dispose of it responsibly.

**Read responsibly. Choose ebooks.**

Made in the USA
Monee, IL
25 February 2023